THE
Dispossession
OF THE
American Indian
1887–1934

THE
Dispossession
OF THE
American Indian
1887–1934

Janet A. McDonnell

INDIANA UNIVERSITY PRESS

Bloomington and Indianapolis

The paper used in this publication meets the minimum requirements of American
National Standard for Information Sciences—Permanence of Paper for Printed
Library Materials, ANSI Z39.48–1984.

Manufactured in the United States of America

Library of Congress Cataloging-in-Publication Data
McDonnell, Janet A., date.
The dispossession of the American Indian, 1887–1934 / Janet A. McDonnell.
p. cm.
Includes bibliographical references and index.
ISBN 0-253-33628-7 (alk. paper)
1. Indians of North America—Land tenure. 2. Indians of North
America—Government relations. I. Title.
E98.L3M43 1991

333.2—dc20   90-44508
CIP
2 3 4 5 95 94 93 92 91

Contents

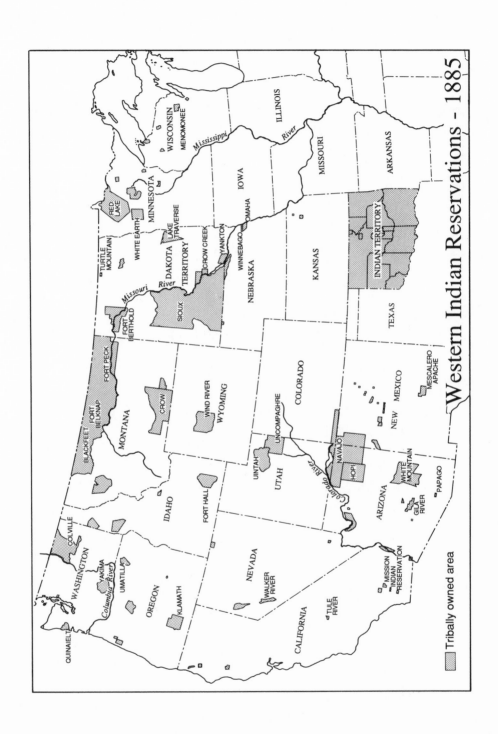

Western Indian Reservations – 1885

Tribally owned area

PREFACE

Land, traditionally the most important issue in Indian-white relations, has been the focus of federal Indian policy. Federal Indian land policy has historically reflected our fundamental assumptions about what Indians should be and do and how they should fit into American society. Each aspect—allotment leases, sales, and fee patents—was part of a general process aimed at "freeing" Indians from government control. I have not attempted to present an exhaustive study of land policy but rather to describe and analyze the formulation, implementation, and effects of certain major aspects of it. Because of the nature of the research materials available, I have focused on the government's administration of land policy rather than the Indian response.

The early twentieth century provides the logical setting for my study. Between the passage of the Dawes Allotment Act in 1887 and the reversal of the allotment policy in the 1934 Indian Reorganization Act, the Indian estate dwindled from 138 to 52 million acres. Historians have noted and lamented the decline, but have not adequately studied or explained the staggering land loss. The questions are perplexing. Why did the Dawes Act fail to create prosperous, independent farmers? Why did Indians become more dependent on the federal government between 1887 and 1934? Who or what was responsible for the shrinkage of the Indian estate during that period? Was federal Indian land policy inherently flawed or simply poorly implemented?

Much has been written about the motives and actions of the reformers and policymakers who drafted and supported the Dawes Act, and there are excellent historical studies of the Dawes Act itself, such as Wilcomb E. Washburn's *The Assault on Indian Tribalism: The General Allotment Act (Dawes Act) of 1887* and D. S. Otis's *The Dawes Act and the Allotment of Indian Lands*. Aside from Otis's book, a straightforward account of the motives of the advocates of allotment and of the effects of the Dawes Act up to 1900, few studies deal with the implementation of the Dawes Act and its impact on Indian landholding.

Just as historians have left an excellent record of the background of the Dawes Act, they have also produced fine studies of Indian affairs in the 1930s, including Graham Taylor's *The New Deal and American Indian Tribalism: The Administration of the Indian Reorganization Act, 1934–1945*, and Kenneth R. Philp's *John Collier's Crusade for Indian Reform, 1920–1954*. Most tribal histories, however, end before the twentieth century or deal with the twentieth century only briefly. Nor do these tribal studies emphasize land issues.

With a few exceptions, historians have failed to study land issues in the period 1887–1934. The most significant study on this topic is J. P. Kinney's *A Continent Lost—A Civilization Won: Indian Land Tenure in America*, but while Kinney provides a valuable compilation of data on land allotment, he offers little analysis or interpretation. In his recent study, *A Final Promise: The*

Campaign to Assimilate Indians, 1880–1920, Frederick E. Hoxie devotes some attention to land issues, but as the title indicates his focus is on assimilation, not land tenure. Leonard A. Carlson's persuasive cliometric study, *Indians, Bureaucrats, and Land: The Dawes Act and the Decline of Indian Farming*, provides ample evidence that allotment benefited whites more than Indians, but it neglects other aspects of land policy. Another scholar, Francis Paul Prucha, devotes one chapter to twentieth century Indian land policy in *The Great Father: The United States Government and the American Indians*.

The period 1887–1934 was marked by the continuation and culmination of the forced assimilation philosophy embodied in the Dawes Act, and the dominant theme was the transfer of Indian lands into white hands. The period was also marked by the development of an extensive bureaucratic structure in the Indian Office to administer the new policies. The major emphasis of my study will be the years after 1900, for it was in the first decade of the twentieth century that the allotment policy peaked. Moreover, the first major leasing legislation was not passed until the 1890s. Not until after 1900 did Congress pass legislation authorizing the sale and promoting the irrigation of Indian land; not until after 1900 did the Indian Office launch its first major effort to promote Indian farming and stockraising. Finally, the practice of issuing fee patents before the trust period provided in the Dawes Act expired did not begin until 1906 and soared to its highest point in the years 1917–1920.

In the first decades of the twentieth century these policies had their greatest impact on reservations in the Northwest and on the Northern Plains, and this was the area of greatest activity. Therefore these regions are the dominant geographical setting for my study; little attention is given to tribes in the East or South. Although tribes in Oklahoma dealt with similar land issues, their circumstances were different. Policymakers treated Oklahoma Indians as special cases, and they were initially exempt from the provisions of the Dawes Act.

Finally, land policy in the early twentieth century is a timely topic, for the Indian land base continues to shrink. The problems of multiple land ownership and the alienation of land through leasing and sales are even more acute today. We must understand the roots of these problems if we are ever to solve them. In a broader sense, the topic tells us much about the tragic effects of forcing one culture on another and about the high cost of "progress."

ACKNOWLEDGMENTS

This is an appropriate time to thank the friends and colleagues who have encouraged and challenged me throughout this project. Lawrence Kelly, Richmond Clow, Martin Ridge, and others whose names I do not know, read various drafts. To these individuals I extend my heartfelt thanks. The manuscript was greatly improved by their keen observations and insights.

I am also grateful for the financial support I received from the graduate school at Marquette University. A series of fellowships and scholarships allowed me to travel to various repositories and devote two years to research and writing. With a fellowship from the National Endowment for the Humanities, I was able to complete the chapter on irrigation.

I would like to thank the staffs of the National Archives and the manuscripts division of the Library of Congress for their assistance. My thanks also to the people of Indiana University Press. They have been efficient, professional, and pleasant. My friend Diane Arms contributed both her time and her considerable skill to produce the index.

My greatest debt is to Paul Prucha. The seed for this project was planted in one of his graduate seminars. Over the years he has read drafts of the manuscript, shared his expertise, offered encouragement, and provided a high standard of professionalism.

ABBREVIATIONS

BIA	Records of the Bureau of Indian Affairs. Record Group 75. National Archives.
BIA-CCF	Central Classified Files. Records of the Bureau of Indian Affairs. Record Group 75. National Archives.
BIC	Records of the Board of Indian Commissioners. Records of the Bureau of Indian Affairs. Record Group 75. National Archives.
BIC Report	*Annual Report of the Board of Indian Commissioners.*
ARCIA	*Annual Report of the Commissioner of Indian Affairs to the Secretary of the Department of Interior.*
IRA Papers	Indian Rights Association Papers. Historical Society of Pennsylvania. Philadelphia (microfilm edition, Glen Rock, N.J.: Microfilming Corporation of America.
IRA Report	*Annual Report of the Executive Committee of the Indian Rights Association.*
SANR	Superintendents' Annual Narrative Reports. Records of the Bureau of Indian Affairs. Record Group 75. National Archives.
SI-CCF	Central Classified Files. Records of the Office of the Secretary of the Interior. Record Group 48. National Archives.
ARSI	*Annual Report of the Secretary of the Interior.*

THE
Dispossession
OF THE
American Indian
1887–1934

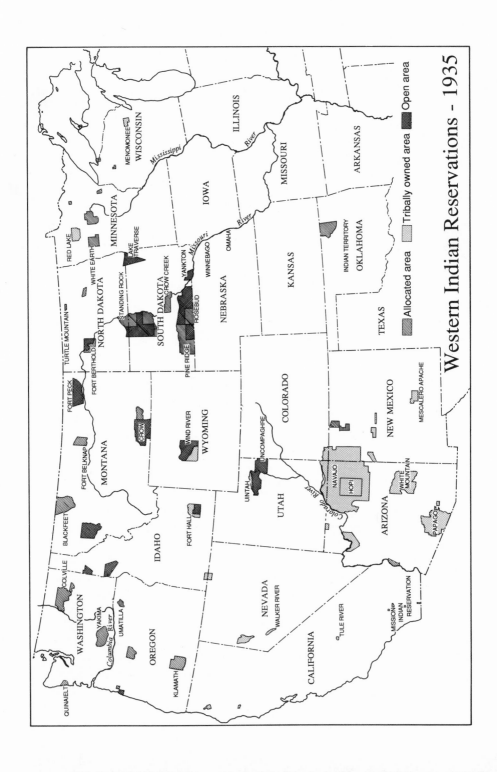

Western Indian Reservations - 1935

Allocated area | Tribally owned area | Open area

Introduction

From the first days of European settlement in North America, Native Americans have retreated as white civilization advanced. In the early nineteenth century, the federal government began removing Indians living in the eastern part of the United States to the region west of the Mississippi River in order to open up Indian land for settlement, to protect the Natives from the corrupting influence of white society, and to promote assimilation. By the 1850s whites were pouring into the trans-Mississippi West, and the federal government adopted a policy of concentrating tribesmen on reservations away from the paths of white migration.

In the late nineteenth century, Americans found that concentrating Indians on reservations had not solved the "Indian problem," the problem of an impoverished, dependent people living in a separate society, and they became increasingly concerned with assimilating the Indians into white society. Reflecting these sentiments, government officials developed policies rooted in two fundamental but erroneous assumptions: that the Indians should give up their tribal existence and become "civilized" and that they should become independent, productive members of white society. Tribal organization was recognized as a defining feature of Native identity, and private ownership of land was seen as a means of civilizing the Indians. By allotting reservation land in severalty policymakers hoped to replace tribal civilization with a white one, protect the Indians from unscrupulous whites, promote progress, and save the federal government money. Native Americans, however, did not view land in the same way as their white neighbors. They did not regard land as real estate to be bought, sold, and developed. Rather, they valued it for the things it produced that sustained life. To Native Americans the land represented existence, identity, and a place of belonging.

Although the roots of allotment extend back to the Colonial period, the Dawes Allotment Act of 1887 was the first comprehensive proposal to replace tribal consciousness with an understanding of the value of private property. The idea was not only to discourage native habits but to encourage Indians to accept the social and economic standards of white society. Americans considered this acceptance essential if the Indians were to survive. Commissioner of Indian Affairs Francis Leupp expressed this Social Darwinist philosophy very well. All primitive peoples, he wrote, were wasteful of their natural resources. As the population of the "civilized" world increased, it was inevitable that the "uncivilized" world would be encroached upon. "Hence the most we can ask of the advanced race is to deal justly with the backward races and give always a fair equivalent for the land it invades."[1]

Historians continue to debate the motives of Leupp and other policymakers. One authority on the Dawes Act, historian D. S. Otis, contends that the leading advocates of allotment were "inspired by the highest motives." Their primary aim, he argues, was to replace tribal culture with white civilization and to protect current landholding. Historian J. P. Kinney is also sympathetic toward policymakers and administrators. He notes that the statements of purposes and policies made by officials were "representative of the sincere aspirations and honest convictions of such officials." Both legislative and executive branches, he concludes, made a concerted effort to protect Indians from land grabbers.[2] Although some of the reformers and legislators who supported the Dawes Act might have been genuinely concerned with protecting Indian interests, evidence indicates that after the Dawes Act was passed pressure from Westerners to open up Indian land increased and lawmakers and administrators became less concerned with protecting Indian landownership than satisfying white land hunger. To understand the allotment policy and its significance, the historian must look beyond motives and rhetoric to the implementation and impact of that policy.

The Dawes Act authorized the president to allot reservation land to individual Indians and specified the amounts of land to be allotted: 160 acres to family heads; 80 acres to each single person over eighteen and each orphan under eighteen; and 40 acres to single persons under eighteen then living or born before the president ordered allotment. After the reservation had been opened, the government could purchase the surplus land and make it available to homesteaders.

Under the act, the government would hold the title to the allotment in trust for twenty-five years to protect the allottee while he learned to use the land and support himself. The law embodied the concept of a trust relationship between the federal government and the Indians that had been evolving since the first days of this nation. Treaties signed in the eighteenth and nineteenth centuries had specified that the federal government would protect Indians in the use and occupancy of the lands they had reserved for themselves. The Dawes Act provided that after an individual selected a piece of tribal land, the government would issue a trust patent which restricted the Indian in the sale and use of that land. At the end of the trust period, when the Indian presumably could support himself and manage his own affairs, the government would replace the trust patent with a fee patent—a deed of unrestricted ownership—and relieve itself of its trust responsibility. Federal officials implemented the Dawes Act with the optimistic faith that Indians could and would adopt white civilization and become prosperous farmers. The logical outcome would be the end of government control over the Indians and the abolition of the Bureau of Indian Affairs. Thus the stated goal of federal Indian

Goal
of
Dawes Act

policy from 1887 to 1934 was to promote the speedy transition of Indians into industrious self-supporting citizens, free from government supervision.

In addition to the goal of promoting assimilation, policymakers were anxious to satisfy white land hunger. After allotting reservation land to individual Indians, the government would be able to open up the surplus land to white settlers. Moreover, when the Indians received unrestricted title to their allotments, they would be able to sell or lease that land to non-Indians. Even the sympathetic Otis concedes that "land seekers and business promoters" exerted strong pressure to open up Indian land and that it was the belief in the efficacy of allotment that made it possible for the government to surrender to these pressures with a clear conscience.[3]

Although the Dawes Act successfully opened up vast acres of surplus land, it did not provide the hoped-for solution to the "Indian problem." Rather, in the early twentieth century disturbed Americans saw that Indians were even more dependent on the federal government and demanded that the federal government relieve itself of its trust responsibility. In a period of accelerating change and growing industrialization and urbanization, the belief was strong that Indians had to surrender to the inexorable force of "progress." As white Americans became less tolerant of people outside the mainstream of society, they demanded that Indians give up their traditional ways and accept the culture and values of the dominant society.

Historian Frederick E. Hoxie argues convincingly that the assimilation campaign consisted of two phases. In the second phase, after 1900, policymakers and administrators continued to use the rhetoric of assimilation but were no longer convinced that Indians could be transformed and achieve complete equality. By the early twentieth century, support for the philosophy of social evolutionism was waning and even the evolutionists themselves concluded that Indians could not advance quickly from one stage of development to another. The complete assimilation envisioned in the late nineteenth century would be neither rapid nor automatic. The allotment and sale of Indian land could now be justified on the grounds that Indians would benefit from an extended period of manual labor under the guidance of white employers.[4]

As disillusionment over the allotment policy grew so did the desire to put Indian land into productive use. The concern that Indians use their land productively was not new. Historian William T. Hagan illustrates that since the seventeenth century, one of the arguments used to justify dispossessing the Indians was that whites would use the land more productively. Since the early days of our nation it had been generally assumed that the needs of whites took precedence over those of the Indians because a prescribed area could support more whites than Indians.[5] As these sentiments grew stronger in the early twentieth century and land resources dwindled, the policy of assimilation shifted to one of exploitation. Congress broke down the safeguard of inalienability surrounding Indian allotments by passing legislation that allowed Indians to lease and sell their allotments during the trust period.

Indians with little training, experience, or credit to buy seeds, implements, and livestock seized the opportunity. The Indian Office emphasized what it called "industrial assistance" to the Indians, which meant introducing better methods of farming, stockraising, and irrigation. Putting the land into productive use became more important than protecting Indian ownership of that land.

Federal Indian land policy was part of a national drive to develop Western water, land, and mineral resources, and the paternalistic attitude of lawmakers and administrators toward Indian land resembled their attitude toward other resources. Indian land policy reflected the two major themes in public land policy in the early twentieth century: development and protection. In this period, Americans became aware that the valuable resources of the West, particularly land, trees, oil, and coal, were diminishing at an alarming pace, while growing industrialization and urbanization increased the demand for them. Westerners, in particular, exerted intense pressure on lawmakers and administrators to allow whites to develop the resources on the public domain and on Indian reservations.[6]

Under President Theodore Roosevelt's conservation policy, the government withdrew valuable land from settlement in order to protect it, but Westerners resented having these resources locked up in untouchable reserves. From 1890 to 1920, the population of the country jumped from 63,000,000 to 106,000,000, a 68-percent increase, prompting settlers to push into the arid and semi-arid regions of the West. As the cost of farmland soared, the "free" land of the public domain and the surplus land on Indian reservations became more appealing. Whites who saw the supply of valuable land shrinking now demanded that Indian land be developed and managed efficiently. It was no longer enough for Indians to accept allotments and surrender the surplus land to whites; they were expected to use their own allotted land profitably or surrender it. Western legislators who took this view gained increasing influence in Congress in the early twentieth century as several new states with large Indian reservations joined the Union.

During the administration of President Woodrow Wilson, policymakers were imbued with the prevailing spirit of optimism, progressivism, and individualism. Thus, they were not only anxious to put Indian land into productive use, but they also believed strongly in the progressive principle that individuals must be forced to "stand on their own two feet." They pushed the Dawes assimilation policy to its extreme limits. During these years, the government completed allotment work on most reservations and moved with alarming speed to "free" the Indians from government control. Humanitarian concerns were all but forgotten as federal officials arbitrarily issued fee patents releasing Indians from guardianship before the twenty-five-year trust period expired and before they were capable of supporting themselves. The Wilson years were a watershed in that the progressive, assimilationist approach to Indian policy reached its peak and would begin to decline.

By 1921 Americans could no longer ignore the disastrous effects of the Wilson administration's policy of removing restrictions on Indian land. Overwhelming evidence indicated that the Indians who received fee patents had become homeless and impoverished. Faced with such tragic evidence federal officials reluctantly conceded that many Indians were ill prepared for complete control over their resources and would have trouble withstanding the pressure to alienate their land. The administrations of Warren G. Harding, Calvin Coolidge, and Herbert Hoover would attempt to reverse the pattern of dispossession set by the Dawes Act. Commissioner of Indian Affairs Charles Burke (1921–29) exercised more caution in issuing fee patents and tried to repair some of the damage caused by his predecessors' liberal policies. Yet Burke continued to work from the same faulty assumption that assimilation was a proper and effective solution to the "Indian problem," and the Indian Office's policy changed little during his tenure. Throughout the 1920s and early 1930s widespread abuse continued in the practice of leasing and selling Indian land, and Indian land continued to fall into white hands at an alarming pace.

During the first decades of the twentieth century, then, legislators and bureaucrats violated their trust responsibility toward their Indian wards by devising what were often flawed policies that jeopardized Indian landholdings and often disregarded Indian rights. Yet even their most enlightened policies were often thwarted by unscrupulous, land-hungry whites. Field officials were often unwilling or unable to implement the established policies fairly and protect the Indians in their landownership. The maladministration of Indian lands by federal officials was a major factor contributing to the disintegration of the Indian estate.

1.

Allotment

The Land Divided

During the first decades of the twentieth century, the assimilation policy embodied in the Dawes Act was pushed to its extreme limit as the government allotted tribal land at an unprecedented rate. Policymakers and administrators in the legislative and executive branches were primarily concerned that allotment work continue unimpeded and thus did little to ensure that allotments were made in a fair and humane manner. Although Indian Office officials sometimes tried to protect Indian interests, more often they submitted to pressure from whites who wanted to acquire Indian land and as a result violated the intent of the Dawes Act by allotting land that was not suitable for farming, land upon which Indians could not possibly succeed as farmers or stockraisers. As the demand for homesteads grew, so did the demand that these officials allot valuable mineral and timber lands on the reservations and open up the surplus to whites. Government officials concluded that it was more important to exploit the Indians' land, mineral, and timber resources quickly and to satisfy white land hunger than to fulfill their trust responsibility by helping Indians become independent, self-supporting farmers and stockraisers.

Every commissioner of Indian affairs who served between 1887 and 1934 endorsed the goal of self-sufficiency and maintained that allotment was the first step toward making the Indians self-supporting, industrious citizens. Thomas J. Morgan (1889–1893), a Baptist minister and educator, called for complete assimilation and the breakup of the tribal system and enthusiastically endorsed the Dawes Act. William Jones (1897–1904), a banker turned politician, contended that Indians had to become useful, self-supporting members of society. Because they lacked the training and ability to compete with whites in commerce and industrial arts, most had to become farmers, stockraisers, and laborers. Jones believed that the allotment system was the "solution of the Indian problem" and called the Dawes Act "a mighty pulverizing engine for breaking up the tribal mass." By establishing individual homesteads it fostered in the Indian a regard for family, he reasoned, and by making each allottee a citizen it sought to replace tribal allegiance with allegiance to the federal government.[1]

Jones's successor, Francis E. Leupp (1905–1909), was a former journalist and civil service reformer with a long commitment to Indian affairs and to the progressive principles of efficiency and economy. He believed that Indians should be taught to work and that reservations should disappear, but was convinced that this could only happen gradually. The government would have to slow the allotment process and continue its wardship responsibilities for another decade or generation.[2] "Moreover, as fast as an Indian of either mixed or full blood is capable of taking care of himself," he argued, "it is our duty to set him upon his feet or sever forever the ties which bind him either to his tribe, in the commercial sense, or to the government. . . . Each Indian must be recognized as an individual and so treated, just as each white man is." The government needed to protect the Indian's property after allotment but as he became self-supporting he should be set "fully free."[3]

Leupp was succeeded by a Harvard-educated reformer, Robert Valentine (1909–1912), who also believed that allotment was the best means of promoting self-support. Although he conceded that not all Indians should become farmers, it was "the best chance of the majority."[4] In 1913 Commissioner Cato Sells (1913–1921), a former Texas banker, warned that the speedy completion of allotment work was the only chance for 70 percent of the Indians to become self-supporting.[5]

After 1887, the Indian Office conducted allotment work under the authority of the Dawes Act, which authorized the president to allot reservation land to individual tribal members. It also allotted reservation land under special acts of Congress applying to specific reservations. Initially the Indian Office used these special acts because under the Dawes Act the land could not always be divided properly or the surplus disposed of to the Indians' advantage. Each allotment bill differed in content depending on the needs and demands of neighboring whites, but if it followed the general guidelines of the Dawes Act and promoted assimilation, it met the government's requirements. When the white community of western Montana proposed legislation opening the Flathead reservation, the Indian Office modified their bill only slightly. The Crow and Flathead allotment bills differed because they were shaped by the different demands of the Billings and Missoula whites.[6]

The procedure for making allotments was time-consuming and complex. First, the General Land Office conducted a detailed survey paid for with money transferred from the Indian Office's appropriations which the Indians were theoretically to repay. After completing the survey, the government prepared a roll of all Indians entitled to allotments, as prescribed by the secretary of the interior.[7] Special allotting agents, appointed by the president, prepared the allotment schedules and directed the allotting process. The Indian Office sometimes employed surveyors to locate allotment boundaries. Usually the Indian selected his own tract of farming or grazing land; the head of a family chose land for his minor children; and the allotting agent or superintendent selected land for orphans. The allotting agent was to encourage Indians to select the best land on the reservation for themselves, and if any Indian had already occupied or improved it, the agent usually recognized his right to that land. After the agent marked the tracts, he forwarded to the Indian Office schedules with the name, age, sex, and family relationship of each allottee, and a description of the allotment.[8]

Under the procedure laid out in the Dawes Act and other allotment legislation, between 1887 and 1900 the government assigned 32,800 allotments, or 3,285,000 acres, and tribes sold or ceded 28,500,000 acres of surplus reservation land after allotment. The government reduced Indian holdings by half. The bulk of the allotment work occurred in areas of rapid white settlement. The Indian Office made large numbers of allotments in Oregon, Washington, Nebraska, and Idaho between 1887 and 1900. White settlement was so rapid in the Northwest and on the Plains that in 1890 Idaho, Montana, North Dakota, South Dakota, Washington, and Wyoming became states. In 1900 the largest number of allotments approved were on the Colville reservation in Washington, Fort Berthold in North Dakota, Klamath in Oregon, Rosebud, South Dakota, and Yakima, Washington.[9]

From 1900 to 1921 the government assigned 85,860 allotments, or 14,300,000 acres, and sold 20,000,000 acres of tribal land. The bulk of the allotment work during this period occurred between 1900 and 1910, principally on reservations in Oklahoma, Montana, the Dakotas, Minnesota, Wyoming, Idaho, Washington, Oregon, and northern California. By 1911, roughly two-thirds of all Indians had received their allotments.[10]

By 1913 when President Woodrow Wilson took office, a large percentage of the allotment work was completed. The government had spent $4,500,000 to allot 34,000,000 acres, an area a third larger than the state of Texas, to 180,000 Indians, leaving 39,000,000 acres for allotment to 120,000 more. Commissioner Sells cheerfully remarked that reservations as Americans knew them were disappearing as Indians took their places on homesteads and allotments and were trying to make a living. As the allotment work declined, so did the congressional appropriations for that work, from $250,000 in 1913 to $50,000 in 1919. Sells, however, refused to break up the large reservations in the arid Southwest because tribes such as the Navajo had to live communally to survive. These nomadic herdsmen who followed the grass and rain could not exist on 80 or even 320 acres.[11]

When President Warren G. Harding took the oath of office on a clear, crisp day in March 1921, a new era began in American politics and in Indian affairs. This distinguished-looking, affable man was determined to do whatever he could to promote business interests in the country and to encourage the development of natural resources. Rather than safeguarding the public trust, the Harding administration opened up some of the nation's most valuable oil reserves to exploitation, including the Teapot Dome oil reserve in California.[12] Harding's commissioner of Indian affairs was Charles Burke (1921–1929) from South Dakota, a practical politician with "the round, hard eyes, and the square jaw and lip smile of a fighter." Burke had been a member of the House of Representatives from 1899 to 1906 and 1909 to 1915 and had gained valuable experience in Indian affairs while serving on the House Indian Affairs Com-

Commissioner of Indian Affairs Charles Burke.
Credit National Archives (photo no. 75-BK-23).

mittee. After an unsuccessful bid for the Senate in 1915, he had returned to his real estate business in Pierre, South Dakota. Reformers were generally pleased with his appointment because of his "experience and pleasant temperament."[13]

Like his predecessors, Burke wanted to promote Indian self-support and assimilation by allotting tribal land. He believed that Indians who had their own tracts of land would cast off their old communal traits and customs, become independent, and embrace white civilization, a process necessary for their survival. Although certain native traits and customs should be honored and perpetuated, Burke argued, "it is not desirable or consistent with the general welfare to promote his tribal characteristics and organization." Only after tribal relations were dissolved could the Indians be assimilated.[14]

By 1921 the era of large scale allotment work was drawing to a close. Farm prices had declined, and much of the remaining reservation land was worthless for agricultural purposes. The Indian Office had completed most of the allotment work except for that involving children who had been born since the original allotment rolls closed on their reservation and who were entitled to allotments. Such was the case on the Crow and Cheyenne River reservations. In the 1920s field service employees and some Indians demanded that unallotted reservation lands be allotted to children born since the previous allotment work was done. As a result, Congress passed legislation in the 1920s under which the government allotted several million acres on the Fort Peck, Fort Berthold, Flathead, Crow, Fort Belknap, Northern Cheyenne, Cheyenne River, Lower Brule, Blackfeet, Umatilla, and Wind River reservations. By 1929, the government had allotted roughly 40,000,000 acres to 207,000 Indians, and about 35,000,000 acres remained to be allotted to 118,000 Indians.[15]

Burke's successor, Charles J. Rhoads (1929–1933), a devout Quaker and former president of the Indian Rights Association, called for the continued individualization of Indian land as a means of making Indians self-supporting. Thus the Indian Office's stated goal of individual land ownership remained firmly fixed even though little reservation land was left for allotment purposes. By 1934, the government had allotted 118 out of 213 reservations and brought over three-fourths of the Indians under the provisions of the Dawes Act. Eighty-two percent of the allotted acreage was in Montana, South Dakota, North Dakota, Oklahoma, and New Mexico.[16]

Most allotment work under the Dawes Act concerned land that the Indian Office considered suitable for farming. When the land was more valuable for mining than for farming, the issue became more complicated. Initially the Indian Office did not allow the Indians to select tracts with mineral deposits or timber for their allotments; rather this land went into the public domain to be reserved for exploitation by whites. As good farming and grazing land became scarce, however, non-Indian mining interests pressured Congress and the Indian Office to allot reservation land containing rich mineral reserves. The demand for mineral land, on and off the reservations, increased dramatically in the early twentieth century as the nation continued its industrial growth, and thus the allotment of mineral land became one of the most controversial aspects of Indian land policy. Although the Dawes Act clearly specified that the government allot only land classified for farming or grazing in order to create self-sufficient farmers, allotting agents began assigning land that was unsuitable for either of these purposes. Government officials allotted mineral land to individuals in order to open up surplus land to whites who were anxious to exploit the mineral wealth. Clearly the primary goal was not to create self-sufficient farmers but rather to exploit the rich mineral resources.

Congress authorized the allotment of valuable mineral lands on the Fort Peck reservation and opened the surplus to whites. Indian Office officials allotted Fort Peck under a 1908 act only to discover that the reservation contained valuable coal deposits. The 1908 act specifically named grazing, timber, and irrigable classes of land, which indicated that Congress did not intend to allot surplus mineral land but rather wanted to dispose of it in a way that would benefit all of the Fort Peck Indians. The presidential proclamation of July 15, 1913, opened surplus land on Fort Peck to homesteaders. When the

Indians saw white homesteaders greedily snatching up their land, they demanded that the government assign allotments to children born since the original allotment roll was closed in 1911. In 1914, when Congress authorized the allotment of surplus land to these children, the controversy over allotting coal land developed.[17]

Although the Indian Office generally supported the practice of withholding coal land from allotment, in this case it favored allotting coal land to those Fort Peck children as long as the coal deposits were reserved for the benefit of the tribe as a whole. Thus, it sought legislation authorizing the disposal of the underlying mineral deposits separately from the surface land. In 1919 Congress agreed to allow the Fort Peck Indians to select coal lands with mineral rights reserved to the federal government, not the tribe, which put the Indians on equal footing with whites who were legally allowed to select coal lands as homesteads.[18]

Beginning in 1922, eligible Indians received allotments either on the lands opened by the 1913 proclamation that were still vacant or on the coal lands opened in 1917 that were vacant and could be used for farming or grazing with the coal deposits reserved for the tribe.[19]

A similar situation developed on the Blackfeet reservation where Congress authorized allotment in 1907 before realizing that the reservation land contained valuable minerals. When the Interior Department uncovered valuable oil and gas deposits on part of the reservation in 1917, it reclassified those tracts as mineral land. What then was the Interior Department to do about the allottees who had already selected the tracts involved? Should it reject those selections or let them stand? The Interior Department solicitor concluded that the government had no legal authority to withhold lands from allotment or to refuse to approve allotment selections on land with valuable minerals because Congress had not intended to withhold mineral land from allotment when it passed the 1907 law. In 1919 Congress authorized the secretary of the interior to allot the mineral land on the Blackfeet reservation.[20]

Allotting reservation land containing valuable timber resources became as controversial as allotting land with mineral deposits. In the social and political climate of the 1920s, which favored the development rather than the preservation of natural resources, both the Harding and Coolidge administrations came under pressure to allot Indian timber land and open the surplus to whites. Lands classified as more valuable for timber than for farming and grazing could not be allotted under the current regulations and laws. Although the authors of the Dawes Act clearly intended that allotments be suitable for homesites, some Indians selected heavily timbered lands that were wholly unfit for farming. If the timber was later cut, they could not make a living off the land. The Indian Office tried to protect Indian interests by refusing to allot valuable timber land, but sometimes Congress and the courts made the protection of Indian rights impossible.

Indians who were anxious to gain control of valuable timber land challenged the Indian Office's policy of withholding this land from allotment. The

Indian Office discontinued allotment work on the Quinaielt reservation in Washington in 1910 because there was no farming or grazing land left, only timber land, and the Dawes Act specifically authorized the allotment of farming and grazing land. Indian Office officials argued that Congress had not intended to protect the rights of the individual at the expense of the tribe as a whole. Rather, the government should sell the timber for the benefit of the whole tribe, reclassify the land for farming or grazing after the timber was removed, and make it available for allotment. Indians on the reservation who had not yet received allotments were outraged by this plan. Thomas Payne, a member of the Quileute tribe, filed suit to force the secretary of the interior to allot him an eighty-acre tract containing valuable timber resources. To make matters worse, Payne's selection, located just one mile from the estuary of the Raft River, would interfere with the sale of timber on the surrounding land.[21]

The district court decision in Payne's favor was a complete reversal of the Indian Office's long-standing policy and practice. Commissioner Burke feared that the Payne decision would not only destroy the tribe's timber operation but also serve as a dangerous precedent on other reservations, preventing timber land from being distributed equitably. At his urging the Interior Department appealed the case, only to face defeat a second time. On April 7, 1924, the Supreme Court upheld the district court decision and forced the Indian Office to allot the land to all eligible Indians on the Quinaielt reservation regardless of the value of the timber.[22] As a result valuable timber lands fell into private hands. Instead of the equal distribution of the income from the timber that would have been possible if the tribe had retained ownership, a great disparity developed in the value of individual holdings.

Meanwhile Indians on the Klamath reservation also challenged the allotment policy. If heavily timbered land would have been suitable for farming once the timber was removed, allotment of the land might have been somewhat justified, but this was not the case on most reservations, especially Klamath. The Klamath reservation in southern Oregon stretched over a million acres of mountainous land, much of it blanketed with virgin yellow pine. Local whites who were anxious to acquire surplus timber land in this lush area pressured Congress for legislation authorizing allotment even though the local superintendent warned that allotment would cause "great loss and injustice." He predicted that once the timber was removed from the land, an allotment would be virtually worthless, and the Indian owner would not be able to earn enough off it to pay the high taxes. The superintendent had the support of the Board of Indian Commissioners, a small body created by Congress in 1869 to offer advice on Indian affairs, which opposed the allotment of timber lands because it believed the allottees would sell the timber to the first bidder who offered them cash. "They will sell their birthright for a mess of pottage," one board member warned, "and eat the pottage as soon as can be." Sadly, the issue created divisions among the Indians themselves. Many of them believed allotting timber lands would be unwise and unjust, so they asked the government to advance $2,000,000 to the tribe in lieu of such allotments to be repaid from the proceeds of the timber sales. Other Indians whose children had not received allotments demanded that the government approve their selections of timber land.[23]

President Harding's secretary of interior, Albert B. Fall, sided with the superintendent and opposed allotting timber lands on the Klamath reservation. Fall had worked in the Southwest as a bookkeeper, cowboy, merchant, miner, timberman, and foreman, and had served as a territorial supreme court justice and attorney general. Some Indians and reformers had vigorously opposed his appointment as interior secretary because he had demonstrated little concern for Indian interests while in the Senate. Fall sympathized with mining and ranching interests and favored the rapid development of Indian natural resources. He reiterated that the Interior Department's official policy was to arrange for the sale of the timber and allow the proceeds to accrue to the benefit of the tribe as a whole. The proposed legislation would, Fall warned, "completely disrupt our long established policy in the matter" and would set a precedent that land with valuable timber had to be allotted. The department's policy, he contended, was more beneficial to the Indians and more equitable.

Faced with such strong opposition from the Interior Department, the Indian Office, and some Indians, Congress rejected the legislation. After the unsuccessful attempts to acquire forested allotments through special legislation in 1927 twenty-nine Klamath Indians filed suit to force the Interior Department to allot them tracts of valuable pine timber lands. The court upheld the government's position in six cases and dismissed the rest, an outcome different than in the Quinaielt case.[24]

Meanwhile Congress authorized the allotment of valuable timber land on the Flathead reservation for children born on the reservation since the original allotments were made. To comply the Indian Office had to allot timber lands, reserving the timber for the benefit of the tribe. This situation, where the children owned the land and the tribe owned the timber, made conflicts and confusion inevitable.[25]

While Congress and the courts struggled with the sensitive problem of allotting mineral and timber land on the reservations, Indians had moved onto nonreservation land belonging to the federal government, the public domain. Threatened with white encroachment, they sought to protect their land holdings by having the federal government formally allot the land to them and issue trust patents. Although Commissioner Sells tried to fulfill his trust responsibility by defending the right of the Indians to receive allotments on the public domain and tried to make it easier for them to do so, he faced strong pressure from whites who for selfish reasons were anxious to keep such Indians from acquiring title to their land.

An Indian could take public domain land in two ways. First, under the act of March 3, 1875, and the 1884 Indian Homestead Law, family heads and single persons over twenty-one who had severed their tribal ties could take homesteads on the public domain under the same regulations as whites without paying the stipulated fees. Second, under section four of the Dawes Act as amended in 1891, any Indian family head or single person over eighteen who was legally entitled to an allotment and who settled vacant public land could have that land allotted and in the same amount.[26] Even Indians who already had allotments could take homesteads provided their reservation allotments were less than 160 acres. Nor did the Indians have to be citizens under the 1884 Indian Homestead Law. Federal policy concerning public domain lands was further refined in the omnibus act of June 25, 1910, which limited public domain allotments to those Indians who were recognized tribal members and who were entitled to allotments on their own reservations if they were available. It also provided that the public domain allotments be made to parents and their minor children in the same manner as reservation allotments.[27]

Although the general provisions for taking allotments on the public domain seemed fairly liberal, the actual procedure proved to be time-consuming and confusing. The Dawes Act did not specify how long applicants had to live on the public domain allotments or what improvements they had to make, but in 1910 the Interior Department decided that the existing rules and regulations governing white settlers on public lands applied to Indians as well. Sells argued, however, that the same standard of continuous settlement should not apply to Indians as to whites because the Indian owner might have to travel for months out of the year to find food for his stock. Each case should be decided on its own merits.[28]

Under Sells's direction in 1914 Indian Office staff investigated the procedures for allotting public domain land and the way in which Indians used the land in order to determine what the requirements for granting allotments should be.[29] The Interior Department approved new regulations on April 15, 1918, which required an Indian who wanted an allotment on the public domain under section four of the Dawes Act to obtain a certificate from the commissioner of Indian affairs indicating that he was entitled to such a land grant. Upon presenting the application to the land office in the district where the land was located, he received a "certificate of allotment." He could claim up to 40 acres of irrigable land, 80 acres of nonirrigable agricultural land, or 160 acres of nonirrigable grazing land as long as that claim was based on the reasonable use or occupancy of that land. Most of the public domain allotments went to Mission Indians in California, Turtle Mountain Indians in North Dakota, and Navajos in New Mexico and Arizona.[30]

The debate over whether or not to allot the public domain intensified when it concerned the arid public lands in New Mexico and Arizona. Many Indians in those states, finding the cramped treaty reservations too small to meet their needs, poured onto public land to find adequate water and grazing areas. By 1913 whites threatened their lands, and if the government did not officially allot the lands to the Indians, they would lose them. Again the Indian Office struggled to uphold its trust responsibility by defending the right of these landless Indians to allotments on the public domain, but strong opposition from local white interests forced it to compromise.

In 1913 Albert Fall, then a senator from New Mexico, introduced an amendment to the Indian appropriation bill for 1914 to stop the allotment of public land in New Mexico and Arizona. After hearing persuasive evidence from Fall and the Indian Office concerning the complaints of local whites, the Senate Committee on Indian Affairs recommended that the government discontinue allotment work in New Mexico and Arizona pending an investigation.[31] In its final form, the Indian appropriation bill for 1914 stipulated that none of the appropriation could be used for assigning land on the public domain to any Indian within the states of New Mexico and Arizona.[32]

The Indian Rights Association, an organization established in 1882 by Herbert Welsh to promote Indian reform, condemned the amendment and demanded that the government protect the Indians on the public domain by giving them allotments as soon as possible. "We cannot conceive of any other course to pursue," S. M. Brosius wrote, "if the government fulfills its promises to these dependent people. And we believe that these promises made in faith will be carried out when the heart of the people is reached."[33] Of the 28,000 Navajos who occupied an area approximately 100 by 300 miles, from the Grand Canyon in the west to Pueblo Bonito, New Mexico, in the east, one-third lived on the public domain. Although the Navajos could graze successfully only 20 sheep on each 160-acre tract, their herds ranged in size from 300 to 2,000 head; so they desperately needed access to the public lands for grazing. To suspend allotment there, Brosius warned, could cripple them economically and would cause overcrowding on the reservation.[34]

When the Fall amendment came up again the next year, the Indian Office agreed to compromise with Fall by assigning the public lands in New Mexico and Arizona only to those Indians who had been living there before June 30, 1913. The Indian Office reasoned that all the Indians who were entitled to allotments on the public domain already lived there and their interests could be protected under this compromise agreement. The rest of the Indians could be cared for on existing reservations. The agreement in effect reversed previous Indian Office policy and left many Navajos landless.[35] By 1918 the Indian Office had approved only 618 of the 2,410 Navajo applications for allotment. Commissioner Sells pleaded with Congress for funds to buy land around Crownpoint, New Mexico, for the Navajos. With the $100,000 he received, he bought 12,000 acres, not nearly enough for 4,000 to 6,000 Indians.[36]

Recognition of the right to public domain land was as critical for the Papagos as it was for the Navajo Indians. Papagos who had settled on the public land in Arizona were threatened with white encroachment. Sells and other concerned individuals urged the president to create special reservations by executive order to protect the Papago land holdings. Treaty reservations were established through an agreement between Congress and the Indians. Executive order reservations, however, were created unilaterally by the president, when he withdrew lands from the public domain for the exclusive use and occupancy of the Indians. The title to treaty reservations was clearly vested in the Indians, but title to executive order reservations was cloudy. In 1914 superintendents H. J. McQuigg and Frank A. Thackery reported on the need for executive order reservations to protect the Papagos, who were living on the public domain in Pima, Pinal, and Maricopa counties in Arizona. These Indians, who depended on the cattle industry for their livelihood, needed at least fifty acres of range land for each head of stock, so any proposed reservation would have to be of adequate size.[37]

The Papagos were confused and angry about their situation. The Papago Indian League pleaded with the Indian Office to set aside the land where they were currently living as an executive order reservation.[38] In 1915 the Papagos requested that the president create such an executive order reservation because white intruders were threatening their cattle industry. After examining a report that verified the findings of McQuigg and Thackery, Sells decided to support the Papagos' request and to visit them to discuss the matter.[39] Meanwhile, McQuigg warned Sells that as Pima land became more valuable with the advent of the railroad and the arrival of more farmers, conflicts would surely erupt. If some of the land was left open, white cattlemen might run their cattle on it to the detriment of the Indians who were just starting their livestock industry.[40]

The Papagos received support not only from within the Indian Office, but also from reform groups. The Board of Indian Commissioners also supported the creation of several executive order reservations for the Papagos. These reservations, it argued, should contain land adjacent to villages, which were needed for farming and grazing purposes and as sources of water for irrigation. If the government did not create a reservation, the board warned, the Papagos would become homeless vagrants.[41]

Reformers clamored so loudly that Sells felt compelled to respond. In 1915 he met with a group of reformers, self-called "Friends of the Indians," who met each year at a resort hotel on Lake Mohonk in New York to hear speakers on various subjects of concern and to discuss Indian reform. In an emotional speech to the conference, Sells poignantly described his recent visit to the Papagos in southern Arizona. No white, he told his hushed audience, could survive under the conditions existing there, and the Indians deserved the government's help. "Nothing affecting any tribe of Indians has aroused my sympathy more," he added, "and I want to assure you that the best efforts of which I am capable will be exerted to permanently establish these Indians in the Papago country."[42]

President Wilson finally responded to the pleas of the Papagos with the executive orders of January 1, 1916, and February 1, 1917, which set aside permanent reservations for their use. The Indian Rights Association congratulated Sells for persuading Wilson to set aside 3,700,000 acres for these Indians.[43] The executive orders, however, angered some whites. When the Tucson Chamber of Commerce tried to get the orders revoked, a hearing ensued in Secretary Lane's office at which Sells skillfully used his firsthand knowledge of the situation to defend the orders.[44]

Despite Sells's victory in the Papago case, opposition from Westerners was so great that Congress blocked the creation of any more executive order reservations. An item in the Indian appropriation act of May 25, 1918, prohibited the president from creating any more executive order reservations in New Mexico and Arizona. The Indian appropriation act of June 30, 1919, extended this prohibition to all the states.[45]

Although Congress resolved the issue of creating executive order reservations in 1919, the controversy about allotting public lands continued. During the 1920s the Indians continued to demand public domain allotments, but Westerners anxious to develop the public lands resisted. In 1928 the Indian Office revised the 1918 regulations governing public domain allotments. They now required proof of tribal membership and the issuance of "certificates of allotment." The government would reject all applications unless they clearly indicated "reasonable use and occupancy" of the land involved and would withhold trust patents for two years so that the applicant could demonstrate his good faith and intentions. Regulations continued to limit the size of public domain allotments to 40 acres of irrigable land, 80 acres of nonirrigable farming land, and 160 acres of nonirrigable grazing land. One new provision stipulated that where an Indian woman was married to a white man or some other person not entitled to an allotment, her right to an allotment on the public domain would be determined not by blood quantum but by whether she was a tribal member or entitled to be one.[46]

The controversy continued to plague the Indian Office during the 1920s, which did little to protect the Indians. Navajos on the public domain in New Mexico and Arizona who had developed some water resources and were raising cattle complained that white ranchers invaded on their land, used their water, and killed their cattle. The 160-acre public domain allotments were, as Hugh Scott of the Board of Indian Commissioners sadly observed, "only a source of trouble."[47]

White cattlemen were anxious to push approximately four thousand Navajos off their allotments and back onto the reservation so that they could use the public domain land themselves. They opposed the government's attempt to lease and purchase public lands with the $100,000 Congress had appropriated in 1921, though they occupied little of the land and the Indians had traditionally used it. The New Mexico Cattle and Horse Growers' Association pushed a bill in Congress that would permit whites to lease at one cent an acre public land which could not be irrigated; if it were enacted, four thousand Navajos in New Mexico as well as several thousand more in Arizona would suffer. A few whites would get control of the range, driving the Indians back on their allotments to starve. "Is it right," asked the Navajo superintendent, "to let the white men have this country just because they are asking for it and trying in every way to get it, regardless of what the Indians may say?" In a chilling warning he said that if nothing was done, "there may be an uprising of the Indians and this will mean that some Indians and whites are going to get killed." White stockmen continued to pressure the government to force the Navajos off the public lands in New Mexico and Arizona.[48]

The Rhoads-Scattergood administration continued to allot land on the public domain, but in small amounts. In 1931 there were 345 allotments on the public domain (54,654 acres) and in 1932 only 1,042 allotments (208,817 acres).[49]

Although the primary justification for allotment was the claim that Indians would become self-supporting farmers, government officials allotted land that was valuable only for its mineral and timber resources, not for farming. The Indian commissioners tried to protect Indian interests with timber land and public land but they were thwarted by the courts, by Congress, and by pressure from local whites. The allotment policy, based on biased and unrealistic assumptions, broke down in implementation.

2.
Allotment
Policy Implementation

Allotment activity on treaty reservations and on the public domain continued at a rapid pace in the first decades of the twentieth century. Unfortunately, Indian Office administrators and the field service failed to implement the allotment policy in a fair, cautious, and efficient manner so as to protect Indian interests. Indeed, their shoddy implementation leads one to question their commitment to Indian self-support. Indian Office officials in Washington and in the field violated the intent of the Dawes Act by failing to insure that Indians received adequate irrigable land of good quality so that they could succeed as farmers or stockraisers. The Fond du Lac and Crow reservations did not contain enough land for all the Indians who were entitled to allotments. Similar land shortages on the Shoshone reservation in Wyoming meant that many Indians who were entitled to 160 acres received only 80, and the allotments were often arid and worthless.

On the Papago reservation, where land without water for irrigation was almost worthless except in large tracts, the Indian Office allotted each Indian only 10 acres of irrigable land. On the Fort Hall and Colorado River reservations too the Indian Office allotted land that was worthless without water. The only land available on the Yakima reservation in Washington for assignment to newly enrolled applicants and to the children of the allottees was in the "Bug infested area," which was rough, rocky land wholly unsuitable for farming and barely tolerable for grazing. On the Pine Ridge reservation, the only land left to allot to the 200 to 250 children born each year was in the Bad Lands, an area "worthless except for scenery." When this parched land ran out, some Indians would go without allotments.[1]

The allotting agents were sometimes directly responsible for the poor quality of some allotments. Although they were obligated to provide each Indian with irrigable, usable land, the land assigned was often of poor quality. Negligent agents assigned land to California Indians that was completely useless. Allotments at the Fort Duchesne reservation in Utah were made hurriedly and haphazardly. Although the land on the reservation was unusable without water, agents made selections on elevated land that could never be irrigated, and they carved allotments on islands in the Duchesne River, which were submerged at flood times and on land so rocky as to be worthless.

Sells conceded that allotments existed where Indians would starve to death and where no whites could be induced to settle, in regions where "one hundred acres would not feed a rabbit," as he observed. Yet whites branded the Indian who did not succeed on this land a failure.[2]

Allotting agents on the Fort McDowell reservation were careless about classifying the land that they allotted. On the Colorado River reservation, agents kept such poor records that many recent selections were "blanketed over" previous allotments. On some reservations agents paid so little attention to the physical conditions that only two to five acres out of every ten allotted could actually be farmed. They made no allowances for main canals, roads, sand dunes, and other physical handicaps. One allotment was situated with half of the land on a sloping mesa wall, at a forty-five-degree angle; another was in the bed of the Colorado River; a third was two miles below the last irrigation ditch.[3]

Some allotting agents were lazy, sloppy, and even corrupt. On the Taholah reservation, they assigned allotments to unqualified persons; 20 percent of the names on the rolls did not belong there. Indians on the Papago reservation complained that officials did everything possible to intimidate them and force them to take allotments, while Pine Ridge Sioux Indians worried about allotting crews who were drunk on the job.[4]

The allotting agent on the Yankton reservation, Henry E. West, assigned allotments on the poorest, hilliest part of the reservation and allotted land to persons without legitimate claims. The Indians were angered by his preferential treatment of the wives and children of "squaw men." Indians on the Yankton reservation were limited to 160 acres for each family head, but some of the women who were married to non-Indians received 320 acres. The Indians also protested that another allotting agent, James E. Hatchett, refused to recognize the claims of Indians to land that they had lived on for years.[5]

It took the allotting agent on the Klamath reservation, Hiram F. White, two years to submit his first allotment schedule, one riddled with inaccuracies. White rarely went into the field, leaving that work to the surveyor. Moreover, he managed his records poorly and left his paperwork uncompleted. In two years he had not scheduled a single allotment. The Indians complained that he assigned valuable tracts of heavily timbered land to those with the least Indian blood. Upon investigation, Indian Office inspector Charles L. Davis conceded that White "must be regarded as quite incompetent for the work he is doing, the most so of any allotting agent I have ever met."[6]

Allotment work on the Yakima reservation suffered because the allotting agent, M. F. Nourse, used slow and expensive methods. Lack of cooperation between Nourse and the agency and several time-consuming surveys also impeded the work. This inexperienced agent spent four months of his two-year tenure in assignments not directly related to allotment. After he failed to meet the deadline for completing the work, Sells dismissed him from the Indian Service.[7]

Although Nourse was apparently guilty of only negligence and laziness, other agents were clearly corrupt. Finch R. Archer, an allotting agent on the Quinaielt reservation, employed John Mitchell as a boatman, laborer, cook, packer, and in other capacities from 1911 to 1912 and paid him with government funds. During this time, Mitchell performed no work for the government; instead he looked after livestock on Archer's ranch. Like Nourse, Archer neglected his work, spending no more than eight days a month at it until Sells fired him. In another instance, the government brought charges against Agent John F. Armstrong for canceling allotments for a fee of $100 and for pretending to have the power to approve allotments while he was on furlough. Moreover, for a month before being furloughed, he spent most of his time at a local land office to find out which Indian allotments would be canceled and then tried to sell that information. In response to the charge that he canceled allotment entries for $100 each, Armstrong replied that this was the usual fee charged to do all the work involved. He claimed that the only information he had been "offering for sale" was his own knowledge of the land laws, decisions, and procedures in contested cases, some of which he had obtained while working for the Indian Office. He contended that he had the right to continue practicing his profession because he received no salary while on furlough and needed the income. Convinced that Armstrong sincerely believed that he had the right to practice his profession while on furlough, Sells agreed to drop the charges against him if he resigned immediately.[8]

Indian Office officials can be faulted for failing to supervise allotting agents effectively or to deal with the problems of laziness and corruption. Indeed, supervision of the agents was minimal; the system provided for few controls over them. Each agent had to submit a monthly report showing the number of acres allotted, the number of Indians receiving this acreage, the amount of money spent, and the number of Indians left to receive allotments. Unless the Indian Office sent a supervisor or special agent to oversee their work, it had no way of knowing what the agents were doing except through these reports. It would be naive to assume that they were all completely accurate and objective. The agents, some with no previous experience, were political appointees rather than part of the civil service system, so they tended to nurse their jobs to extend their employment.[9] The fact that they were political appointees as well as their physical distance from Washington no doubt also made them more sensitive to pressure from local whites.

Some members of Congress recognized this problem. At a Senate hearing in 1914 Senator Harry Lane conceded that most allotting agents performed badly because they were appointed through political influence. Assistant Commissioner Meritt acknowledged that the Indian Office had some problems with its agents and that some of them knew nothing about the work when they were appointed, but he quickly assured the committee that the Indian Office was gradually weeding out the poor agents and the rest were doing better work.[10]

Given the poor quality both of some allotments and some allotting agents, Indian resistance was inevitable. The Red Lake Indians in Minnesota angrily protested the allotment of their land. No doubt expressing the fears of many Indians, they wrote, "We have seen the White Earth Reservation despoiled, the Indians cheated and defrauded of their lands, and both the old and young men, and even women, debased and degraded by the use of whiskey." They feared that the same thing would happen to them if their reservation was carved up. "Our land is sacred to us," they explained; "we want to keep it till we die for our children and their children." Having already surrendered three million acres to whites, they clung tenaciously to the little land that remained. On the Yuma reservation the agent jailed nine old men who refused to accept their allotments and threatened others who resisted with the same punishment. "We have never wanted allotments," a delegation of Yuma Indians sadly complained, "and all our troubles have come since we had it." When allotting agent James E. Hatchett arrived at the Yankton agency he was met with resistance. Tribal officials ordered him to leave.[11]

In 1903 allotting agent William A. Winder reported that there were 350 "kickers" on the Rosebud reservation who refused to select allotments. When special allotting agent Charles H. Bates began work on Pine Ridge in 1904, he found several camps of "old, non progressive and troublesome full-blood Indians" who resisted allotment. Disputes over prior claims to certain land, especially along the more desirable creeks, hampered his work. Sometimes as many as four families lived on the same section and disputes had to be resolved. "It has taken much time and patience," Bates reported, to get them to agree to a division of the land so as to give them their home and water and the balance of their allotment elsewhere. Thus most of the allotments of family members were scattered. One old man, frustrated by the allotment process, went home, put on his breechclout and paint, and started for the survey outfit with his gun until the police intervened. Another distraught Indian whose claim was not recognized hired a lawyer and took his case to court.[12]

Perhaps one of the most publicized and controversial instances of resistance occurred on the Mission Indian reservations in southern California where Commissioner Burke tried to force angry Indians to accept allotments. Burke implemented his policy over the objections of the Indians because he believed allotments were necessary for their advancement and because he wanted to make the surplus reservation land available to non-Indians. Eventually the public outcry in support of the Mission Indians would become so strong that Burke would have to back down.

In 1922 Burke ordered an allotting agent to begin work on the most conciliatory Mission reservations, particularly the Torres-Martinez, Cabazon, and Augustine reservations. When the allotting agent encountered resistance on Palm Springs reservation where the Indians had lived as peaceful farmers for thirty-six years, Burke refused to suspend the field work, contending that the consent of the Indians was unnecessary. Allotment, he responded to his critics, would promote the progress of the Palm Springs Indians by encouraging them to develop irrigation projects and to establish permanent homes. The Indian Office was not trying to take their land away, he argued, but rather to help them make better use of it. Tension mounted when Indian leaders at Palm Springs refused to let the surveyors continue. Burke threatened to call in the U.S. marshal if necessary so that the surveyors could complete their work.[13]

Burke's policy toward the Indians at Palm Springs outraged reformers. In an effort to arouse public sympathy reformer-writer Elizabeth Green argued that allotment meant only "injustice and misfortune." Each Indian would be allotted forty acres inaccessible to water, out in the desert. Thousands of acres would be left over which Green charged the Indian Office would sell very cheaply, regardless of what the Indians wanted.[14] Another influential reformer, the fiery John Collier, spoke out in support of the Palm Springs Indians. Despite the small number of Indians directly involved—only fifty-five—he believed the situation revealed much about the Indian Office. "If the stubborn brainlessness of the Indian Office system deals with Palm Springs as here described," he wrote, "what may it be expected to do with the business and educational problems of 340,000 Indians and with the Indian property, equal in area to the whole of Japan proper and worth billions of dollars?" To him these small cases represented the most serious indictment of the Indian Office because Congress was not pressuring the Indian Office and public sentiment rested with the Indians.[15]

Such stinging criticism drew a quick response from Interior Secretary Hubert Work, an industrious Colorado doctor turned politician who had been Harding's postmaster general. Work assured Collier's group that field officials had taken every precaution to protect the rights of the Palm Springs Indians. Like Burke, Work believed that the object of allotment was to encourage Indians to become independent property owners and to promote assimilation. "The future well-being of the Indian," he explained, "lies in his ability to become a member of the civilized structure which the times had built up around him."[16] In response to public pressure, the Indian Office agreed to withhold approval of the Palm Springs allotment schedule until November 1, 1925, in order to give the opposition a chance to investigate and prepare its evidence.[17]

In 1924 resistance spread to other Mission reservations where determined residents struggled to retain their communal lifestyle. These Indians received support from the Mission Indian Federation, an organization rooted in opposition to allotment. When disgruntled Indians halted the work of the General Land Office surveyors on La Jolla, the Indian Office sent in the Indian police to oversee completion of the work. Protests from Indian and white organizations delayed the approval of the Rincon and La Jolla allotment schedules, as well as those of Augustine, Cabazon, and Palm Springs.[18]

Sensitive to the growing protests from Indians and reform organizations, Work agreed to correct any abuses that might be found and sent Dr. Samuel Blair to investigate. The Indians complained to Blair that the proposed allotments would separate families and disturb the orchards that they had carefully nurtured for years. In his final report, Blair recommended that the government postpone allotment work on Palm Springs but not discontinue it because then the government would lose its "control" over the Indians. Moreover, Blair concluded that the demand of the Indians on Augustine reservation for enough water to irrigate the whole area of each allotment was unreasonable because the water was not available, and he recommended that the government approve the current Augustine schedule.[19]

Burke's rigid stance on the Mission allotments slowly softened, in part because of the constant pressure in the press. Burke sent Assistant Commissioner Edgar Meritt to California to observe the situation first hand. This experienced bureaucrat was responsible for much of the day-to-day administration of Indian Affairs. Indeed, in the 1920s some reformers considered Meritt to be one of the most influential figures in Indian administration, and he became a prime target for their attacks. On Meritt's advice, Burke decided to remove from the pending allotment schedules the names and selections of those Indians who did not want allotments and to present the revised schedules to the Interior Department for the issuance of trust patents. He directed the allotting agent to proceed with his work on the unallotted Mission reservation so that each Indian would receive at least five acres of irrigable land if available or any other suitable tract. In January 1927 the Indian Office adopted a policy of allotting land only to those Indians who applied in writing.[20]

By the mid-1920s critics of the allotment policy were gaining strength. Reformers and government officials were becoming increasingly disillusioned with an allotment policy that apparently only encouraged dependency. John Collier, one of the Indian Office's most vociferous critics, called the allotment policy "the greatest single practical evil." The purpose of the laws creating trust allotment, he complained, had been defeated by the actual working of those laws. Congress had intended to give the Indians a twenty-five-year period in which they would be exempt from taxes and the temptations of private ownership so that they could become like white farmers and stockmen. Instead, "the trust allotted Indian has found himself less free not more free than before he was allotted; more completely prohibited from taking initiative, assuming responsibility, or in any fashion standing upright as a man." Collier charged that often the amount of land allotted was inadequate or the quality was poor. The allotment laws combined with the Indian Office's administration of those laws had created physical and financial handicaps "which no farmers however expert or persistent could overcome." In closing, Collier suggested that the government give the Indians the option of organizing in some corporate manner to administer their land cooperatively, either on an allotted or an unallotted basis.[21]

John Collier was not the only reformer to become disillusioned and disgusted with the allotment policy. At its 1926 meeting in Philadelphia, the Indian Rights Association called for a "thorough and impartial" survey of the situation to determine how well the allotment policy had prepared the Indians for citizenship so that the government could decide whether to continue it.[22]

Policymakers themselves become more doubtful that the allotment policy would ever fulfill their expectations. In 1928 Meritt confessed with some embarrassment to a House committee that the Indian Office was concerned that so many allottees rapidly disposed of their lands. While visiting fifty schools and agencies, he had been shocked by the amount of land that had sifted through Indian hands. He noted that as much as 50 percent of the land on the Crow Creek and Lower Brule reservations had been lost. The plight of the dispossessed allottees, he conceded, was becoming a "real problem." Even Burke, one of the last great believers in allotment, became disillusioned. With striking honesty and bluntness he confided to the House Indian Affairs Committee: "Those who were responsible for the allotment act were not farseeing. They did not realize that it was, in the last analysis, going to work out by leaving the Indian landless."[23]

Dissatisfaction with the Indian Bureau prompted several major investigations during the 1920s by Congress and by various agencies. One of the most significant and most revealing investigations was led by Lewis Meriam and his staff from the Institute for Government Research, a private research organization. Meriam submitted his report to Secretary of Interior Work on February 21, 1928. It was only one of a series prepared by professional specialists in public health, irrigation, and education in the late 1920s that blamed flaws in the social and economic system rather than individuals for the current social problems. The so-called Meriam report contained stern criticisms of federal Indian policy and marked a significant step in the move away from the Dawes allotment policy.

The report argued persuasively that allotment had caused Indians to lose much of their land without improving their economic ability. The allotment policy had failed to achieve its original goal of promoting Indian initiative and self-support, the report explained, because the government had relied too heavily on the effect of individual land ownership and had done nothing to educate the Indians in the use of the land. The government, it added, often allotted land under pressure from the Indians or neighboring whites before the Indians were ready to accept the responsibility for holding and developing it. The report suggested that the government individualize property through a corporate form of organization so that it would be maintained intact and the Indian's interest would be represented by shares of stock in the corporation.[24]

Every commissioner of Indian affairs between 1887 and 1934 upheld the belief that if Indians received individual plots of land, they would learn to support themselves and gradually adopt white ways. Convinced that allotment would solve the "Indian problem," they allotted reservation lands to Indians without their consent. Sometimes, as in the case of the Mission Indians, they were willing to use force. Moreover, negligent and corrupt field service employees implemented that policy badly. Often it was not the Indians but whites who benefited from the allotment policy because it opened up surplus reservation land for settlement. Whites successfully manipulated allotting agents to gain control of good quality land. Despite the problems, every commissioner between 1887 and 1934 regarded allotment as a beginning, not an end in itself. The next step was putting the land into productive use.

3.

Putting the Land
to Work

Indian Farming and Stockraising

As the first decade of the twentieth century passed and the bulk of the allotment work was completed, Indian land policy no longer focused primarily on the issue of opening large tribal holdings. Rather, it chiefly concerned itself with the management and efficient use of lands that had already been allotted. Reflecting popular sentiment, Indian Office administrators insisted that Indian land be put into productive use and that development of that land was more important than ownership. As part of their effort to promote Indian industry (the willingness and ability to work) and to develop Indian land they implemented extensive farming and stockraising programs. Such programs met with some success, but the commissioners and their staffs failed to provide enough training, equipment, and capital to prevent thousands of Indian farmers and stockraisers from sinking into poverty.

Although early proponents of the allotment policy believed in training Indians as farmers, they could not persuade either Congress or the Indian Office to provide the necessary means. In the years after the Dawes Act shortsighted legislators apparently expected Indians to farm their allotments successfully without adequate training, tools, or equipment, for their initial appropriations to promote farming were pitifully small. In 1888 Congress appropriated only $30,000 for seed, farm implements, and other necessary items, which amounted to less than ten dollars for each allottee. In 1889 lawmakers again appropriated $30,000 but dropped that amount to $15,000 in 1891, 1892, and 1893. From 1894 to 1911 they appropriated nothing. In 1911 Congress established a loan fund known as the "Industry among Indians" appropriation. The $250,000, or $1.50 for each Indian, set aside in the fund was woefully inadequate. By 1934, the government would loan $5,000,000 from this fund, of which the Indians had repaid $2,000,000. The 1934 Wheeler-Howard Act authorized $10,000,000 for a revolving loan fund. Although this sum was still inadequate, it signified the first substantial recognition of the Indians' need for financial credit.[1]

When it came to promoting Indian industry, Indian Office officials limited their assistance to the appointment of government farmers and stockraisers. They employed experienced farmers to teach Indians the principles of modern farming and stockraising. The first duty of the government farmers was to visit Indians at their own farms, teach them modern farming methods, and advise them about the livestock industry and facilities for marketing their products. Government farmers also studied soil, climate, and water conditions to determine the best crops to be introduced and the proper fertilizing and weeding procedures. Government farmers were expected to know all the farmers in their districts personally and to report regularly on their needs and resources. There were never enough qualified farmers to meet the demand. In 1900, for example, there were only 320 farmers to serve 185,790 Indians, exclusive of the Five Civilized Tribes.[2]

Initially, the Indian Office had no formal regulations to govern the work of its farmers and stockmen. At many agencies these employees acted as stable men or errand men or served as laborers around the agency and school grounds. Under Commissioners Valentine and Sells, however, the Indian Office developed general guidelines, which stressed that the primary reason for employing farmers and stockmen was to provide teachers and business agents for the Indians and administrative representatives for the superintendents. The first duty of the farmers and stockmen was to familiarize themselves with each Indian family and home, their resources and needs, and then to interest them in a suitable agricultural pursuit. The guidelines specified that they be paid from agency funds and located close to the Indians they served.

The Indian Office divided large reservations into districts with one farmer each. These district farmers acted as the superintendent's administrative representatives in many matters, their authority coming from the superintendent. The Indian Office expected a great deal from them. They were to encourage and instruct Indians in all matters related to gardening, farming, and stockraising; supervise the business affairs of incompetent Indians; care for the sick and dependent; insure that lessees complied with the terms of their contracts; and "discharge such administrative duties as the superintendent may direct." They were also to maintain order and discipline within their districts; promote and maintain good will among the Indians and between the Indians and their white neighbors; suppress drunkenness and liquor traffic; and enforce federal regulations.

The Indian Office encouraged its farmers to focus most of their effort on the more "primitive" Indians and then pull back as they became self-supporting, giving them as much freedom as their level of competency justified. They were to adapt their methods to local conditions and make their instruction "elementary and practical" in nature rather than technical and scientific, so that the Indians could understand them.[3]

In addition to employing expert farmers, the Indian Office established model farms on many reservations for demonstration purposes. The Indian Office again emphasized simplicity, reminding field officials that the goal of the demonstration farms was not to compete for "showy agricultural results" or to experiment with unusual fruits, grains, and vegetables that Indians would not be able to duplicate on their own allotments. Rather, these farms should demonstrate to the Indians the best methods of planting, cultivating, harvesting, and rotating crops and furnish them with good seed and high quality stock to upgrade the reservation stock. The farms should be as nearly self-supporting as possible.

Indian Office administrators instructed the farmers not to tolerate any resistance. If gentle encouragement proved ineffective, they were to use a thinly veiled threat. "The Indian does not consider his tomorrow, but he does think a great deal of his domain," the guidelines noted. "When it is explained that vast tracts of idle lands sooner or later are sure to pass into the hands of whites unless he makes use of them, it is believed that something will result. To withstand the invasion of the white man the Indian will find thriving farms of more effect than delegations to Congress."[4]

Field officials for the most part responded to the new policy with enthusiasm. The Crow Creek superintendent directed his government farmers to gather information from the federal and state experiment stations in the area. On the Winnebago reservation, the superintendent met with struggling farmers each month to discuss their work and plan activities for the following month. An even more zealous official, Superintendent William A. Lee at Fort Apache, actually plowed and planted part of the crop of any Indian who showed interest in farming to demonstrate the proper methods. The superintendent of the Mission reservations, Marion E. Waite, suggested combining traditional fiestas with an agricultural fair. He also suggested the formation of farmers' clubs and rewarding successful Indians with credit.[5]

Despite the enthusiasm of some officials, their efforts had mixed results. The success of the farming program varied from one reservation to the next. In 1912 Northern Cheyenne Indians on the Tongue River reservation faithfully reimbursed 33⅓ percent of the $12,000 that had been allocated for seed, implements, and livestock a year earlier. On other reservations, severe problems plagued the program: lack of interest; tribal tradition and custom; poor climate; and lack of proper equipment. Indians whose crops failed became discouraged. Some resisted giving up their traditional farming methods. Twenty-five to thirty-five percent of the Indians at the Uintah and Ouray reservation remained "hostilely opposed" to any industrial scheme. Indians who found that they could survive with rations or revenue from sale and lease of their land showed little interest in farming.[6]

Climatic conditions on some reservations hampered farming. After experiencing two consecutive years of crop failure, the disheartened Crow Creek superintendent complained that his reservation was too dry for farming. The government, he said, expected the Indians to succeed where white farmers under the same conditions were "starved out." The land on the Turtle Mountain reservation in North Dakota was covered with oak stumps and brush and much of it was rocky and hilly. Many Indians had no choice but to work for neighboring white farmers for small wages. Nor did the Indians have the tools and equipment that they needed. An Indian from the Omaha reservation stated the problem: "While some of we Indians are trying to follow out the advice given out by the Indian Office, and have found out that our salvation is work, we are striving to do that, but when our implements get out of order we have no place to go to have them repaired, and we Indians don't have money in our pockets every day." The Natives diligently struggled to raise wheat and oats only to discover that they had no threshing machine.[7]

Despite these problems, during Woodrow Wilson's administration the Indian Office not only continued the practice of maintaining Indian farmers and experimental farms on the reservations, but also introduced new programs to promote Indian farming and stockraising. As the supply of valuable farm land in the country shrunk, the American public became less willing to let Indian land remain idle. Expressing the popular sentiment, Wilson's secretary of the interior, Franklin K. Lane, warned that "Idle Indians on idle land must lead to the sale of the lands, for the pressing populations of the West will not long look upon resources unused without strenuous and effective protest." Indians, he argued, were no more entitled to idle lands than whites.[8]

Franklin Lane, a native Canadian who was raised in California, had been a restless young man of progressive political leanings. "Plump, well-fed, and well groomed," he had moved between the east and west coasts, between journalism, politics, and the law. His support for Teddy Roosevelt in the 1904 election won him a position on the Interstate Commerce Commission where he remained for ten years until Wilson named him secretary of the interior in 1913.[9]

Soon after taking office, the secretary wrote that he faced two of the greatest problems ever presented to the American people. The first problem, he said, was how to develop American lands and still preserve the interest of the nation in them. "Second, and I think perhaps this should be first, is the Indian problem," he continued. "Here we have thousands of Indians, as large a population as composes some of the States, owning hundreds of millions of dollars' worth of property which is rapidly rising in value. I am their guardian. I must see that they are protected."[10]

As a fervid progressive, Lane advocated the orderly development and efficient management of all natural resources, especially land. In 1913 he announced his intention to promote the fuller and freer use of natural resources. He noted that there was a growing feeling in the West that its affairs and needs had not been given enough consideration by the federal government. Lane sympathized with Westerners who did not understand why the resources of their region had not been developed. "We have called a halt on methods of spoliation which existed, to the great benefit of many," he argued, "but we have failed to substitute methods, sane, healthful, and progressive, by which the normal enterprise of an ambitious people can make full use of their own resources." He noted that a new concept had evolved in the public mind, that the land should be used for the purpose to which it was best fitted and that the government should keep this in mind when disposing of it.[11]

Lane, then, reflected the two dominant themes in public land policy and Indian land policy in the early twentieth century—development and protection. Feeling strong pressure to protect and develop land on the public domain and on Indian reservations, he had to steer a middle course between the extreme conservationists and an anti-conservationist coalition of Westerners and powerful private interests. The conservationists were one of the most vocal and powerful groups in the country, but there were also powerful oil, timber, and livestock interests that wanted to exploit the public domain and the reservations.

Conservationists applauded Lane's appointment as secretary of the interior because they believed he was a man of integrity, with a devotion to conservation. Although Lane skillfully maintained this image, his record in office, especially on the oil land questions, and his stand on mineral leasing eventually alienated the conservationists.[12] Congressional hearings in the 1920s would reveal that Edward Doheny, the multimillionaire president of the Pan American Petroleum Company, made contributions to Democrats as well as Republicans and, at one time or another, to Lane and other members of Wilson's cabinet. Lane would leave his position as secretary to accept a very lucrative spot with Pan American Petroleum—reportedly at a salary of $50,000 a year.[13]

Historian John Ise argues convincingly that Lane was not consistently and sincerely interested in conservation and that he worked to promote the interests of big business, particularly oil, at the expense of the public interest. Ise calls Lane "one of the most dangerous men that have ever held the office of Secretary of Interior" because, while working to promote the ends of the exploiting interests, he also made speeches and wrote articles on conservation and preserved an impenetrable facade of sincerity and respectability.[14] Lane held a Western view of conservation; he favored rapid development of the public domain. Historian E. Louise Peffer asserts that in his public land policy Lane was "one of the most reactionary of all twentieth-century Secretaries of Interior."[15]

Lane's belief in the principles of efficiency, order, and progress, his materialistic values, and his unceasing optimism greatly influenced his policies as secretary of the interior. This energetic secretary maintained that people were basically selfish, vain, and lazy, and that work was the first stepping stone toward achievement. "It is only by work that man realizes himself," he noted. "All civilization is the product of work." Lane believed that man advanced toward the civilized state when he became obsessed with the desire to have his wife dressed as well as the next man's or his children fitted in shoes that were just as good as anyone else's. If a man did not have these ambitions, he said, something was wrong. A new day was dawning in America, he proclaimed, in which classes would be obliterated and each man would be evaluated for his usefulness.[16]

Lane enthusiastically embraced the doctrine that Indians, through industry and self-support, would progress in orderly stages toward independence and citizenship. He did not for a moment doubt that the adoption of white materialistic values was the proper goal for the Indians, and was willing to use force to get them to accept those values. In 1913 the secretary told a group of businessmen that the government had done everything possible to force the Indians to become independent. It had educated them, irrigated their land, and taught them to farm, but without success. The government could try one more experiment. "We can," he said, "give that man an education and then we can turn him loose and say to him 'You have an admixture of American blood. We have given you all of the advantages that civilization can give to anyone. There is only one thing that distinguishes one man from another, and that is his willingness to work and his ability to control himself. Now, it is up to you to make a man out of yourself.'" If the government tried the experiment, Lane conceded, many would go under but thousands would become independent, productive citizens. Lacking any sympathy for the Indian who refused to see the value of white American civilization and who clung tenaciously to his own traditions, Lane argued that the government had to destroy that Indian's culture and replace it with a better one if he was going to adopt a new life.[17]

In Cato Sells, a fellow progressive Democrat, Lane found a comrade who shared his views. Sells, too, anxiously anticipated the destruction of tribal life. Little in Sells's background as a lawyer and politician qualified him for managing Indian affairs. As one of Woodrow Wilson's earliest supporters in 1912, the energetic Sells had been instrumental in getting a majority of the seats in the Texas state convention for Wilson and holding the Texas delegation for Wilson during the forty-six roll calls at the national Democratic convention. After Wilson's nomination, Sells became his chief fundraiser in Texas, and in 1913 Wilson rewarded him with an appointment as commissioner of Indian affairs.[18]

Wilson readily turned decisions on Indian policy over to his subordinates, for he had no interest in fighting for reforms that might alienate his supporters in Congress. With the appointment of Sells and Lane, he firmly placed Indian affairs in the hands of Democrats and Westerners. Wilson came to office with a limited view of the proper function of government and no program of social reform. At heart a states rights Democrat, he believed federal power should be used only to dismantle barriers to individual effort.[19] Thus he would not interfere with any plan Lane and Sells might devise to relieve the government of its trust responsibility toward the Indians and force them to become independent.

Lane reflected popular sentiment when he argued that Indians were no more entitled to idle lands than whites. Both he and Sells believed strongly that farming and stockraising provided the best means the Indians had of becoming self-supporting, of advancing toward civilization, and that their rich agricultural lands, vast acres of grass land, and great forests should be used as instruments for their civilization. "I hold it to be an economic and social crime," Sells observed, "in this age and under modern conditions, to permit thousands of acres of fertile land belonging to the Indians and capable of great industrial development to lie in unproductive idleness." Farm prices were high in the prewar years and Sells was anxious that Indians share in the prosperity that other farmers were experiencing.[20]

The Indian Rights Association agreed that the government should encourage the Indians to work industriously and should advance any available funds belonging to individual Indians so that they could "help themselves." Warren Moorehead of the Board of Indian Commissioners, who strongly supported Sells's policy, called the reimbursable appropriations and the encouragement of industry "two of the most hopeful signs of Indian progress."[21] A reimbursable appropriation was an advance by the federal government that would be reimbursed out of tribal funds. A gratuity appropriation, in contrast, did not have to be reimbursed. Congress made the latter appropriation not on the basis of any specific treaty or agreement but in recognition of the general responsibility of the government to improve the social, economic, or physical condition of the Indians.

With enthusiastic support from the reformers, then, the Indian Office used reimbursable tribal funds to buy livestock and farming implements for impoverished Indians and successfully encouraged them to develop their own herds. Believing that the Indians' basic problem was lack of capital with which to purchase blooded stock and to develop their pastures, Sells persuaded Congress to appropriate large amounts for reimbursable loans, which enabled Indians to use their own lands effectively. Although Sells also promoted the use of loans for land improvement and implements, his efforts in this area were less successful.[22]

In 1914 as part of its program to promote Indian self-support and labor the Indian Office put 450 government farmers in the field. When Sells later discovered that despite earlier guidelines these farmers had become merely clerical assistants for superintendents, he ordered them to spend more time in the field helping the Indians and less time in the office doing paperwork. Nor did the superintendents escape his censure, for Sells issued a stern warning that his administration would no longer tolerate negligence and mismanagement in cultivating soil, breeding stock, and handling grazing land.[23]

The Indian Office also began to pay special attention to the quality of Indian livestock. Rather than doling out appropriations for promoting Indian farming and stockraising to individuals, in 1914 the government began buying large tribal herds for some reservations. Whites would manage these herds while the Indians learned how to care for the animals. Individuals would borrow breeding stock from the tribal herds, and when they became self-supporting, the tribal herds would be liquidated and the debts repaid. In this way, the Indian Office hoped to put a large number of acres of idle grazing land to use, teach the Indians the livestock industry, and provide a market for their hay. From 1914 to 1918 the government would spend $1,500,000 in gratuity appropriations for this purpose.[24]

Despite Sells's determination and his ambitious policy the agricultural industry program faltered on some reservations, especially on the Northern Plains with its extreme temperatures and harsh climate. Hot winds and drought withered what had promised to be bumper crops and the parched soil became so hard that new crops could not be planted. Some Indians such as those on the Standing Rock reservation understandably lost interest in farming after seeing the products of their hard labor shrivel up and die, but on other reservations Indians continued to plant with grim determination, much to the surprise of their superintendents. Conditions were so desperate that in 1915 a joint commission concluded that farming and stockraising programs on the reservations were failing.[25]

Over the next few years, as farming conditions improved, field reports from the Northern Plains became more encouraging. In 1915 and 1916 Indians on the Cheyenne River reservation began to plant gardens and to demonstrate a renewed interest in farming with impressive results. On the Crow reservation within one year 100 percent more land was sown to grain, and the superintendent predicted that 400 to 500 percent more land would be sown to winter wheat. In 1916 farmers on the Pine Ridge reservation cultivated an additional two thousand acres and most families planted gardens. Indians farmed more land and produced more crops in 1916 than ever before. In 1911, 24,489 Indians had farmed 383,025 acres and produced crops valued at $1,951,672, but in 1916, 35,825 Indians farmed 678,527 acres and produced crops worth $5,293,719. By 1920 nearly 37,000 Indians were farming about 1,000,000 acres and 47,000 were raising stock. "The Indian's transformation from a game hunter and a wanderer to a settled landholder and home builder," Sells boasted, "is everywhere evident."[26]

World War I increased the pressures on Indian land, for wartime demand for food, fuel, and raw materials intensified the drive to promote Indian labor and to encourage Indians to lease or sell their idle land. The war provided new opportunities for the exploitation of Indian land and gave the Indian Office an excuse to step up its policy of dispossession. The result was a further disintegration of the Indian estate—and at a rapid pace.

Anxious to increase wartime grain production, in 1917 the Senate became interested in the feasibility of cultivating parts of the unused public domain as well as unused Indian land. To cultivate the remaining unreserved public domain was, in fact, impractical because that land was largely rough, mountainous, or more suited for grazing. Unused Indian land, however, provided an attractive alternative because roughly 112,000 acres of irrigable land and 50,000 acres of dry farm land on reservations in Arizona, Montana, and Wyoming could be cultivated with the proper authority and funding. Specifically, the Pima, Colorado River, Salt River, Fort Peck, and Shoshone reservations contained large areas of cultivable land.[27]

Responding to the Senate's keen interest, the Interior Department drafted a bill to appropriate money for cultivating unused Indian land. As Senator Edwin Johnson of South Dakota stood on the Senate floor to introduce the bill, he argued persuasively that hundreds of thousands of acres of fertile land lay idle while half the world was starving and that if the government leased these unused lands, it would get back two dollars for every dollar that it spent.[28]

Despite pressure from Congress and a direct order from Commissioner Sells in January 1917, superintendents hesitated to sell the Indians more seeds and implements on the reimbursable plan when their record of repayment was poor. The Leech Lake superintendent, for one, complained that the policy of issuing seeds had actually been detrimental because the Indians knew that the seed was paid for out of tribal funds and thus felt no compulsion to pay for it. Nonetheless, most superintendents promised to obey Sells's instructions or claimed they were already taking steps to procure seeds and implements for their Indians.[29]

In March the commissioner instructed the superintendents to redouble their efforts. Most field officials apparently supplied seeds and implements as Sells directed, but they had not taken the necessary steps to insure that the Indians actually used them effectively. They spent most of their time helping the more intelligent and progressive Indians in order to make a good showing while neglecting those who really needed their advice and encouragement. Sells was not overly concerned about this biased approach, for a month later he boasted, "There is every indication that the Indian Service employees and the Indians are responding beyond expectations; that they have a patriotic sympathy with the Government in the present emergency; and that their activities in the way of increased production will be a material factor in the country's food supply."[30]

On April 9, 1917, a week after Congress passed a resolution recognizing a state of war between the United States and Germany, Sells instructed superintendents to enlist the patriotic cooperation of leading Indians in cultivating every tillable acre on their reservations so as to meet the wartime demand for wheat, beans, potatoes, corn, and meat. Supervisors, inspectors, superintendents of irrigation and others received similar instructions, and they responded enthusiastically. One superintendent was "much gratified" by the effort the Indians made.[31] Though pleased with the encouraging replies, Sells did not ease up. With the entry of the United States into the war, he explained, "the importance of an increased food supply cannot be overestimated. We must sacrifice every non-essential along other lines for this supreme object." He reminded Indian Service farmers to spend long hours in the field, to enlist the cooperation of lessees and white farmers in the vicinity, and to appeal to the patriotism of the Indians.[32]

Although the field reports indicated that almost every reservation had successful agricultural activities underway, much cultivable land on the reservations remained idle, and many able-bodied males were not working. The commissioner tried to make Indian Service employees and the Indians themselves aware of the emergency. As part of this effort, Sells sent some of his most experienced agents to help the superintendents, farmers, and other employees in aggressively carrying out the program for increased food production.[33]

The commissioner optimistically maintained that the Indians would significantly increase the country's food supply during the war and that the war would promote Indian progress. The wartime farming activity would "materially hasten the final solution of the Indian problem," Sells contended, for through it the Indians would develop better business judgment in handling and disposing of their products and gradually achieve self-support and become independent. As evidence of this, Sells noted that in 1917 Indians on seventy-three reservations farmed 472,156 acres, as compared to 358,796 acres the previous year—an increase of 11,360 acres or 31.6 percent.[34]

The Indian Office's wartime campaign succeeded. Most superintendents had energetic farming campaigns underway, often with the support of the Indians themselves.[35] During 1919 Indians cultivated 759,933 acres, as compared with 676,691 acres in 1917, and food production on the reservations increased 5 to 100 percent. Although the Indian Service had lost many of its farmers and stockmen to war service, the acreage farmed by the Indians increased substantially. Since 1913 it had almost doubled; and Indians had quadrupled the value of the crops and livestock produced and sold.[36]

The Indian Office struggled to maintain the high level of food production during the postwar period in order to feed the allies and to keep domestic food prices from soaring. In 1919 Sells predicted that the world would need an additional fifteen million tons of food to carry it over to the next crop. Millions of hungry people would have to be fed. "We are at the entrance of a new industrial era," he explained, "which will demand not only greater and more varied domestic supplies but vastly larger efforts than ever before. War gardens have convinced us of the necessity of peace gardens."[37]

Sells's successor, Charles Burke, preached the same gospel of self-support and endorsed Sells's farming and stockraising activities: "An Indian should be made to understand that he must help himself, and that if he expects the Government to give him assistance he must do something to meet the government at least part way."[38] Believing that the best opportunity adult Indians had of becoming self-supporting was in the productive use of their lands, Burke continued the Indian Office's policy of promoting progress through farming and stockraising programs. Although Burke did not favor indiscriminately forcing all Indians to farm or raise stock, he maintained that with the expected growing demand for food in the postwar period the nation had to make each acre, including acres of Indian land, yield as much as possible. In 1921, 49,926 Indians farmed 890,700 acres and produced crops worth $11,921,366. In a time of fiscal stringency, it was perhaps the secretary of the interior, Hubert Work, who provided the most convincing argument in support of a program to promote Indian farming and stockraising industries. He pointed out that as more Indians became self-supporting under such a program the government would be able to cut its Indian appropriations.[39]

Burke's program to encourage Indian farming and stockraising was crippled by the general depression in the nation's farm economy after the war. Favorable conditions before the war had led farmers throughout the country to expect a growing demand for their products, rising prices, and continued prosperity, so they had invested heavily in farmland, much of it marginal, and the value of that land was inflated. When the demand for foodstuffs dropped after the war, farmers did nothing to restrict production. Farm prices plummeted in May and June of 1920 with the onset of the depression, and through the 1920s they remained far below what they had been between 1890 and 1920.[40]

The depressed farm prices only spurred Burke to push harder in his efforts to encourage farming, and he enlisted the help of the superintendents. When he discovered that many Indian Service farmers were again spending most of their time on clerical work and other duties not directly related to farming, he ordered the superintendents to impress upon them that their primary duty was to instruct the Indians in farming. During the crop season, they were to spend long hours in the field and make sure that the Indians followed their instructions. Meanwhile, Indian farmers should be provided with good seed and adequate farming equipment, and encouraged to incresae their acreage, while Indian stockmen should be encouraged to build up their herds and care for them properly.[41]

Burke was apparently not yet satisfied, because his directives to the field service continued. After scrutinizing various reports and visiting a number of reservations, the commissioner concluded that the successful superintendent was the one who took a personal interest in his Indians, who visited their homes and farms to discuss plans for agricultural advancement. The usual excuse for not making such visits was lack of time, but Burke responded that the superintendents who really wanted to visit their Indians would find the time. In March 1922 he warned the superintendents to work very actively among the Indians during the coming spring and summer and to submit by May 15 an outline of the measures they would take to promote farming. After completing their outline, they were to report on the homes visited, the conditions found, and the plans formulated. Despite Burke's worthy efforts, in 1924 Indians still did not use large areas of irrigable land for which water had been provided.[42]

The Indian livestock industry, like Indian farming, suffered as a result of the postwar depression. The number of Indian cattle, which had increased markedly before the war, dropped significantly. During the war and immediately after, the Indian Office had pressured the Indians to sell their herds and lease their grazing lands to whites, and some of this grazing land was converted to small grain production. When livestock prices fell in the 1920s, however, white cattlemen who had leased Indian land could not pay their rents, and the Indian Office, sympathetic to their plight, lowered their fees, leaving the Indian lessors to absorb the loss. As a result, Indian landowners lost many of the advances they had made before 1920.[43]

Industrial parade on the Pine Ridge reservation in South Dakota. *Credit National Archives (photo no. 75-BK-21).*

This pattern of failure was especially true on the Northern Plains. The Pine Ridge Sioux, for example, prospered as cattlemen before the war, but in 1917 at the superintendent's urging they sold their herds and leased their land to whites. With the high cattle prices the inducement to sell was so great that within a year almost all the arable land on the reservation came under white control. The loss of the herds spelled disaster for the Indians who quickly squandered the proceeds. After 1921 when wheat and cattle prices dropped and the frantic lessees demanded that their rentals be reduced, the Indian Office agreed. In 1922 several cattle companies had to abandon their pastures; other lessees were unable to pay their rent because they could not finance their operations.

A similar pattern developed on the Standing Rock reservation where the Indians found it increasingly difficult to resist selling their cattle as more whites pushed onto the reservation. "They are beset at every turn," the superintendent complained, "by the unscrupulous white man who first sets up a desire for something and immediately provides a means of its attainment by the sacrifices of stock." When the tribal herd on the Fort Hall reservation was sold off, the Indians received only four or four and a half cents a pound for steers that had originally cost them seven or eight cents a pound.[44]

On some reservations the livestock industry, already reeling from low prices, suffered an added blow because of natural disasters. Drought conditions plagued Montana and other parts of the Northwest in the summer of 1918, followed by the most severe winter experienced in that area. Indians on the Blackfeet reservation who had prospered during the war now found their crops destroyed by two years of drought. With no hay for winter feed, they were forced to watch helplessly as thousands of cattle and horses starved to death on an overstocked range during the winter of 1919–1920. The tribal herd of five thousand was sold down to about six hundred because feed was in short supply. The extreme drought and severe winter of 1919–1920 wiped out Indian and white cattlemen on both the Blackfeet and Crow reservations. Much of the Crow land had been leased because of war conditions, but the drought had hurt the lessees so badly financially that they could not pay their rent.[45]

In 1921 a grim Charles Burke conceded that the Indian livestock industry, like stock interests throughout the country, had during the past three years faced "the most trying and disastrous period in its history."[46] Despite a general improvement during the fall of 1922, farming and stockraising conditions on the reservations for the most part remained poor. Convinced now that some sort of major program was needed to improve food production on the reservations, the Indian Office began to study a plan used on the Blackfeet reservation. In March 1921 the Blackfeet superintendent had launched a "Five Year Program" to promote Indian labor on his reservation. The program had almost instant success, for nearly all of the able-bodied adults on the reservation became self-supporting, and with its success the Indian Office began to see the possibilities of planned economic development.

Blackfeet Indian exhibits at the midwinter fair, Browning, Montana, in 1925. *Credit National Archives (photo no. 75-EXB-3-10).*

As the first step toward formulating and implementing a general Five Year Program the Indian Office asked the superintendents of three reservations to outline what they perceived to be a practical program for economic development on their reservations over the next five years. Then Burke, who believed the acceptance of a definite economic program was essential for solving the Indian problem, sent all the superintendents copies of the outlines of the programs adopted for the Fort Hall and Pine Ridge reservations for their careful consideration as a guide for their own plans.[47]

By 1923 the Indian Office had studied roughly half of the reservations to determine the exact situation of the Indians as well as their needs and resources. After completing similar surveys on the remainder, it would develop a definite, systematic economic program for each of them, extending over a five year period. Under these so-called Five Year Programs, the superintendents visited each home on the reservations to discuss plans for improving food production, to encourage the individual families, and, perhaps most important, to forge a bond of common interest. Five Year Programs also included such things as farm clubs, where the Indians themselves conducted extension services and community development programs, and women's clubs for canning, gardening, and other purposes. The programs provided the farmer with credit, supplies, and implements to establish a home and farm.[48]

The programs improved farm conditions dramatically on some reservations. After the superintendent introduced the Five Year Program on Pine Ridge in 1923, for example, corn production jumped 75 percent, potato acreage increased 300 percent, and the entire crop production rose 25 percent. On Standing Rock most of the Indians faithfully planted one acre of potatoes, one acre of garden, and ten acres of corn as the program stipulated. In general, the year 1923 marked a substantial increase in the number of Indians farming, acreage cultivated, use of modern implements and machinery, and adoption of successful methods. This was due in part, no doubt, to the fact that the livestock market had recovered from the depression of 1918–1921, for the spiraling prices sparked the Indians' interest. By 1927 Five Year Programs were in effect on fifty-five reservations, which led to an even greater increase in the number of Indians farming and the total acreage under cultivation. Approximately 27,500 Indians farmed 610,500 acres, and 31,725 Indians used 20,423,762 acres for stockraising.[49]

Although on some reservations the Five Year Programs had remarkable success, on others they failed miserably. The problem was simply too severe. Indians on the Cheyenne River reservation ignored many of the provisions of their Five Year Program because, as their frustrated superintendent explained, the government had made them so dependent that they could not function without constant supervision. The Crow superintendent drafted a program along the lines recommended by the Indian Office only to discover that it could not be followed with a group of four hundred to five hundred Indian farmers because, while such a program might have good results with some farmers, it would fail with others.

By the end of the decade conditions on some reservations were what can only be described as tragic. According to some accounts, Indians on the Fort Peck and Flathead reservations survived largely on prairie gophers and horsemeat, and were close to starvation. The government apparently had purchased cattle for the Indians and then leased their reservation to a large cattle company, leaving them with no money or crops to see them through the winter. "Now," one tribesman pleaded, "we can't stand it much longer under the present administration." On the Blackfeet reservation, the high altitude and cold climate hampered farming efforts. Crops were good in only one year out of four, so despite government irrigation and stockraising programs, many Indian suffered. Weakened by poor diet, they fell easy victims to cold and disease.[50]

In 1928 many Indians had difficulty supporting themselves and their families on trust allotments. The government's experience in reclamation work for white farmers had demonstrated that they needed a minimum capital of $2,000 and two years of farming experience if they expected to make a living on the federally irrigated farms of the West. Yet Indians who had no farming experience or capital were placed upon the raw land and expected to support themselves immediately. The government had been appropriating reimbursable funds to help the Indians buy farm implements, livestock, and seeds, so they could use their allotments. Although the record of repayment was "remarkable," there was only enough money to help six thousand Indians.[51]

Despite their limited success, Burke pushed his farming and stockraising programs even more fiercely, perhaps because he saw no other solution. He sent the superintendents form letters about the need for work in the Indian's scheme of existence, which they were to mail or hand to any Indian they thought needed them. In these stern letters, Burke asked the recipient whether he was one of the Indians who worked and prospered or one of those who did not. If he belonged to the latter group, he should have his superintendent or government farmer put him on the right path. "We do not want to make farmers of all Indians," the letter continued, "but we do want every Indian to do his best, no matter what his occupation." Burke also ordered the superintendents to try harder to visit Indian families to "hammer into their minds" the doctrine of work. Meritt followed up on the form letter by ordering the superintendents to submit before December 1 a report for the 1927 crop year indicating the acreage farmed, the crops produced, the improved methods, and the effects of the letter in encouraging farming efforts.[52]

By late 1928 some reservations were far into their Five Year Programs, one or two had already completed one five-year period, and others had not yet begun programs. The Indian Office planned for a general review to determine the status of each Five Year Program; to study the results of the program and where necessary to modify them; and to create programs on reservations that did not have them. It asked each superintendent to submit a report describing his Five Year Program and its results no later than January 10, 1929.[53] Burke's farming and stockraising programs failed to meet white standards of success in part because the Indians had neither the capital nor the experience necessary for the programs to work effectively. To make matters worse, farmers on the Northern Plains suffered from low prices and drought.

The Indian Office employed 137 farmers in 1931, and Commissioner Rhoads asked Congress for $315,000 for the development of farming and stockraising. Although farming and stockraising were essential for their livelihood, he explained, Indians as a race were not "naturally inclined" to that work, so they needed "constant, systematic, and sympathetic advice, instruction, and supervision" to apply modern methods successfully.[54] His words, echoing those of Secretary Lane years earlier, seem to indicate that the Indian Office's fundamental philosophy had changed little.

On March 9, 1931, Rhoads reorganized the Indian Office in order to decentralize operations and make them more responsive to the needs of the field. In the process he created a division of agricultural extension and industry. The extension field staff included a director, 4 supervisors, 23 agricultural extension agents, 10 home extension agents, 221 farm agents or farmers, 62 stockmen, and 40 dairymen. In 1932 Indians planted more gardens and field crops than in the previous ten years. The lack of outside employment, along with losses from drought and crop pests, had forced the Indians to take more interest in farming. In 1932 Indians on 24 reservations planted 138,281 acres in field crops; extension agents gave 2,127 demonstrations on better farming and helped 1,175 Indians acquire better livestock. Five Year Programs had increased the number and size of gardens on the Blackfeet, Fort Hall, Pine Ridge, and Chippewa reservations, and had improved the livestock industry on the Blackfeet, Fort Peck, and Standing Rock reservations.[55]

Although the Indian Office's administrative and policy changes had some success, in 1934 many Indians remained unable or unwilling to use their land constructively. Lack of adquate money, training, and equipment, poor climate and soil conditions, as well as cultural factors continued to hamper economic self-sufficiency on the reservations.

What are 5 Yr. programs?

4.

Leasing
A Policy Unfolds

In the first decades of the twentieth century as the Indian Office became more concerned with the management and efficient use of Indian lands that had been allotted, in addition to launching Indian farming and stockraising programs, it encouraged the Indians to lease their unused lands. Reflecting popular sentiment, aggressive administrators insisted that Indians who could or would not use their land efficiently must lease or sell it to non-Indians; leasing would benefit the Indians by providing them with a steady income while they learned to support themselves and by bringing them into contact with whites who could teach them self-reliance.

Although the Dawes Act prohibited leasing during the trust period so that the allottees would learn to support themselves on their land, policymakers soon discovered that some allottees were physically incapable of using their land even if they wanted to, so leasing was a necessity. Congress gradually broke down the safeguard of inalienability surrounding the trust allotments by passing a series of increasingly liberal leasing laws.

The first of these applied only to Indians with specific disabilities that prevented them from using their land, but gradually Congress liberalized the laws, extending leasing to able-bodied Indians who could or would not use their land. The act of February 28, 1891, authorized any Indian who "by reason of age or other disability" was unable to occupy and improve his allotment himself to lease it for three years for farming and grazing purposes or ten years for mining. The law greatly benefited Western land seekers and business interests who had been pressuring the Indian Office. In 1894 Congress enlarged the class of Indians who could lease by adding "inability" to age and disability as the criteria for leasing allotments, and it extended the lease period to five years for farming and grazing and to ten years for mining and "business purposes." Moreover, the 1894 law permitted tribal "council" leaders to lease surplus tribal lands for farming and grazing purposes. The maximum lease period for allotments was reduced in 1897 to three years for farming and grazing and five years for mining and "business purposes" and the word "inability" was dropped. Before 1894 the Indian Office approved only 6 leases; in 1894 it approved 300, and between 1895 and 1900 it approved 2,500 leases a year.[1]

Congress vacillated when it came to determining the appropriate length of the lease period. In 1900 it again raised the lease period for farming purposes to five years although it left the other limits intact. Commissioner of Indian Affairs William Jones condemned the 1900 act because he believed it defeated the purpose of allotment and impeded the process of assimilation. "The Indian," he complained, "has been allotted and then allowed to turn over his land to whites and go his aimless way. This pernicious practice is the direct growth of vicious legislation." By taking away the incentive to work, Jones wrote, it defeated the object of the allotment policy.[2]

Many Eastern philanthropists also opposed the leasing of Indian land. The Board of Indian Commissioners objected because it would prevent the Indians from becoming self-supporting, aptly predicting that large tracts would be leased without adequate notice or safeguards for the Indian owners. "The Department does not and can not make careful investigation of the circumstances in each application for permission to lease individual holdings of land," the board noted, "but is compelled to depend upon recommendations which are too often colored by interest or influenced by local pressure to get the best Indian lands at the lowest prices and by the desire of lazy Indians to escape work." No able-bodied Indians who could work their land should be allowed to lease them. The Lake Mohonk Conference also opposed leasing because it transformed the Indian from an "industrious worker" into an "idle and improvident landlord." Only the disabled or infirm should be allowed to lease, it concluded.[3]

Although Commissioner Jones publicly objected to the leasing legislation, he had already turned to a policy which ultimately forced some Indians to lease their land. Jones slashed the amount of rations that the government distributed to Indians on the reservations and ordered that able-bodied Indians be given rations only if employed. He justified the reduction of the ration rolls as a "humane" act to stimulate "self-help," arguing that the policy of reducing rations would not only relieve the government of an enormous burden but would solve the "Indian problem" within one generation. To Jones leasing and rations presented the greatest obstacles to Indian independence and self-support, while cutting rations forced many Indians to turn to leasing as their only source of revenue.[4]

Early leasing regulations often stipulated that leases contain specific provisions for improvements by lessees such as groundbreaking or constructing fences and barns; the Indian Office believed such improvements would benefit the allottees and increase land values. In 1900 the Interior Department limited leases with no provisions for improvements, for money payment only, to two years for farming and farming and grazing leases, and one year for grazing alone, but it allowed leases for three years for farming and farming and grazing and two years for grazing if there were improvements. Interior Department regulations in 1907 provided for the same leasing terms, two and three years respectively, and reaffirmed the principle that leases should provide for specific improvements.[5] However, white lessees who preferred not to improve the land could get around the law simply by renewing their leases each year.

The Indian Office's commitment to leasing was firmly established in the first decades of the twentieth century. Commissioner Francis E. Leupp believed that since Indians wasted their natural resources, whites would inevitably encroach on their land. Leupp's official policy was to discourage leasing by able-bodied Indians. The leasing laws, he said, applied only to invalids, children, cripples, women, and the aged, but some able-bodied Indians who were lazy abused the law. On some reservations, he conceded, the agents were too busy or shorthanded to keep a proper vigil, so the allotment-leasing system became "more noteworthy for its abuses than for its benefits."[6]

All the early leasing laws and regulations made the secretary of the interior responsible for determining who should be able to lease on the basis of age and disability or inability to improve or occupy the land. The Interior Department formulated regulations to prevent mistakes, to help old and disabled Indians lease their land, and to discourage leasing by Indians who were capable of using their land. The 1907 regulations provided a clear statement of the Interior Department's opposition to indiscriminate leasing. They stipulated that the chief job of the Indian agent was to encourage able-bodied Indians to work. The regulations defined "disabled" as those Indians eighteen or under; elderly Indians; widows with no sons over eighteen; allottees with chronic illness or physical defects; married women with sick husbands; and the mentally disturbed. The regulations also outlined a procedure to make leasing more efficient and successful. Indians who preferred to lease their land applied first to their agent who in turn forwarded their application to the Indian Office for approval. Tribal leases were not to exceed five years for grazing and ten years for farming purposes. The agents would determine the quantities, terms, and conditions of these tribal leases but the leases were ultimately subject to the approval of the secretary of the interior.[7]

Although the Indian Office still maintained that old and disabled Indians should have help leasing their land, in 1907 it also began to give "progressive," able-bodied Indians more freedom in managing their allotments, specifically allowing them to lease their own land without the approval of the Interior Department and to collect their own rentals if they could prove that they deserved that privilege. The agents and superintendents supplied the Indian Office with the names of the lessee and lessor, a description of each lease and the character of the land leased, the extent of the business carried on by the lessee, and the reason the lessor could not work the land, along with his own recommendations, so that the Indian Office would have as much information as possible in deciding whether or not to approve the lease.[8]

Leupp's successor, Robert Valentine, became the first commissioner of Indian affairs to try to resolve the difficult problem of administering a vast estate for Indians who were trying to live off their rentals. In 1909 he introduced a system of sealed bids administered directly by the commissioner's office instead of local superintendents. This practice increased the Indians' revenue from leasing but also increased the cost of administering the leasing policy. Valentine believed the Indian was being threatened by being put in the position of landlord and receiving rents for which he had done no work himself. Much of the laziness and idleness of the Indians, he argued, resulted from easily acquired leasing money. Leasing as it had been practiced hurt the Indians by destroying their incentive to work. A steady rental provided a good excuse not to farm. Thus he favored leasing only in very narrow and specific cases: when an Indian who was already farming part of his land successfully had neither the capital nor labor to farm the rest; when the Indian had adopted some industrial pursuit other than farming; and when the Indian was incapacitated. Although Valentine personally preferred to limit leasing to these specific cases, as the price of the rapidly shrinking public domain land increased the pressure to lease Indian land to whites intensified.[9]

In 1910 the Interior Department adopted new regulations which stipulated that the proceeds from leases be paid to the allottees or their heirs or expended for their benefit. Under these regulations, allottees would be classified as competent or incompetent, and although the competent Indians would be permitted to make their own leases and collect their own rentals, the agency office would continue negotiating leases for the incompetent ones and disburse their rental money. Thus, by 1910 the basic framework of a leasing policy had been established. Subsequent legislation would change only the details, not the fundamental nature of the policy. Indian Office officials would continue to encourage competent Indians who would or could not use their land to lease it and use the rental money wisely. Yet they remained torn by the dilemma that leasing could be beneficial when the allottee had adopted another pursuit or when the revenue from leasing surplus land could be used to improve the remaining land, but it could also harm the Natives by enabling them to live off rentals rather than farm.[10]

Expanding on the 1910 regulations, in 1915 Assistant Commissioner Edgar Meritt ordered the superintendents to give each allottee who had the leasing privilege a reasonable opportunity to demonstrate his competency but not to approve any lease if they believed the Indian would suffer. If the lease was fair and made with a lessee whom the superintendent believed was a "fit person to live in the Indian community," the superintendent should approve it.[11] Meritt believed the government should continue to hold Indian land in trust until the owners had acquired enough business experience to lease it themselves, but Congress would not enact legislation upholding this principle until 1921.[12]

To protect Indian interests, on July 1, 1916, the Interior Department approved regulations limiting the leasing of allotments for farming and grazing to three years. These regulations also limited the leasing of allotments of deceased Indians for which heirs had not been determined to one year and those of minors until they reached the age of majority. These regulations made leasing difficult; prospective lessees often selected tracts to lease for the usual full term, but when they discovered that the tracts included undetermined heirship land or the allotments of minors, they backed out.[13]

Commissioner Cato Sells ordered the superintendents to submit these cases to the Indian Office with all the information and their recommendations. Where the proposed leases involved the allotments of minors, the Indian Office had to be sure that the particular situation justified leasing beyond the age of majority. After reiterating that superintendents should encourage Indians to farm as much of their land as possible, he ordered the superintendents to consider each case carefully so as to preserve Indian interests. Some of the superintendents were already implementing leasing policies so that the unused land would be cultivated.[14]

World War I gave the Indian Office an excellent excuse to expand its leasing policy, and it fell back on its traditional argument that leasing would not only put Indian land in use but would also promote Indian progress. Because many leases provided for improvements, the Indian would supposedly benefit from the lease money as well as from an improved farm and home when the lease expired. The push for leasing was an important part of the general push by whites for control of Indian land during the war. In the name of wartime emergency the Indian Office approved leases to large cattle companies and beet sugar companies that violated Indian rights. Moreover, these leases, often forced on the Indians as essential war measures, were left in place after the war ended.

During the war government officials took new aggressive steps to lease the surplus Indian land and liberalized leasing regulations to permit long term leases.[15] The act of May 18, 1916, permitted an allottee to rent irrigated lands for ten years if he or she was too old or disabled to live on or improve the allotment. Indian Office administrators hoped to attract white farmers to remote areas of the reservations so that they would preserve the allottee's water rights by using the irrigation ditches and would give the Indians an example of industrious farming. Yet the Indian Office's official stance was to urge allottees to establish homes and work their land rather than to depend on rentals.[16]

The commitment of Lane and Sells to a liberal leasing policy became even more apparent in 1919 when it pushed for an amendment to the act of May 18, 1916, which would permit a longer leasing period by applying the ten-year limit for leases on irrigable allotted land to unallotted reservation land as well. This legislation was especially important for the Western reservations where much land remained idle. After noting that such legislation would benefit the Indians and increase food production, Meritt assured members of Congress that the Indian Office would use the authority provided in the bill only when it was in the best interests of the Indians to do so.[17]

The new leasing laws apparently were effective, for the acreage under cultivation increased markedly, contributing to an increase in wartime food production. After the war Sells expected the Indians to maintain the same standard of accomplishment. Although the patriotic fervor for increased food production had subsided, he observed, "there are definite signs that many of the Indians are acquiring the 'habit' of sustained industry, which will give permanence to their progress along industrial lines."[18] Secretary Lane agreed that the leasing policy not only added to the general food supply but also developed individual responsibility among those Indians who managed their own leases and rental money. Approximately 40,000 leases were made in 1920, covering 4,500,000 acres and bringing $8,000,000 in rent.[19]

In the 1920s Indian Commissioner Charles Burke and his staff continued to encourage leasing under certain circumstances.[20] Although Burke realized that leasing subverted the Indian Office's goals of progress and self-support, he conceded that the policy was necessary because not all Indians would successfully farm their own land, even with government assistance and encouragement: "I do not see how we can get away from the leasing proposition without being charged with being derelict in not getting for the Indian the most return for what he possesses." To critics, he responded, "We would not lease the Indians' land if there were any way we could compel them to make use of it. We do not encourage them to lease where they can farm."[21]

During his first years in office, Commissioner Burke began turning more responsibility for leasing over to the superintendents, presumably so that decisions could be made by local officials who knew the allottees personally. Superintendents and other field officials began granting certificates of competency to Indians who were qualified to negotiate leases rather than submitting these lease applications to the Indian Office for approval as they had done in the past. Then, in 1921, the superintendents received authority to approve all farming and grazing leases without submitting them to the Indian Office. The Indian Office enacted new regulations that permitted the superintendent to approve and retain at his agency all these leases, except the disputed ones which were sent to the Indian Office for settlement. Although the 1921 act relieved the Washington office of burdensome paperwork, it added to the confusion in the field and caused disparity in leasing practices.[22] Moreover, it created a dangerous situation because superintendents could be more easily pressured and manipulated by local whites who wanted leases than distant Washington officials.

In the 1920s Indian Office administrators became even more concerned than their predecessors that the lessees make improvements on the land for the benefit of the Indian lessor. Thus in 1923 they formulated new regulations that limited leases for money consideration alone to one year for grazing and to two years for farming or for farming and grazing purposes, but where payment came in forms other than cash, the leases could be made for two or three years. Indian Office regulations insisted that one of the main reasons for leasing should be to provide permanent improvements, such as fences and walls, that would help the allottee become self-sufficient when he reoccupied his land, so it was now stipulated that each lease provide for some specific improvement. If a minor planned to occupy the land later, the leases were to provide improvements necessary for a home by the time the minor was expected to need one. Finally, to protect the Indians from exploitation, the rules provided that no person or corporation could lease more than 640 acres of farmland, but they set no limit on the amount of grazing land that non-Indians could lease.[23]

With the approval of the secretary of the interior, Burke amended the 1923 regulations by adding the phrase, after the word "improvements" in section twenty, "and for the planting of such crops, crop rotation and methods of cultivation, including the use of fertilizers, as may be deemed necessary to conserve the fertility of the soil." Thus, leases had to include proper measures to conserve the soil. The new regulations were significant, for superintendents now had the power to force lessees to provide for conservation measures whereas before many leases contained no provision for soil conservation so the fertility of soil was depleted by the end of the lease period.[24]

Determined to put the land into use as well as provide improvements, again with Interior Department approval, Assistant Commissioner Meritt amended the 1923 regulations to give the superintendents more control over Indians who resisted farming. Under the 1923 regulations a superintendent could sign leases for only those resisting Indians who were "mentally incompetent," but the amendment authorized him to sign leases for allottees who were "clearly incapable of acting for their best interests by refusing to lease their lands." This vague wording gave superintendents powerful discretionary authority to coerce resisting Indians into signing leases. Indian Office officials reasoned that sometimes adult allottees were clearly incapable of understanding the benefit of having their land leased and improved. If the need for leasing was exceptionally great and the superintendent could not induce the allottee to sign, he was to turn the matter over to the Indian Office with all the pertinent facts and his recommendation that he be allowed to sign on behalf of the allottee. The superintendent was not, however, to submit cases unless the facts were "exceptional" and the lease was "absolutely necessary" so that the Indian Office could properly protect the Indian's interests.[25] Thus Charles Burke was the first commissioner to authorize superintendents to lease allotments without the approval of the Indian owners.

In the 1920s Commissioner Burke encouraged parents to sign leases for their minor children as a another means of putting Indian land into productive use. He also ordered superintendents to make leases regardless of what the parents wanted. Any allottee with enough knowledge, experience, and "business capacity," the commissioner warned, had the privilege to make his own lease and those of his minor children and to collect rentals for them with the superintendent's approval, but if the leasing privilege was abused, the Indian Office could revoke it.[26]

Despite the regulations and Burke's pleas for caution, pressure from local whites and superintendents and the promise of easy cash in the form of rentals prompted more Indians to resort to leasing each year. In 1925 over 40,000 farming and grazing leases were made on approximately 4,000,000 acres of allotted land for which the Indians received a cash rental of roughly $5,000,000, or $1.25 an acre, plus other benefits. The superintendents were to return leased lands to the Indians at the end of the lease period if there was evidence that the Indians would exert "reasonable and practical" efforts to develop the land and improve their conditions; if not, they were to lease the lands for another term.[27]

Although non-Indians leased more land each year, they remained dissatisfied because they wanted a longer lease period than the regulations provided. One field service employee encouraged the Indian Office to lease unallotted Indian land for terms long enough to enable lessees to farm such land successfully. Long term leases, he argued, allowed the lessees to develop Indian land to the point where it could be used for homes and farms or produce revenue from continued leasing. Many of the lessors worked as hired help on their own land, so they received both a steady income and valuable experience.[28] The Interior Department responded to these complaints by pushing for an extension of the lease period. The 1894 law had limited farm leases on tribal land to five years, a period that Secretary Work believed was too short because much of the "rough, unbroken sage-brush" land was costly to cultivate. The five-year limit, he charged, had seriously handicapped Interior Department efforts to make surplus reservation land productive.[29] On July 3, 1926, at Work's urging, Congress authorized the secretary to lease unallotted irrigable lands on any reservation for farming for ten years with the consent of the tribal council, business committee, or other representative body.[30]

The Indian Office's leasing policy encompassed not only grazing and farming land but also land with valuable mineral deposits. Indian-owned mineral lands were developed without the Indians' permission and with little economic benefit to them, and federal officials would justify the process on the basis of the Indians' inability to manage these resources "efficiently." The formal policy of leasing mineral lands began in 1891 when Congress authorized mining leases on treaty reservations for up to ten years. It reduced this period to five years in 1897. As the demand for oil and other resources grew in the early twentieth century and as new mineral deposits were uncovered in the Southwest, the call for more liberal leasing legislation grew louder. Congressmen from Arizona and New Mexico who wanted to develop their states pressed for the authority to lease tribal lands to miners. In 1915 Senator Henry Ashurst of Arizona, reflecting the sentiments of many Westerners, proposed a general bill to allow the secretary to grant mineral entry on reservations on the same terms as on the public domain. The Interior Department supported the bill, arguing that without it non-Indians could not develop the valuable mineral deposits on Western reservations, despite the current high prices for metals. Nor did the Indians have the knowledge and the capital for extensive mining operations.[31]

Ashurst's bill failed to pass, but when he introduced a similar one in June 1918, again with Western support, Congress responded more favorably. With war now raging in Europe, Democrats argued persuasively that the bill was essential to increase the output of important metals and that the Indians were unable to manage their own resources efficiently. After a stormy three-day debate in the Senate and frustrating delays in the House the bill became law on June 30, 1919. Not once during the debates had the opponents of the bill questioned the basic assumption that the federal government had complete authority over Indian land. The law authorized the secretary of the interior to lease reservation land in Arizona, California, Idaho, Montana, Nevada, New Mexico, Oregon, Washington, and Wyoming for the mining of metalliferous minerals.[32] Although the legislation was initially conceived during the war as a means of increasing the production of certain minerals, it ultimately allowed non-Indians to exploit the mineral resources on Indian land and sometimes gain control of that land.

Before the war, the Wilson administration had followed a policy of withholding public lands containing valuable mineral deposits from sale or lease in order to conserve them, but with the growing wartime demand for raw materials, it now came under intense pressure to lease those lands. Secretary Lane personally favored the exploitation of mineral resources through leasing, provided the Western states received a share of the royalties, but he had not been able to get legislation allowing him to lease mineral-rich public lands because of opposition from concerned conservationists. Without such legislation, he could do little but experiment with leasing on Indian reservations.

When Democrats introduced a mineral leasing bill in 1918, it was defeated because it failed to satisfy Western demands. Eventually both houses agreed on a mineral leasing bill signed by the president on February 29, 1920, which recognized the right of the United States to hold public land in trust permanently rather than turning it over to the states. The bill, which marked the acceptance of leasing as a general policy, gave Lane's development policy a tremendous boost. The Wilson administration had clearly retreated from its conservation principles.[33]

As the supply of good land diminished in the early twentieth century, the Indian Office and Interior Department came under pressure to lease not only valuable mineral lands on treaty reservations, but also land on executive order reservations. The 1891 act had authorized the Interior Department to lease lands within treaty reservations, but not lands within reservations created by executive order or by an act of Congress. Interior Department and Indian Office officials, however, believed current leasing laws deprived Indians of income and impeded the development of their land, so they pushed for legislation to permit the secretary to lease for farming and grazing purposes unallotted lands on executive order reservations. Meritt went so far as to call the legislation "very desirable . . . from the Indian standpoint."[34] He and the other officials were anxious to lease executive order land because it contained valuable mineral deposits. Congress held the exploiting interests at bay temporarily by refusing to act on the Indian Office's proposal, but the issue did not die.[35]

The controversy became even greater in the 1920s, specifically because of the fierce disagreement that developed over whether the General Leasing Act of February 25, 1920, applied to the executive order reservations. The General Leasing Act authorized the leasing of the public domain, under the direction of the General Land Office, with 52.5 percent of the leasing proceeds going to the reclamation fund, 37.5 percent to the states, and 10 percent to the U.S. Treasury.[36]

The battle over leasing began when one E. M. Harrison applied for a prospecting permit covering part of the Navajo executive order reservation. Harrison applied to the General Land Office rather than the Indian Office because he believed executive order reservations were part of the public domain, not part of the Navajo reservation, and that the General Leasing Act therefore applied. On January 4, 1922, the General Land Office rejected Harrison's application on the basis that it had no jurisdiction over Indian lands and that the Interior Department had ruled that the 1891 leasing act covered oil and gas mining on treaty reservations only.[37] Harrison then appealed to the secretary of the interior, who was sympathetic to the mining interests. On June 9, 1922, Secretary Albert Fall made an administrative decision that the General Leasing Act did apply to executive order reservations because these lands were owned by the federal government, not by the Indians. In the past, he noted, presidents had restored various reservations to the public domain, proof that they were only temporarily in the Indians' custody.[38]

The Indian Rights Association angrily challenged the Fall decision by arguing that the government had for thirty years considered Indian title to land within executive order reservations as secure as title to land within treaty reservations. Fall's departure from that policy would seriously undermine Indian title to land on executive order reservations and would discourage industrious Indians from building homes and improving their land. Finally, the association contended that since the General Leasing Act applied only to government land, not to reservations, the Fall decision should be reversed.[39]

Although the Indian Office opposed the Fall order, its hands were tied until Hubert Work replaced Fall in March 1923. Work at first indicated that he would not implement Fall's order until Congress met in December 1923, but later he informed Burke that he would uphold the Fall decision. When Burke, surprised and angered, strode into Work's office demanding an explanation, the secretary calmly assured him that there had been a misunderstanding and promised to recommend legislation giving the proceeds from the oil leases on executive order reservations to the Indians.[40]

On December 6, 1923, Work recommended legislation to permit leasing on executive order reservations under the General Leasing Act, with the proceeds from such leases to be deposited in the U.S. Treasury to the credit of the tribe for which the reservation was created. In this way Work hoped to placate both the General Land Office and the Indian Office. The General Land Office would control the leasing process, but the Indians would receive all of the proceeds.[41] On February 15, 1924, Work ordered the commissioner of the General Land Office to stop issuing or approving permits for leases on executive order land.

This order froze about four hundred applications that had been made since the Fall decision.[42]

Attorney General Harlan Stone determined on May 27 that the General Leasing Act did not apply to executive order reservations and recommended that all pending applications be rejected automatically. The Indian Rights Association proclaimed a great victory, for Stone had upheld their argument that the executive order reservations were not part of the public domain.[43] As a result of the Stone decision, in July 1924, the government brought suit in the federal district court of Utah to cancel the permits that had been issued under the Fall order on the grounds that the secretary had had no power to issue them. The court, however, held that the General Leasing Act did apply and dismissed the case. The government then appealed the case to the circuit court of appeals, eighth circuit, which in turn submitted it to the Supreme Court for answers to two questions: (1) Did the secretary have the authority to issue leasing permits on executive order reservations under the General Leasing Act, and (2) if the General Leasing Act did apply, did the government have to stop its suit to cancel the permits?[44]

Meanwhile the Senate approved the Work bill. Both the Senate and the House agreed that executive order reservations should be leased under the General Leasing Act, but they differed on the percentage of taxation the states should get. The House maintained that taxation should be the same as on treaty reservations, but the Senate wanted the percentage to be the same as under the General Leasing Act. The House amended the Work bill to permit the states to levy a production tax on the oil extracted from the land, as the 1924 Indian Oil Leasing Act provided. The Indian Oil Leasing Act of May 29, 1924, had amended the 1891 leasing act to extend the leasing period on treaty reservations from ten years to as long as oil and gas were found in paying quantities, and it had authorized each state to levy a production tax and to tax as it saw fit. The Senate later amended the Work bill to provide that 37.5 percent of the proceeds be paid to the state where the reservation was located in lieu of taxes.[45]

The Indian Rights Association vehemently opposed the Work bill; by turning such a large part of the proceeds, 37.5 percent, over to the states the government was actually denying the Indians' title to the land involved. Nor was Burke pleased. With the cooperation of the Indian Rights Association, he succeeded in having the bill killed on a point of order.[46] Burke believed that the same law should apply to leasing executive order reservations that applied to treaty reservations, that all royalties and rentals should go to the U.S. Treasury for the benefit of the Indians, and that permits issued under the Fall order should not be recognized.[47]

After defeating Work's plan, Congress devised a compromise measure. In 1926 Representative Carl Hayden introduced a bill putting leasing on executive order reservations under the 1924 Indian Oil Leasing Act. Instead of a production tax, the state in which the reservation was located would get 37.5 percent of the rentals and royalties, provided the money was used for roads within the reservation and for public schools attended by the Indians, and the Indians would receive the remaining 62.5 percent directly. The House amended the bill to recognize the rights of both the applicants for permits and the permit holders.[48]

Burke supported the Hayden bill because his main concern was that the Indian Office, not the General Land Office, administer the leasing policy, and by placing leasing under the Indian Oil Leasing Act the bill insured Indian Office control. Now doubtful that any legislation would pass giving 100 percent of the proceeds to the Indians, Burke was willing to let the states have 37.5 percent provided that they spent the money for the benefit of the Indians. Moreover, the Hayden compromise would at least protect Indian rights on executive order reservations. Although it supported the Hayden bill, the Indian Office still refused to recognize the rights of the approximately twenty applicants who had actually received permits.[49]

The American Indian Defense Association condemned Burke for supporting a bill that would turn a large part of the Indians' income over to the states.[50] Echoing this sentiment, Representative James A. Frear of Wisconsin criticized Burke for defending a bill that would deprive the Indians of 37.5 percent of their revenue, exempt oil companies from a production tax, and compromise the Indians' title to 22,500,000 acres of executive order land. Rather than helping the Indians, charged Frear, Burke had recommended a measure "more profoundly destructive to Indian rights" than any which had been before Congress in the past twenty-five years. Under pressure from John Collier, a congressional committee amended the bill to provide for a production tax.[51]

The Hayden bill faced stiff opposition in the Senate until senators Samuel G. Bratton and A. A. Jones of New Mexico introduced new bills modifying it. In testifying on the new measures, Burke took the same position he had taken on the original Hayden bill. Although he was willing to compromise, he opposed the provisions in both the Jones and Bratton bills recognizing some or all of the applicants for permits because these people had not received the department's permission to prospect, had not lost any money prospecting, and therefore deserved no compensation.[52] A heated floor fight ensued during which Senator Ralph Cameron introduced a fourth bill which provided that the Indians get 100 percent of the royalties, subject to state tax, as Collier and Frear wanted. The Hayden bill was later amended with some of the provisions of the Cameron bill and sent to President Coolidge. Coolidge vetoed it because he believed it discriminated in favor of the twenty people who had received permits before the Fall decision was reversed and against the four hundred who had applied for permits.[53]

The next year, the Senate amended the Cameron bill to put those who had actually received permits under the General Leasing Act on an equal basis. Only section five of the Hayden bill, concerning the rights of permit holders and applicants, had to be amended to meet the president's objections. The Cameron bill provided that executive order reservations would come under the same leasing law as treaty reservations, that all the oil and gas mining lease revenue would be deposited in the U.S. Treasury to the credit of the Indians, that states could tax oil and gas production directly, and that permit holders or applicants who had spent money prospecting for oil and gas under the General Leasing Act would receive relief.[54] Frear conceded that the bill was "the best that we can get." Indians with interests in executive order reservations would benefit, he said, because the bill would validate their title to these reservations and settle the question for all time.[55]

The Indian Oil Leasing bill, which the president signed on March 3, 1927, was one of the most significant pieces of legislation concerning Indians passed in the 1920s because it recognized the Indians' title to executive order lands and their rights to the proceeds of mineral leases. The boundaries of executive order reservations could no longer be changed except by an act of Congress, and the Indians were to be consulted about the expenditure of their tribal funds.[56]

While the Indian Office hammered out procedures to allow Indians to lease their valuable farmland and mineral lands, it actively encouraged other Indians to sell their land. The rationale for both policies was the same—to provide Indians with an income and to put the land into productive use. Yet land sales, like the leasing policy, contradicted the goal of self-support and violated the intent of the Dawes Act: Indians tended to live off the sale proceeds, then, when the money was gone, move in with friends or relatives. The policy made it easier for whites to acquire Indian land, but the Indians themselves reaped few benefits.

The Dawes Act stipulated that land remain in trust for twenty-five years so that the Indian owner could not sell it, but Congress soon began chipping away at the safeguard of inalienability surrounding trust allotments. By 1900 many of the original allottees had died and their land was in the hands of heirs who lacked the capital to develop it or were too old or disabled. Often inherited lands could not be partitioned successfully, so the only way to make the land productive or to get the money needed to develop other land holdings was to let the heirs sell it. This, however, proved to be disastrous for the Indians, for the sale of inherited lands meant that the third generation—heirs of the allottee's heirs—would be left landless.[57]

In a May 27, 1902, act, Congress authorized the secretary of the interior to permit heirs to sell trust lands instead of partitioning them and to distribute the proceeds among the heirs. The law stipulated that the government appraise all tracts for sale and establish a minimum price, and that a court-appointed guardian supervise the sale when the beneficiaries were minors. The justification given was that the heirs could use the proceeds from the sale to improve their own allotments. The 1902 law opened the floodgate for the wholesale dissipation of the Indian landed estate. Land sales before 1902 amounted to only 10,291 acres. From 1902 to 1910, however, Indians sold 775,000 acres of inherited land, and by 1920, 1,373,000 acres had passed to white hands under the provisions of this act. Reports from field agents in 1904 indicated that speculators purchased much of it. "Under present conditions,"

Commissioner Jones reported, "the sale of these lands produces few beneficial results, but, on the contrary, has brought about conditions so detrimental to the Indians' welfare and so demoralizing to the community in general as to call for immediate and serious consideration." Congress later modified the 1902 act to provide a more orderly method of determining heirs, principally by the acts of May 8, 1906, and June 25, 1910.[58]

After dealing with the problem of inherited trust lands, Congress turned its attention to the sale of allotments by their original owners. The act of March 1, 1907, authorized sick, disabled, and incompetent Indians to sell their interest in any land with restricted title under rules and regulations prescribed by the secretary. The law was ostensibly intended to provide relief for elderly Indians who could not work and risked starvation. Although the language implied that it would affect only those with specific disabilities, Commissioner Leupp urged that it be applied to all cases where Indians were unable to develop their allotments. Leupp's interpretation aside, Congress was at least acknowledging that in certain cases Indians should be allowed to sell all or part of their allotments. Supporters were clearly anxious to promote the rapid sale and development of Indian land, and the bill led effectively to dispossession as speculators used the law to acquire valuable allotments. From 1908 to 1920, 720,000 acres passed into white hands under the provisions of this law. By 1934, under the 1902 and 1907 acts, another 3,700,000 acres of trust land was alienated from Indian ownership, bringing the Indians total proceeds of $68,671,976.[59]

Leupp's successor, Robert Valentine, also favored the sale of Indian land, but only in certain situations. The Indian's land was of two sorts, he said, that which he actually needed to raise crops and that which was simply valuable as property. Valentine favored selling the surplus property as quickly as possible to open thousands of acres to development and bring in non-Indians. This would put more land on the tax rolls and lead to better school facilities and other social advantages. Selling the land, Valentine concluded, would benefit both the states and the Indians.[60]

In 1910 the Indian Office issued regulations for the sale of Indian land which stipulated that the lands covered by the trust patents were under government supervision and could be sold only when it was in the Indians' best interests. An Indian who wanted to sell his land first petitioned the commissioner of Indian affairs through his superintendent or some other official who had jurisdiction over the land. After receiving the petition and verifying the information, the superintendent would appraise the land, post a notice of the sale in a conspicuous place for sixty days, and advertise the land in one or more local newspapers once a week for eight weeks. The sale was made to the highest bidder; then it went to the secretary of the interior for approval, along with the original petition for sale, the appraisals, all the bids, and a report from the superintendent.[61] Section five of the 1910 regulations made it illegal to induce Indians to execute any contract, deed, mortgage, or any other instrument of conveyance for trust land. The Indian Office warned superintendents to watch out for violators and report them to the Indian Office promptly. The Indian Office sent out notices to be posted in the agency offices which warned the public about section five.[62]

Because of the Indian Office's casualness about enforcing the regulations, many whites robbed the Natives of the full value of their land. Appraisals were often far below the true value, but even in cases where the appraisal was fair, there was abuse. Although he had no proof, the Crow superintendent charged that a few purchasers, after discovering the appraised value of land in the advertisements, apportioned the advertised land among themselves and bid them in at a few dollars above the appraised value. On the Uintah and Ouray reservation, where lands were to be sold in tracts of not more than 640 acres, individuals used fictitious names to purchase more than one tract and they conspired to lessen competition in bidding and to merge the land into large individual holdings.[63]

With the growing demand for food during World War I, the Indian Office placed new emphasis on its practice of pressuring Indians to sell a portion of their allotments to raise the capital and buy the stock and machinery that they needed to improve and develop their remaining land.[64] As part of the nation-wide effort to put as much land into cultivation as possible, in 1917 Sells suggested that the government allow a buyer to take immediate possession of the land without waiting for the secretary's approval because the approval might come too late for that year's crop. If the Interior Department ultimately rejected the sale, the prospective purchaser would have the land at least for the crop season, and the Indian would receive the rental fee for that period.[65] Land prices had risen during the war because of the increased demand throughout "Indian Country," especially in Nebraska, the Dakotas, and Oklahoma. Appraisals on the reservations averaged about $40 per acre, but some allotments sold for over $300 per acre on competitive bids.[66]

As the Indian Office intensified its drive to sell unused Indian land during and immediately after the war, more Indians surrendered their land to whites and relied on friends, relatives, or the federal government for their support. In 1921 a new Republican administration inherited the problem of a shrinking Indian estate. Indian Commissioner Charles Burke encouraged Indian families to sell their original allotment and live on an inherited tract or to relocate in a neighboring town with the proceeds from the sale. He also urged old and incompetent Indians to sell part of their land and to use the proceeds for living expenses, while encouraging minors to sell their surplus land and use the proceeds for education, health care, and other benefits. The results of this policy, however, were disappointing because of a postwar depression. In 1921 the number of sales and the acreage sold declined markedly because of the general collapse of farm prices and the resulting agricultural distress as well as the general depression in business conditions in the country. The Indians received lower prices for their land than they had in 1920 because of decreased demand, and the Indian Office sometimes had to give purchasers extensions on their notes.[67]

Depressed conditions existed throughout the country, but the low demand made it especially hard to sell land in Montana and the Dakotas.[68] In an effort to ameliorate the depressed market conditions, the Indian Office permitted installment payments. This was part of a nationwide trend to buy on credit in the 1920s. In 1923, 1,328 tracts, covering 171,715 acres, were sold on installment. Although many buyers diligently made their payments, the Indian Office occasionally was forced to grant extensions. The extensions, however, were to be given only with the consent of the Indian involved and upon payment of the interest due. Over the next few years the government placed restrictions on installment payments such as requiring 25 percent down to prevent abuse.[69] In 1930, Indians sold 71,684 acres of original allotments and inherited land for $666,524. Many payments were deferred for another year because of the depressed economic conditions in the country and the shortage of available credit. The following year 69,795 acres sold for $1,008,538.[70]

In practice, non-Indians violated laws and regulations governing Indian land sales as aggressively as they violated the leasing laws and regulations. Companies used unscrupulous methods to grab up large blocks of Indian land. One buyer, Frye and Company, managed to acquire 90 percent of the land sold on the Fort Peck reservation by using questionable, if not dishonest, methods to purchase certain tracts. It reportedly paid advances to certain Indians before their land was advertised or approved for sale by the secretary, thus forcing the Indians to sell their land for less than its real value.[71]

The Indian Office staff and the superintendents violated their trust responsibility by failing to protect their wards from abuse and to insure that they received fair compensation for their land. In a less than reassuring letter to a resident of Martin, South Dakota, who was disturbed by white land-grabbing, Commissioner Burke admitted the weakness of his policy. The fact that speculators were buying up large tracts of Indian land was "unfortunate," he conceded, but it was "a hard thing to control." A sixty-eight-year-old full blood from Fort Peck, Circling Eagle, charged that the agent had sold his 320-acre allotment without his consent and against his wishes. Although he received a two-room house as compensation, he could not discover what his land had sold for, what the house cost, or if there was any balance due him; nor had he ever been paid any money for the land. Florence Lambert Shield and her mother, also from Fort Peck, complained that in six years they had received only one-fifth of the sale price on their inherited allotment. Although Shield was unemployed and desperately needed the money, the superintendent ignored her pleas and made no effort to collect from the seemingly prosperous buyer.[72] Many superintendents simply refused to report cases where the purchasers of Indian allotments defaulted on their payments despite regulations requiring them to do so.[73]

Policymakers in the Interior Department, the Indian Office, and Congress gradually broke down the safeguards surrounding allotments and actively encouraged their sale or lease in order to make Indian land as productive as possible. In fact, the leasing and sales policies subverted the goals of allotment, contradicted the stated objectives of these policymakers, and made a mockery of the claim that Indians would use the trust period to improve their farming skills. Rather than promoting self-support and industry, these policies encouraged the Indians to live off lease rentals or revenue from land sales. Moreover, field service employees failed to enforce the laws and regulations effectively and to protect Indian rights adequately. As a result, hundreds of thousands of acres of Indian land fell into white hands, and in the 1930s the government would have to deal with the problem of restoring that land to Indian ownership.

5.
Leasing
Problems and Abuses

The government's ambitious policy of leasing Indian land led to widespread abuse. The rights of Indian landowners were often violated because Indian Office officials administered the leasing policy badly and ignored their trust responsibility. The most serious problem with the policy was that, despite the professed good intentions of policymakers in the executive and legislative branches, leasing defeated the purpose of the Dawes Act. Rather than promoting the goals of self-support and assimilation, leasing encouraged dependency among Indians who tended to live off their lease rentals rather than work. Moreover, leasing often became the first step toward the sale of Indian land and thus led directly to the shrinkage of the Indian estate.

The Indian commissioners often turned a deaf ear to the numerous field officials who complained that leasing encouraged dependency and demoralized Indian landowners. One critic, for example, explained that by leasing to whites the Fort Hall full bloods "loose [sic] their best opportunity to have that responsibility upon themselves (the care and management of their own lands) which is essential to their development." Too often, he complained, the Indian Office allowed the Indians to lease their land throughout the trust period only to end up less competent than they were before it began.[1] One Indian Office inspector, while admitting that the lands on Pine Ridge were good only for grazing and that the Indians would make little use of them, opposed leasing because the Indians would live off their lease checks rather than go to work. The Indians themselves expressed the same concern. The Pimas, for example, objected to leasing on the Gila River reservation because it would "demoralize [the Indian's] ownership, his sense of appreciation of land value and will also undermine his responsibility as a homemaker and producer." It would, they argued, cause him to sell his land and become a pauper, a burden on the government and his community.[2]

In response to such stinging criticism, the government's supporters argued that leasing was sometimes necessary because the Indians lacked the expensive equipment needed to compete with large farmers. They were unable to cultivate all of their farmland or did not have enough stock to use their grazing land. Without government aid, supporters charged, Indians would lack the necessary capital to make the land produce. The Pine Ridge superintendent, for one, argued that although the lease payments for individual Indians were not large, the total of all payments amounted to many thousands of dollars that would otherwise be lost to the Indians. Moreover, the rich grass on the reservation would otherwise be wasted. Lessees employed many Indians as ranch hands and farm hands, whereas before the Indians had to leave the reservation to find employment.[3]

Critics of leasing also complained that the lessees destroyed the fertility of the soil. Since the land did not belong to them, lessees concerned themselves with short term use, not the future quality of the land. They refused to practice the intelligent crop rotation necessary to keep the land at a high level of productivity. For example, most lessees on the Flathead reservation raised a single crop—wheat, which depleted the soil.[4]

Whether one believed that leasing encouraged or discouraged self-support, the fact that it led to abuse could not be denied. As a direct result of the government's leasing policy, Indian rights were violated and their property was destroyed. Indians rarely received fair compensation for the lease of their land or for damage to that land. On the Crow reservation, some allottees were not compensated at all for the use of their unfenced grazing land. Lessees on the Cheyenne River reservation let their cattle graze outside the lease area, where they broke down fences and destroyed Indian hay, causing so much damage that an Indian Office inspector pleaded with his superiors to stop leasing the grazing land there altogether. From the same reservation came the complaint that lessees stripped the land of its minerals and reduced its value by planting flax, wheat, and oats. On Standing Rock as well lessees made no effort to confine their large herds, thus destroying the Indians' fences, their land, and, more important, their ambition and interest. The cattle companies cost the Indians huge sums of money, and although the Indians pleaded that these cattle be removed from their land, they were ignored. "They feel that the 'Great Father' in Washington is asleep and has forgotten them," the superintendent complained, "and certainly it would appear that they were not wholly incorrect in this assumption."[5]

Non-Indians sometimes used questionable methods including threats and phony promises to secure leases. The Indian Office relied on the "integrity and good work" of its agents in implementing its leasing policy because it could not witness the situation in the field first hand. It almost always approved leases made by agents and selected 90 percent of its agents from the locality they served. In a subtle admission that agents could not be objective, Commissioner Jones conceded that the agents were anxious to stay on friendly terms with their non-Indian neighbors, so they usually granted their requests for leases. The superintendent on the Yuma reservation in California falsely certified three old Indians as councilmen so that they could sign a lease of tribal lands to a white speculator, and he reportedly leased land to lawyers, merchants, and real estate men, rather than to farmers. Agency officials were not immune to local pressures. The Yankton superintendent showed favoritism in leasing by rejecting leases made by those not of his "political faith." He also leased land for eight to ten cents an acre when a fair price would have been at least twenty-five cents an acre.[6]

Occasionally Indians themselves were responsible for the abuse when they leased land to whites illegally. Indians on the Sisseton reservation promised to lease their lands to two or more persons for the same season. Over 50 percent of the allotted lands leased on the Santee reservation was leased illegally by Indians to whites to get money in advance for immediate use, for payment of debts, and for securing loans or credit. Non-Indians around the Sisseton reservation told the Indians that they had the right to lease their allotments without obtaining Indian Office approval. As a result, the Indians made so many illegal private leases that the superintendent recommended that the Indian Office take drastic measures. In all these cases the Indians ultimately became the "victims" for they paid enormous interest for loans and received pitifully small lease payments. Often they received only the advance payment, not the balance. Moreover, many young able-bodied Indians who leased their land reportedly became idle "drunkards."[7]

With the rise in farm prices during World War I abuse in leasing increased and the Indian Office became less vigilant. As part of its effort to encourage leasing and promote the war effort, the Indian Office waived certain regulations, especially those making the lessor responsible for improvements on the leased land.[8] During the war the Indian Office leased huge tracts of land to individuals and corporations, and the Indians sometimes suffered from its enthusiastic leasing practices. The Indian Office made these large leases without the consent of the Indians and then closed its eyes as lessors violated the terms of those leases. In 1919 Commissioner Sells authorized W. R. Elliot of Phoenix, Arizona, to lease five thousand acres on the arid Gila River reservation for ten years. In return, Elliot was to leave one-fourth of each tract seeded with alfalfa at the end of the lease period, provide wells for irrigation, and provide electricity to operate them. The only support for the Pimas who opposed the lease arrangement came from the Indian Rights Association which demanded that the secretary rescind the lease agreement because it had been made in secrecy, "by dark lantern methods," and because the Pimas were unanimously opposed to it.[9]

When the House Committee on Indian Affairs challenged the lease, Sells responded that without water the land was worthless and when irrigation plans failed leasing was the only solution. He stressed that planting alfalfa would be expensive for Elliot. The advance knowledge and consent of the Indians was unnecessary in the Elliot case, he explained, because he had only signed an agreement authorizing Elliot to negotiate for leases, not an actual lease. Sells's persuasive arguments apparently impressed Chairman Homer Snyder, for he concluded that the agreement looked like "a splendid proposition for the Indians themselves," and that if Elliot followed the guidelines, the Indians would benefit in the long run.[10]

Despite the committee's decision, the Indian Rights Association continued to fight the lease. It argued that aside from having his ten-acre tract cleared,

One of Campbell's wheat fields on the Crow Reservation in Montana. *Credit National Archives (photo no. 75-BK-64).*

leveled, and ditched, all the Indian owner would get out of the lease, after going without rentals for ten years, would be $1.25 an acre, or 12.5 cents an acre per year. Elliot, however, would reap a huge profit by renting land for much less than its actual value. To make an arrangement so favorable to Elliot and so damaging to the Indians, the association charged, violated the government's trust responsibility. If the government gave the Indians the water it had promised, it concluded, they could farm the land themselves. Indian resistance made it hard for Elliot to secure leases. Under the agreement, if Elliot did not obtain leases within twelve months, the secretary of the interior could cancel the agreement, and when the twelve-month period ended on November 22, 1920, he did so.[11]

Indians on the Umatilla reservation complained that the superintendent showed favoritism instead of awarding leases to the highest bidder and that he enabled certain lessees to enrich themselves at the expense of the Indians. Indeed some men leased more than the eight hundred acres allowed and became wealthy within a few years. Moreover, these lessees refused to make the substantial improvements provided for in the leases. To improve the situation, the Indian Office ordered the Umatilla superintendent to appraise the lands at their lease value, advertise them at a specified time, and force the Indian owner to accept the highest bid, thereby destroying any chance for graft. Sells also decided to reduce the acreage of lessees who held more than eight hundred acres where it could be done without damaging them or the lessors.[12]

On the Crow reservation, too, lessors violated Indian rights. Thousands of acres of good, irrigated land sat idle in 1917, and people in southern Montana generally believed that one way or another whites would ultimately own the unallotted grazing lands on the reservation. The Indians were too poor to purchase cattle, so their only hope was to farm. They had neither the desire nor the capacity to farm a large part of their land, but if they leased, whites would farm the land for them. In April 1918, Secretary Lane made an agreement allowing Thomas D. Campbell to lease their land, and members of the tribal business committee approved it because they believed the land would be leased with or without their consent. A month later, Sells informed the Crow superintendent that he wanted every acre not being farmed by the Indians to be leased but only after he had insured that the Indian had enough land to live on. The commissioner's priorities were clear. The government had a responsibility to protect Indian interests, he explained, but more important was its duty to promote any plan to make idle land productive. The Indian Office implemented a liberal leasing policy on that reservation, and within one year it had made several large leases to the Sheridan Sugar Company and the Montana Farming Corporation. Through these leases the production of much-needed wartime commodities, such as beef, flour, and sugar, increased.[13]

Some Crow tribal members, however, vehemently opposed the leases. The Montana Farming Corporation lease had been presented to them as a necessary wartime measure, and the Indians had agreed to it out of a sense of patriotism. They therefore understandably expected the lease to terminate when the war ended. As plans evolved to expand its terms, the lease began to seem more and more like a plot to exploit the Indians. When the corporation plowed up the land of unsuspecting Indians, they received little sympathy from the superintendent, who coolly remarked, "As long as it has been plowed, you better sign a lease." The corporation acted so forcefully that the Indians felt coerced into signing the leases whether they wanted them or not and would agree to almost anything that the corporation did. After the war ended, the corporation continued to negotiate leases and sublet the Indian land to outsiders for 30 percent of the crop's value, while the Indian owners received only 10 percent.[14]

Complaints about the abusive leasing practices on the Crow reservation finally prompted Congress to investigate. In September 1919 Thomas L. Sloan, an outspoken Indian lawyer, testified that the Crow superintendent often leased the Indians' lands without their knowledge and consent. "In some instances," he continued, "they found their fences had been torn down and land leased, and when they went to the office to inquire about it they were told the agent had the authority to make the lease and nothing could be done about it." The Indians claimed that they were abused and mistreated whenever they opposed the agency administration. They feared retribution from the agent if they complained. According to Sloan the superintendent controlled the land in heirship cases, and when an allottee died the superintendent could lease his land and prevent the heirs from receiving it for many years. Sloan cited the case of Jesse Morris, who owned a 160-acre allotment, an 80-acre inheritance from his son, and 80 acres from his deceased father. In his will, Morris left everything to his wife, but she was deprived of any income from the estate and died in poverty. Sloan alluded to other cases where the lessors received no compensation at all.[15]

In the face of growing criticism, Lane was now called to defend the lease agreement at a congressional hearing. The conditions on the Crow reservation had been "disgraceful," he explained, with only 6,000 to 8,000 acres out of 75,000 acres of irrigable land under cultivation. Thus when Thomas Campbell approached him early in 1918 and promised to plant vast quantities of wheat if the Indians leased him the land, Lane made an agreement even though it violated department regulations because he considered it a patriotic as well as a commercial venture to increase food production. He denied charges that the Campbell Corporation forcibly dispossessed the Indians, saying that the Crow Indian council formally approved the lease. The secretary's agreement did not obligate the allottee to lease; many allottees, in fact, refused to lease and no lands were taken without their consent. As his last defense, Lane argued, "it was a perfect crime to have that land lying out there unused."[16]

During the war Indians continued to have trouble collecting their rent payments. Pine Ridge Sioux who signed leases out of a patriotic desire to help the war effort complained that they did not receive their lease money. Although the regulations required the superintendent to distribute the money to the lessors every six months, some of them waited one to two years for payment or died of starvation and neglect because they could not get the lease money when they needed it. The lessors were not the only Indians on Pine Ridge who were hurt. Young, able-bodied men who had farmed successfully before the war now found their land overrun by white lessees who allowed their cattle to trespass and trample their crops, and when the Indian owners attempted to protect their property by driving out the cattle, local officials threw them in jail. "It is pretty hard for us on the reservation," explained James H. Red Cloud, grandson of the famous Chief Red Cloud. "The reservation is covered with cattle like a whole lot of worms on it. I cannot raise any garden and cannot do anything." Conveniently ignoring these abuses, an Indian Office inspector upheld the leases.[17]

When the abuses were made public, Meritt dutifully defended the Indian Office's actions by noting that during the war that office had been under great pressure to use every acre of grazing land, and since thousands of acres of land on Pine Ridge had been idle Meritt had felt compelled to lease them. The lease terms favored the Indians in that the cattlemen agreed to pay fifteen to thirty cents an acre and to make improvements such as digging wells, making reservoirs, and building fences. Meritt blamed the superintendent's office for delays in distributing lease money, and he blamed war conditions for the fact that non-Indians violated their leasing agreements.[18]

Leasing abuses, specifically the problem of collecting rent, worsened in the 1920s because of low farm prices and because of the Indian Office's refusal to make every possible effort to collect delinquent payments. The Indian Office had a long-standing arrangement with the Justice Department that allowed the superintendents to refer cases involving delinquent rentals directly to the U.S. district attorney for the district in which the reservation was located, but in 1921 the Indian Office ordered the superintendents to submit only those cases where the lessee owed a large amount or had no good reason for not paying. Instead of submitting cases where the lessee was unable to pay, they were to arrange for the lessee to pay the past rentals in installments. Evidently the superintendents ignored the order, for they submitted many cases to district attorneys who subsequently found the lessees to be impecunious.[19] Burke clearly sympathized more with the non-Indian lessee who could or would not pay his rent than with the Indian owner.

Although field service employees were responsible for protecting Indian interests when leasing their land, they neglected their trust responsibilities and Indian Office officials in Washington were so lenient toward delinquent or negligent lessees that some Indians received no rental money at all. The case of Blanche Kokoom, an Indian from Hobart, Oklahoma, was all too common. Kokoom complained in 1930 that her husband had never received the second half of his lease money. Although the lessee had left around 1922 without paying, the government never filed suit or did anything to retrieve the money that Kakoom needed so desperately. When she located the lessee herself and went to the agency to ask the clerks to take action, they laughed at her. Her superintendent estimated that the Indian Office would be lucky to collect 40 or 50 percent of the lease money owed to the Indians.[20]

Indian rights were also violated on the Yakima reservation where Indians found themselves unable to collect their rentals because whites simply did not have the money. Although the number of such cases was small, the destitute lessors could ill afford the loss. The Yakima superintendent attempted to collect, but hesitated to bring suits against delinquent lessees because he did not know who would pay the filing fees and did not believe the rental money could be recovered.[21]

Collecting rents also posed a problem on the Crow reservation where only 3 of the 143 delinquent leases were reported for suit. A combination of poor crops and hard times prevented non-Indian farmers and stockmen from paying their rent, and the government often gave them extensions, if the lessor agreed. Plans were made to extend the leases on over a million acres of tribal grazing land to bring the tribe the revenue and to keep the land in use.[22]

Unlike some of the other tribes which relied on the Indian Office to protect their interests, the Blackfeet Indians chose to handle the problem of delinquent leases themselves by canceling all grazing leases to lessees who failed to meet their payments. Again siding with the non-Indian lessees, Burke opposed arbitrarily canceling all of the leases and permits on the reservation because most lessees wanted to continue using the land, even though they could not afford the payments. He wanted to grant them an extension until July 1, 1922, to prove that they intended to continue their work and would act in good faith. If they made a good showing by that date, he said, the Indian Office would consider giving them more time to meet their payments. Because of the poor grazing conditions on a range that was infested with gophers and Indian ponies, the commissioner was willing to cancel 60 percent of the principal due from each delinquent lessee and all of the accrued interest to date. He would not, however, cancel the entire principal because the contracts were valid ones, which had been entered into in good faith on both sides. Despite poor range conditions, he added, the lessee could usually use at least part of the land, so the government expected the delinquent lessees to pay the remaining 40 percent of the principal soon.[23]

The problem of collecting rents only worsened as farm prices continued to plummet in the 1920s. In 1928 the percentage of delinquency was alarmingly high, one report showing $30,000 delinquent on a single reservation. Perhaps jarred by these figures, Meritt issued a stern warning to superintendents that although bad crops or financial conditions sometimes justified delinquency, the money belonged to the Indians and without it they would be seriously handicapped. Therefore the superintendents were to refer the delinquency cases to the district attorney. Many lessees also failed to make the stipulated improvements within the specified time or did not make them at all, and the superintendents were to check such leases closely. They were to report before July 1 the amount of delinquent rentals at their agencies and the efforts they were making to collect them.[24]

Although the courts ordered the lessees on the Uintah and Ouray reservation to pay $13,071.96 in delinquent rentals, the superintendent found it impossible to collect the money because the lessees were insolvent, had left the country, or had died and left no estate. The Yakima superintendent turned some cases over to the district attorney, but more often he accepted notes and mortgages with such success that only $13,824 of the $1,250,000 total cash rental between 1925 and 1927 was still outstanding. Few cases on the Crow reservation went to court because the record of repayment was good, with only $2,002 of the $300,000 total rentals, two-thirds of 1 percent, delinquent.[25]

Some superintendents in the 1920s were lax in dealing with defaulting lessees; others violated Indian rights in more serious ways. Negligent and sometimes corrupt field service employees did little to enforce leasing regulations and to protect their wards from leasing abuses. Agency employees on the Yakima reservation coerced Indians into leasing rather than encouraging them to farm. They approved lessees different than those the allottees selected and failed to ensure that able-bodied Indians kept part of their allotments as the regulations stipulated. Although department regulations prohibited leasing more than 640 acres of irrigated land to any one individual, firm, or corporation without special permission from the commissioner, the superintendent approved seventeen leases, covering one thousand acres, to one investment company and to individuals who were financed through that company.[26]

The administration of leasing matters on the Yakima reservation was careless at best. Agency employees treated certain lessees with leniency and favoritism and ignored regulations. When Burke heard of these abuses, he ordered Superintendent Estep to devise instructions for every aspect of the leasing procedure and give them to the various employees. He reprimanded Estep for not emphasizing improvements enough in the leases. "In some instances," Burke conceded, "it would appear that the interests of some lessee or his bondsman have been given greater consideration than that of the Indian. Our first duty is toward the Indian." Estep forced some Yakima Indians who wanted to farm their allotments to lease them. In one case the callous Yakima superintendent altered the name of the lessee on the lease without informing the allottee, and in other cases he leased the allottees' land to men whom they did not want to have it. One angry allottee charged that the superintendent threatened to withhold much-needed irrigation water from his land unless he agreed to lease it, but Burke ignored his plea for help.[27]

On the Crow reservation, the tribal council unanimously passed a resolution requesting the removal of Superintendent Calvin Asbury and the cancellation of all oil leases made without the owner's consent. The Crows, who had been offered more favorable leases than those arranged by Asbury, believed that Asbury had, as one Indian phrased it, "been crooked with them."[28] One

Indian observed that cars came to Asbury's home at all hours of the night and charged that he accepted cash payments in return for favors. Indians who denounced him were threatened with jail or beatings. If Asbury was not a crook, the Indian concluded, "then he is so incompetent as to appear one." So angry were the Crows that they approved oil leases to two Washington attorneys and repudiated the leases made by Asbury. The Crow business committee, however, later reversed itself and approved the Asbury leases in hopes that it could put itself in a position to get rid of him sooner.[29]

The Yuma superintendent, too, violated Indian rights. Although he promised Indian landowners that at the end of a five-year lease period lessees would leave behind fields of alfalfa, cement headgates, a three-wire fence, and fifteen fruit trees to every acre, the lessees made none of these improvements. Although he stipulated that the lessees would leave the houses they built for the Indian owners, they sold them to each other and removed them. According to the agreement, lessees had to have the landowners' approval to renew at the end of five years, but the Yuma superintendent renewed many leases without informing the owners. Nor would he tell them when their leases expired or how much money they should receive. The superintendent would lock the agency door and disappear so that he would not have to answer their questions. Sometimes the Indians received their lease money; sometimes they did not. Indians who complained to the superintendent rarely received their money. In 1921, non-Indians leased 71 percent of the reservation, but the Indian owners had consented to most of the leases.[30]

Rather than uphold his trust responsibility, the superintendent apparently did nothing about whites who left before their five-year period expired without making the stipulated improvements. One powerful lessee, E. F. Sanguinetti, forced the Indians to lease. Sanguinetti leased the allotments of Patrick Miguel's children after promising to make improvements, but he failed to do so by the time the lease expired. The superintendent did nothing except assure Miguel that Sanguinetti did not intend to use the land again. In late spring, however, a startled Miguel found teams working the land and upon investigation discovered that Sanguinetti had leased the allotments for three more years. Miguel had no recourse but to file a suit which he had little chance of winning. The superintendent continued to lease the Indians' land to Sanguinetti without their consent even though Sanguinetti made no improvements until by 1924 this speculator and his agents controlled 75 percent of the original reservation land. Through the use of intimidation, Sanguinetti managed to lease land for five dollars an acre that should have been leased for twenty-five dollars.[31] When the Yumas requested that the Indian Office investigate the unscrupulous leasing practices of their superintendent, it dragged its feet until finally the Indian Rights Association intervened and sent Matthew K. Sniffen to investigate. The association asked President Coolidge not to approve or renew any leases until the investigation was completed. Now under pressure, Burke directed the Yuma superintendent to cooperate with Sniffen.[32]

Perhaps even more serious than the problem of abuses in the leasing policy was the fact that in the late 1920s and early 1930s the leasing policy continued to fall short of its stated objectives. Although the Indian commissioners continued to argue that the purpose of leasing was to enable Indians who could not use their lands to become self-sufficient it clearly had the opposite effect. Allottees generally preferred to accept the comparatively small income from leasing rather than learn to work the land themselves. Leasing on the Sisseton reservation actually discouraged work among the Indians because they could reap a greater return from leasing their allotments than from farming them without risking loss from crop failures.[33]

Policymakers failed to realize that a fundamental cultural change on the part of the Indians was necessary before the leasing program could succeed. At the Devils Lake reservation, leasing produced what one member of the Board of Indian Commissioners called "a race of non-competent landlords." "So long as his scale of living calls for only enough flour and beef to ward off starvation," she wrote, "a single outfit of clothing with no thought of change or repair or laundry, for only enough heat and shelter to permit ten or a dozen people to crowd around the stove in a single airtight room—so long as these conditions satisfy his soul and even a small allowance of lease money will provide them—just so long will the forethought and prudence and industry of the farmer remain an unrealized and uncomprehended ideal." Therefore, to continue the current leasing system, she argued, would hamper progress.[34]

Commissioners Sells and Burke adopted a liberal leasing policy that benefited whites more than Indians and discouraged Indian self-support. Their flawed policy was often poorly implemented by negligent or corrupt field service employees who were more concerned about the needs and desires of local whites than with protecting Indian landowners. Indian Office officials, however, were not entirely to blame for the harm caused by their leasing policies. Non-Indians exerted intense pressure to make Indian land available and to put it into use. Moreover, the prospect of no work, no risk, a steady income, and the promise of improved land was simply too attractive for many Indians to resist.

6.

Land and Water
Federal Irrigation Projects
on Indian Reservations

In the first decades of the twentieth century the federal government spent millions on elaborate irrigation projects on Indian reservations with disappointing results. The federal irrigation program was not only unfair to Indian landowners, it was economically unsound. Moreover, federal officials violated their trust responsibility toward Indians by using Indian money to construct and maintain expensive irrigation projects that they did not want and could not use.

Although the federal government did not devise a formal irrigation policy until the 1880s, Indians themselves had long been using effective irrigation techniques. Evidence in arid regions of the West indicates that Indians had been practicing irrigation since prehistoric times. Complete irrigation systems with ditches were common in the Southwest, as was the practice of planting in soils which were naturally irrigated by waters from overflowing streams. This floodplain agriculture was important to the Yuma tribes of the lower Colorado River. In other parts of the Southwest where large streams were absent, farmers planted crops at the foot of mesas or in washes where the run-off from an occasional shower provided moisture. They sometimes constructed dikes or dams to control the natural run-off.[1]

Until the end of the nineteenth century, irrigation was pursued on an ad hoc basis. The first federal venture in Indian irrigation construction was authorized by the act of March 2, 1867, which appropriated $50,000 for locating Indians on the Colorado River reservation in Arizona and constructing a canal for irrigating the reservation. Congress made the first general appropriation for irrigation work on the reservations in 1884, and after 1893 it made these general appropriations annually.[2]

Indian Office officials worried about losing authority over Indian irrigation to the War Department or the U.S. Geological Survey, for both agencies had staffs of hydraulic engineers. In the 1880s and 1890s, as Westerners pushed for a federal reclamation program, Commissioner of Indian Affairs Thomas Morgan and his successors repeatedly appealed to Congress for money to hire skilled engineers. The principal opposition to irrigation appropriations came from Constantine B. Kilgore of Texas, Thomas R. Stockdale of Mississippi, and other states' rights Democrats, and the principal support came from Westerners like Territorial Delegate Mark Smith of Arizona and Senator Fred Dubois of Idaho.[3]

The matter received increasing attention after 1900 as irrigation became an integral part of the Indian Office's drive to promote Indian self-sufficiency and the productive use of Indian lands. Chief Irrigation Engineer William Reed argued that Indians would profit more from the government's irrigation activities than from any other activity in its program to "civilize" Indians.

The federal government needed to provide water on newly assigned allotments in the Pacific Northwest and the Rocky Mountain regions so that Indians could farm. Many Indian tracts were in arid and semi-arid regions that could not be developed to full capacity without water, so the Indian Office began constructing irrigation projects. Policymakers were sensitive to the glaring contradiction in spending thousands of dollars to turn Indians into farmers but not providing the one element essential to successful farming—water. "If the Indians are considered as owning these lands," noted Frederick H. Newell, the Hydrographer of the U.S. Geological Survey, "and the Government is acting as trustee it is certainly a breach of trust not to give these lands their greatest value." The Indian Office considered irrigation work an important part of its efforts to promote Indian industry because it provided Indians with employment as farmers and ensured them a fair return for their labors. Irrigation provided a valuable means of teaching the Indians the habits of industry and civilization not only because it forced them to work consistently but also because it meant fewer discouraging crop failures.[4]

In addition to promoting self-support, another motive for developing irrigation on Indian reservations was to protect Indian water rights. As the West developed, state governments began to allocate scarce water resources to residents using the principles of prior appropriation and beneficial use. The first applicants got priority in their claim to the water but they had to use their water rights constructively within a set time period. Water could not be reserved for future use.

The same principle of beneficial use governed Indian access to water on reservations. Allottees who would not or could not farm risked losing their water to their more aggressive white neighbors. Thus Indian Office officials concluded that the best way to develop idle allotments and protect the water right was to lease the land. Indian Commissioner Francis Leupp, for example, asked Congress for the power to grant long-term leases at the Uintah and Wind River reservations. Congress agreed to ten-year rentals on the Uintah reservation and twenty-year agreements at Wind River. Long-term leases were also signed at the Yakima, Flathead, and Blackfeet agencies.[5]

Commissioner Leupp conceded that the actual irrigation of Indian lands was not always the primary object, although the Indian office viewed it as a valuable by-product. Before the Newlands Reclamation Act of 1902, which established the first major federal reclamation program, and the new emphasis

Irrigating the beanfield of Antonio Ortega. *Credit National Archives (photo no. 75-EXA-3-9).*

on prior appropriation, he said, no one questioned the power of the federal government to appropriate enough water on reservations to meet the needs of the Indians. Now these rights were being denied. Even when the government had specifically promised to protect Indian water rights and spent thousands of dollars to construct an irrigation system, he added, opponents had argued before the courts, Congress, and the Interior Department that the Indian had no such rights. Leupp contended that if Congress could appropriate all unused waters of the public domain for purposes of the Reclamation Act, it could surely appropriate the waters in Indian reservations for the use and benefit of Indian occupants of those reservations.[6]

After 1902 the Indian Office competed with the newly created Reclamation Service for control of Indian land and water. A 1904 law authorized the Reclamation Service to reclaim and dispose of reservation land as long as each Indian received an irrigated farm. That policy was later applied to non-reservation allotments. A 1907 agreement between the Indian Service and the Reclamation Service empowered the latter to construct irrigation facilities on the Fort Peck, Flathead, and Blackfeet reservations in Montana and on the Pima and Yuma reservations in Arizona. The Reclamation Service would retain control of these facilities until 1924 when Congress returned the responsibility to the Indian Office.[7]

The Reclamation Service upheld the principles of beneficial use and prior appropriation. During the Roosevelt and Taft administrations, the Indian Office deferred to the Reclamation Service, thus hoping to increase the Indian water supply through the storage of surplus water flow rather than claiming already appropriated stream flow.

The conflict between the two agencies over water rights intensified with the Winters case. In an 1888 treaty the government set aside Fort Belknap reservation in Montana for the Gross Ventres and Assiniboine bands. Farming in this region was impossible without irrigation. In 1900 white farmers upstream began diverting water from the Milk River until by the spring of 1905 the river dried up before reaching the parched reservation. The Fort Belknap agent asked the Indian Office to file suit on the ground that he had filed a claim for 11,000 miners inches of water in 1898 before the white farmers had appropriated it. The U.S. district attorney expanded the government's claim to argue that the entire flow of the Milk River had been reserved for the Indians. Much to the dismay of other federal agencies that were committed to the prior appropriation doctrine, he invoked riparian rights. Under the principle of riparian rights the owners of property adjacent to a water source have the rights to that water as long as their diversion of it does not deprive other riparian properties of water.

In the 1908 *Winters v. United States* decision, the Supreme Court held that prior appropriation by the U.S. and beneficial use by Indians was unnecessary because of an implied reservation of water in the treaty. The court based its finding that reservations had inherent rights to water on the premise that Congress intended the Indians to farm their lands. Thus Winters rights existed irrelevant of usage, while prior appropriation rights were determined through usage. Winters rights were established by the federal government, while prior appropriation rights were granted by state governments. After 1908 the Indian office no longer had to rely on prior appropriation as its only weapon in the battle to defend Indian water rights.

The Winters decision, however, was ambiguous. The court did not recognize a specific tribal share of the river or clarify the federal government's power over opened portions of the reservation. Nor did it indicate how the decision should be implemented. As a result the Indian Office had much freedom in interpreting the decision. Despite the Winters doctrine the Indian Office did not adopt a consistent policy to protect Indian rights, and Indian claims to water for future use remained in jeopardy. It continued to lease irrigable land on the assumption that tribes had to use the lands constructively like whites. The Indian Office maintained an ad hoc approach for five years. No official policy or doctrine evolved until 1913. The Indian Office interpreted the Winters doctrine narrowly and assumed that it applied only to unallotted land. From the Indian Office's perspective the doctrine was a temporary strategy to use only until the Indians began farming their allotments.[8]

In his thorough analysis of Indian irrigation, historian Daniel McCool finds little evidence that the Indian Office believed that the tribes had reserved water rights or placed much importance on the Winters doctrine. "It is of vital importance to the future welfare of the Indian," explained Chief Engineer William H. Code, "that his water right be insured through beneficial use. In most instances it is only through leasing that he can effect proper final proof." Thus, the Indian Office took a defensive stance rather than expanding Indian claims under the Winters doctrine. Although it invoked the doctrine occasionally, more often it relied on state prior appropriation laws. The Indian Office's reluctance to use the Winters doctrine ultimately damaged its effectiveness.[9]

With or without the Winters decision, the Indian Office remained determined to make arid land productive and to protect Indian water rights. In the first decades of the twentieth century it advanced its irrigation program in order to meet these goals. Initially the Indian Office used field officers to promote irrigation. The Indian Appropriation bill for 1900 authorized the secretary of the interior to employ two superintendents of irrigation who were skilled irrigation engineers. Projects remained under the supervision of the agency superintendents until 1905 when a small corps of engineers was created in the Indian Service to supervise irrigation projects that served Indian land. A 1905 act authorized the appointment of two engineers as inspectors and designated one of them as chief. Soon after, Inspector William H. Code became the first chief engineer.[10]

The land division in the Indian Office was responsible for irrigation until 1907, when that responsibility shifted briefly to the field work division. In 1909 irrigation activities moved back to the land division. The irrigation section of the Indian Service was identified with other field services rather than with the central office until 1934 when a separate irrigation division was established.

To better organize its irrigation program, the Indian Office divided the arid regions of the United States into five irrigation districts. The field organization included a chief inspector of irrigation, who acted as chief engineer; one assistant inspector, who acted as assistant chief engineer; seven superintendents of irrigation, five of whom supervised the various irrigation districts, one who supervised the "purely mechanical work" in all the districts, and one who was an attorney with special knowledge of irrigation law charged with protecting Indian water rights. Under the superintendent of each irrigation district were engineers, assistant engineers, and their assistants.[11]

As the organizational structure took shape, Congress increased the funding for irrigation projects. In March 1905 Congress approved the use of money derived from the sale of Shoshone and Arapaho land at Wind River reservation in Wyoming for a system of ditches and canals that would irrigate 45,000 acres of the reservation. With these projects policymakers planned to transform the reservation into productive farmland. Similar projects quickly followed on other reservations. In 1906 Congress authorized a 200,000-acre project for the newly opened Uintah reservation in eastern Utah, and it included the Yakima agency in a large system being built on the Yakima River. In 1907, the government allocated $300,000 from Blackfeet funds for the tribe's water system, and the following year it began a project on the Flathead reservation. During that same decade irrigation work was also under way on the Crow, Fort Hall, Mission, Navajo, Pueblo, Wind River, Zuni, Fort Belknap, Tongue River, and Walker River reservations. Appropriations for the construction of ditches and reservoirs, the purchase and use of irrigating tools and appliances, and the purchase of water rights on Indian reservations soared from $50,000 in 1900 to $200,000 in 1909.[12]

By 1910 roughly 160,000 acres were being irrigated—118,640 by Indians and 42,080 by white lessees and purchasers. The federal government had spent over five million dollars to bring 300,000 acres of Indian land under the ditch. By 1916 the completed projects supplied water for 490,000 acres and over 220,000 acres were being farmed. The major projects were located on reservations in the Pacific Northwest, the Southwest, and the Rocky Mountain regions (Yakima, Washington; Klamath and Fort Hall, Idaho; Wind River, Wyoming; Blackfeet, Fort Belknap, Flathead, and Crow, Montana; Colorado River, Arizona). There was, however, growing concern that the Indian Office was constructing too many projects too quickly. Critics warned that it took experience for white farmers to succeed on irrigated land and it was unfair to expect Indians who had never farmed before to go on land under an irrigation project and succeed where white farmers had failed.[13]

From the very beginning the government's irrigation program was plagued with serious problems. Irrigation projects were economically unsound and difficult to finance. Moreover, whites, not Indians, used and benefited from these expensive projects on the reservations. These problems of financing and non-use were intricately related. On Indian reservations, as on the public domain, the federal government constructed projects faster than anyone could use or pay for them. Beginning in 1884 Congress provided money for Indian irrigation either in general Indian appropriation acts with the entire cost borne by the federal government or in special appropriations for specific projects to be reimbursed out of tribal funds on the theory that irrigation benefited the tribe as a whole, not just the individual landowners. This policy was unfair because in most cases the irrigation projects included only a part of the reservation so some Indians reaped no benefit. Yet each tribal member had to pay an equal part of the cost.

In making the gratuity appropriation Congress assumed that a tribe's excess land would be sold quickly and that the allottees would keep their homesteads, so it provided that the proceeds of the surplus sales cover the cost of building dams and ditches. It later became clear that uncertainty over water rights and frustrating delays in construction had discouraged whites from buying the surplus land. Moreover, many Indians who had received fee patents were willing to sell their land, so whites could buy allotments where water was already available and avoid the cost of settling unoccupied land. The tribe received no revenue from the sale of these fee patented allotments and thus could not reimburse the government for its expenditures.[14]

As the problem of financing the irrigation projects worsened after 1900, pressure mounted to require the individuals who benefited from the projects to pay for their maintenance and operation. After visiting the Crow reservation in 1913, Chief Irrigation Engineer Reed warned that the irrigation system had to be changed. The Indian Rights Association argued that tribal funds should not be used to construct large irrigation projects where the lands were opened to settlement. Only those Indians who actually benefited from it should pay the cost, not the whole tribe.

The secretary of the Board of Indian Commissioners, Frederick Abbott, recommended that the government stop the gratuitous use of tribal and government funds in the construction and maintenance of irrigation projects and give the Indians a voice in the matter. Seven million of the nine million dollars that had been spent for the irrigation of Indian lands, he noted, had been charged to tribal funds and the rest came from gratuity appropriations made by Congress although the Indians actually used only 100,000 of the 600,000 acres being irrigated. Therefore he recommended legislation that would charge the cost of construction and maintenance to the individual benefited, payable out of his share of the tribal funds. Abbott also suggested that the government make reimbursable appropriations immediately for all the reservations where the Indians had been unable to use their irrigated land for lack of sufficient funds.[15]

Recognizing the problem, Indian Office officials proposed legislation that would give them the authority to charge Indians for their irrigation projects. This legislation, the office argued, would end the unfair practice of using tribal funds to reimburse the government when only part of the tribe benefited from the project. They maintained that whites on the reservation who benefited from the irrigation projects should pay their share of the cost. Congress responded with the act of August 1, 1914, which provided that irrigation funded by general appropriations acts past, present, and future would be repaid by Indian tribes according to their ability to pay, and that projects authorized by special acts would be apportioned among tribal members on the basis of the benefits they received. The government would now prorate the cost among the individual Indians whose land obtained water, thus placing the burden on those directly benefited. Guaranteed repayments would supposedly facilitate future appropriations, while the individualization of costs would make the allottees more responsible in managing their funds.

Although requiring repayment appeared to be a good way to teach the Indians self-support and industry, the 1914 act also forced Indians to pay for projects they had not wanted in the first place. As a result of the 1914 act, the roughly three million dollars that had been spent since 1884, then considered a gratuity, became a reimbursable charge. One of the strongest objections to the 1914 act was this retroactive reimbursable feature.[16]

Making individual Indians liable for the cost did not solve the problem of financing the projects, for the 1914 act proved difficult to enforce. To compute costs on projects most of which were unfinished was no easy task. For several years after 1914, the Indian Office took no step to apportion irrigation costs as the law prescribed, claiming that it would not know the costs until the irrigation systems were completed and that often the irrigated property had passed into white hands so the money could not be collected. Also, the Indians themselves were often too poor to pay the reimbursement charges. There would be no general legislation specifically authorizing and requiring the collection of construction charges until 1920. The debate over financing continued in the Senate and the House for several years after 1914. One group of legislators called for increased appropriations and the speedy completion of the projects and the other favored reduced spending so that the Indians would not sink any further into debt. The constant bickering in Congress meant too little money and too many delays.[17]

The debate over who should pay became more heated as evidence mounted that the Indians did not benefit from the projects. In 1919 Indians actually farmed 104,000 acres by irrigation; 43,000 acres were leased and farmed by whites; and 34,000 acres had been sold to whites and were being irrigated from Indian irrigation systems. Although the Indian Service had spent $12,000,000 on irrigation construction, it required another $27,000,000 to develop the existing projects on the reservations up to their capacity. Yet supporters argued that the Indians would ultimately profit more from the government's irrigation activities than from any other activity in its program to "civilize" the Indians. In response to criticism that it was unfair to use Indian money for projects that primarily benefited whites, supporters noted that the Indian would benefit from working alongside successful whites.[18]

Congressional critics who favored the amendment or repeal of the 1914 act condemned the irrigation policy in 1919 and 1920, noting that 90 percent of the land cultivated and used under the projects was being cultivated and used by whites. The government was in fact building projects for the direct benefit of whites, not Indians. Some legislators, however, had little faith in the Indians' capacity to use the projects successfully for they believed Indian farmers were less intelligent and less industrious than white farmers. Thus, it was only natural, they reasoned, for whites to benefit more. Critics charged, in addition, that the government had developed irrigation projects far beyond the present needs of the Indians. In response to this charge and the argument that it was illegal to require payment from Indians for what they originally had received as a gift, the secretary of the interior coolly replied that if a group of whites or Indians could not use their land without water the government had a responsibility to develop irrigation so that they could produce crops.[19]

The discussions in Congress resulted in stronger reimbursement requirements. The act of February 14, 1920, authorized the secretary of the interior to require all owners of irrigable land, Indian or white, under any irrigation system constructed for the benefit of Indians to begin partial reimbursement or the appropriations for the particular project would be cut off. To implement the 1920 act, the Interior Department approved regulations on June 21, 1920, that required each owner of irrigable land under an irrigation system to pay on or before November 15, 5 percent of the per-acre cost of construction as of June 30. Thus, for the first time, the government forced the Indians to pay for the irrigation facilities with their personal funds.[20]

Soon after Congress passed the 1920 act, Commissioner Sells asked the superintendents to suggest ways to implement the law. The law permitted the secretary to determine when and how much should be collected, and Sells insisted that the collections be made as quickly as possible. Superintendents who responded to Sells's inquiry warned of impending disaster because the Indians were not yet capable of repaying the construction costs, and if the government forced them to do so, they would become discouraged and abandon their land.[21] Farmers on the Flathead reservation, for example, had just begun to build their homes and to develop their land. With the increasing cost of farm labor, machinery, and supplies, the superintendent continued, they were "struggling to keep afloat" and could not possibly pay even 2 percent of the estimated construction cost. The Nevada School superintendent warned that his Indians would consider repayment a great hardship because they had been told that they would not have to make the payments. The superintendent on the Walker River reservation cautioned that if pressed for payment 75 to 95 percent of the Indians would resist. They would stop making improvements and would abandon their homes. The Indians had spent roughly $200 an acre to buy and clear their land and were just getting started, he explained, so any plan for reimbursement would discourage them.[22]

Other superintendents protested that it was unfair, if not illegal, to require reimbursement because the money for the projects had been appropriated as a gratuity and the Indians were never consulted about the projects or told that the money would have to be repaid. The law provided that allotments be free from all encumbrances during the twenty-five-year trust period, so the Indians should be exempt from construction costs. Several irrigation engineers agreed with these superintendents that it would be unfair to charge the Indians for the projects when no prior agreement had been made about repayment, and they argued that the Indians could not afford the costs. "The trouble with all our projects," one irrigation engineer shrewdly observed, "is that construction has proceeded a good deal faster than developement [sic], and I do not see any possibility of getting any returns from idle land."[23]

The problems of financing and using Indian irrigation projects worsened after 1920. Indian Service projects struggled with some of the same problems that were facing Reclamation Service projects. As crop prices and real estate values dropped after World War I an increasing number of white farmers found themselves unable to make their irrigation payments to the Reclamation Service. By 1923 four out of ten project farmers were delinquent in their water construction payments. As of 1923 only 11 percent of the $143 million spent on federal reclamation had been repaid. The Reclamation Service, by now frustrated and discredited, returned reservation water projects to the Indian office in 1924. In the 1920s discontent permeated all federal reclamation projects, not just those on Indian reservations. As the cost of federal projects climbed, white settlers fell further behind in their payments, and the reclamation fund established under the Newlands Act in 1902 did not revolve. Federal reclamation failed to pay its own way. In the 1920s, a decade that glorified efficiency and economy, Republicans found the crisis intolerable. The political climate was right for reform in reclamation, both on public land and on Indian reservations.[24]

In 1920 Secretary of Interior Albert Fall acknowledged a fact already apparent to many: the reclamation program had failed. Most Indians were not yet ready to live a sedentary farming existence, he explained, so whites controlled much of the cultivable land under irrigation projects. Although Indians had not repaid the irrigation costs, much of the arid land of the West and Southwest had been put into cultivation through the development of irrigation projects, and some of those lands had increased from $400 to $500 an acre in value. The Indian Office, however, continued to argue that even though Indians had not repaid the irrigation costs, irrigation was a good thing because it provided the only opportunity some Indians had to make a living.[25]

Despite the staggering financial problems, federal officials remained committed to reclamation on Indian reservations and on the public domain. In a decade of plummeting farm prices, there was no simple solution. When Hubert Work replaced Fall in 1923, he immediately began reforming the Reclamation Service to cut expenses. Only one out of every twenty-eight federal projects constructed or under construction met all the repayment requirements, and many projects were insolvent, so there was little hope of ever recovering the money invested. He therefore created a special Fact Finder's Committee to investigate the irrigation situation, planning to submit the committee's report to the president with his own recommendations on how to prevent further financial loss and give relief to the water users. Although Work retained faith in the fundamental soundness of the reclamation system, he was also convinced that the government needed a policy that would permit the reclamation of the arid lands of the West in a more orderly and businesslike manner. The Fact Finder's Committee reported that settlers on the federal reclamation projects paid less than 50 percent of the construction charges and only 54 percent of the operation and maintenance costs. As Work tightened regulations concerning repayment, the situation gradually improved.[26]

Meanwhile Congress finally acknowledged that the government had built more irrigation projects than the Indians could use or afford and became more lenient about repayment. In 1924 it authorized landowners within Indian irrigation projects to defer paying charges. New department regulations gave water users an extension to March 1, 1927, on all operation and maintenance or water rental costs that had accrued before March 2, 1924, while 5 percent per annum interest would be charged on the deferred payments instead of any existing penalty. Although Commissioner Burke favored this concession, he refused to give up completely on repayment and reminded the superintendents that the Indian Office was legally obligated to seek repayment of construction, operation, and maintenance charges.[27]

The Indian Office continued to have difficulty collecting in 1926 and 1927, so the irrigation construction charges accrued against the land. Allottees found it difficult to sell their land because prospective purchasers were reluctant to pay the accrued and future irrigation charges as the regulations required. In dealing with specific projects in the Indian Service and all Reclamation Service projects, the government's policy had been to extend payments of such charges over a longer period of years. The Indian Office now modified its regulations to stretch out the payments so that 2.5 percent of the total amount still due would be due on November 15 of each year until further notice.[28]

Despite the repayment problems, the number of major Indian irrigation projects had increased from 62 in 1913 to 150 in 1927. During that time the government had spent approximately $27,500,000 on construction and $8,500,000 on maintenance and operation. It would spend a total of $49,000,000 by 1936, and roughly half this expenditure would benefit lands acquired by non-Indians either before or after the construction of the projects.[29]

While lawmakers and bureaucrats took steps to deal with the problem of financing expensive irrigation projects, the problem of Indian nonuse persisted. The pattern changed little from one reservation to another. On the Yakima reservation there was little increase in the number of irrigated acres farmed by the Indians and the value of crops per acre farmed by tribal members declined relative to whites. Profitable irrigation farming in the West was a high-technology, resource-intensive form of agriculture that was foreign to the Yakima Indians so they shifted their efforts to cattle ranching, nonirrigated farming, or fishing. In 1921, of the 75,963 acres irrigated on the

Yakima reservation under the Indian Service, 43.6 percent was owned and farmed by whites, 9.5 percent was farmed by Indians, and the rest was owned by Indians but farmed by whites.[30]

The Blackfeet Indians were no more willing to farm the irrigated land than the Yakimas. Despite the fact that the Blackfeet displayed little interest in farming and opposed the construction of an irrigation project, the government had begun constructing extensive irrigation projects on the reservation in 1908. The Interior Department employed Indian men in construction but it could not induce them to farm the irrigated lands. In a moment of striking honesty in 1916, Assistant Commissioner Meritt conceded to a congressional committee that the Blackfeet project should never have been built. "If it were purely a white man's project," he explained, "it might be made a success; but we must realize that the Indians do not come up to the white man's standard of industry and effort." Irrigation engineer Reed echoed this sentiment. The Indians on the Blackfeet reservation chose to avoid irrigated farming in favor of cattle ranching, which more closely resembled their traditional lifestyle. In 1926 Blackfeet Indians farmed only 306 acres, a little over 1 percent of the 21,341 acres that had been irrigated at a cost of $1,100,000. A member of the Board of Indian Commissioners, Frank Knox, condemned the irrigation experiment on the Blackfeet reservation as "a monument to the unthinking enthusiasm with which this country twenty years ago embarked upon its reclamation projects."[31]

On April 23, 1904, Congress passed a law confirming the allotment of the Flathead reservation and the opening of that land to whites. Many of the Indians raised cattle and horses, but farming was virtually nonexistent on the reservation because of the lack of irrigation facilities. Whites who moved onto the reservation soon discovered that the land was unsuitable for farming, so they clamored for an irrigation project. In 1908, at the request of whites who wanted to settle the Flathead lands, Congress authorized an irrigation project to be paid for out of funds received by the tribe for the sale of the lands the whites were about to enter. When the irrigation project was completed, whites poured into the ceded land of the Flatheads with major influxes in 1908 and 1910, and the number of acres that the Indian residents farmed dropped dramatically. By 1919 four-fifths of the land on the Flathead project was owned, controlled, and worked by whites. The government justified this by saying that Indians would benefit from working alongside white farmers. In 1927 the Indians irrigated a pitiful 452 acres or 1.3 percent of the 34,441 acres of irrigated land on the reservation.[32]

On the Klamath reservation as well Natives failed to use the irrigation projects. As early as 1884 the agent had advocated constructing an irrigation ditch to water four thousand acres, and the Modoc Point canal was dug from 1901 to 1903. The government completed the Modoc Point, Sand Creek, and Spring Creek units between 1912 and 1920, even though many Indians served by those projects preferred dry farming. A congressional act authorizing the Modoc Point project had stipulated that the tribe pay the cost of construction, but a number of Indians petitioned to have the cost assessed on an acreage basis against the land served. In response, the Interior Department imposed a construction charge of thirty dollars an acre and an annual operation and maintenance charge of one dollar an acre which made Indians whose lands were within the project area reluctant to irrigate. The Modoc Point farmers objected to paying these charges because the project was built without their consent and they did not believe they should be responsible for its financial failure. In 1926 only 300 out of 6,000 acres in the project were under irrigation. There was no effort to enlist tribal support by involving tribal members in the fundamental decisions; nor was there sufficient training of the farmers to be affected in irrigation techniques. Thus, the Indians continued to use dry farming.[33]

The problem of nonuse extended to other reservations as well. In 1927 the Indians on the Wind River reservation irrigated 6,697 out of 21,491 acres being irrigated. On Fort Hall reservation, Indians irrigated 7,338 out of a total of 27,055 irrigated acres, and on the Uintah reservation Indians used 15,243 out of 58,290 acres in irrigation.[34]

The failure of the federal Indian irrigation program could no longer be ignored when the Institute for Government Research submitted its findings in February 1928. The Meriam report did not deal with each irrigation project in depth, in part because there was no expert irrigation engineer on the staff, but it did make some specific recommendations. In dealing with the financial problems and the problem of nonuse, the report raised two significant questions: Was it fair to convert an appropriation made originally as a gratuity into a reimbursable debt by subsequent legislation? And, were the large completed irrigation projects economically sound? The report answered a resounding "no" to both questions and recommended that the government consider canceling gratuity appropriations that had been turned into reimbursable debts. It found much evidence that the government undertook some projects because they were feasible from an engineering standpoint without taking into account whether the land could produce enough to pay for the construction and operating costs and yield the farmer a fair return for his labor. Moreover, when the question of return was considered it was calculated on the basis of high prices for farm products, not the low ones of the late 1920s, which made it difficult for even skilled, experienced white farmers to get a reasonable return on some projects.

As the Indians' guardian the government had a responsibility, the report went on, to protect them from two dangers: the sale and leasing of their land and the loss of their water rights to non-Indians, but it had not fulfilled its trust. In closing, the report recommended that the government construct no new projects until it considered the cost and determined that those projects were economically sound for the Indians. In cases where the Indians could never pay the operation and maintenance costs, the government should write them off or adjust them so that the Indians would not become discouraged by the heavy indebtedness and give up.[35]

The Indian Office's policy suffered an even more damaging blow in 1928 with the submission of another major report which provided indisputable evidence that the Indian irrigation program had been a costly failure. On March 15, 1927, Secretary Work had ordered Ray P. Feele, an agricultural economist in the Agriculture Department; Porter J. Preston, an engineer in the Bureau of Reclamation; and Charles A. Engle, a supervising engineer of the Indian Service, to survey and prepare a report on various Indian irrigation projects. Their report, the so-called Preston-Engle report, included information on irrigation methods, construction costs and returns, the failure to make repayments to the government of the capital invested, the use made of the irrigated lands by the Indians, purchasers, and lessees, and the use and settlement of former Indian lands by homesteaders. The report provided overwhelming evidence that federal officials had violated their trust responsibility by building irrigation projects with Indian money that the Indians did not want and could not use.

Preston and Engle found that there were 150 irrigation projects located on Indian reservations in the West, and of the 692,057 acres susceptible of irrigation on all Indian projects, 484,050 acres or about 70 percent belonged to whites. On the projects covered by the report, Indians owned 452,927 acres, of which they irrigated only 77,990 acres or 16 percent, while whites owned 198,000 acres, of which they irrigated 131,427 or 66 percent. The report revealed that on many so-called Indian projects most of the farming was done by non-Indians, either lessees or owners. The acreage used by Indians had continually shrunk, while that used by whites expanded. Indians, especially on the northern projects, received very small returns from their irrigable land, in part because the government failed to provide them with the technical and financial assistance they needed to become successful farmers and to use the irrigation projects productively.

The Preston-Engle report indicated that the government's policy discouraged rather than encouraged Indian use of the land. The laws requiring reimbursement, especially the 1920 law, often caused Indians to lose interest in developing their irrigated lands. Bitter and disillusioned, they saw the policy as a government scheme to confiscate their land by accruing irrigation charges against it until they exceeded the value of the land. The government had expended $27,140,782 for the construction of irrigation works on all Indian irrigation projects up to June 30, 1927, but it had collected only $979,860, or 3.5 percent.[36] Unfortunately, neither Congress nor the Interior Department ever publicized the Preston-Engle report or attempted to implement its suggestions.

By 1931 the construction cost of Indian irrigation works totaled $40,000,000. Uncollected and unassessed expenditures for operation and maintenance for a period of forty-seven years amounted to $7,500,000. Indians irrigated 126,970 acres; lessees irrigated 105,958 acres; and whites owned 188,573 acres. Only 31 percent of the irrigated land was used by Indians.[37]

Commissioner Rhoads inherited the formidable problem of collecting irrigation costs. He reported that the government had expended money on two hundred projects, which encompassed an area of approximately 1,361,768 acres, of which 361,708 acres were actually irrigated in 1929. The estimated per-acre cost on the projects varied from $6 to $216, and based on an average per-acre cost of $50, the per-acre amount of accrued charges equaled $21.25. Rhoads supported legislation to defer the collection of construction costs. Such legislation, he argued, would aid the Indian Office in its efforts to "keep the Indians upon the soil, and to use the water to irrigate their lands" without canceling construction costs.[38]

In 1930 legislation to eliminate reimbursable charges was introduced in the House, but the House Appropriations Committee rejected it. Assistant Commissioner of Indian Affairs J. Henry Scattergood testified on behalf of the legislation and pointed to cases on the Flathead reservation and other reservations where the irrigation charges amounted to more than the actual sale value of the land. The ultimate goal was to have Indians use their land productively, but charges mounted until its value was wiped out.[39]

In 1932 Congress passed the Leavitt Act, named after Rep. Scott Leavitt of Montana, which stipulated that no assessments for construction costs would be made against Indian-owned lands within federal irrigation projects until Indian title had been extinguished. It also canceled uncollected construction assessments that had been previously levied against Indian land. Rhoads called the legislation "one of the most important Indian items enacted during the past session of Congress."[40]

During his tenure, Rhoads not only eliminated over $3,000,000 in reimbursable debts, he also made fundamental changes in the organization of the irrigation division. In 1931 he organized the irrigation division under the supervision of Major William S. Post, who was appointed director of irrigation on March 21, 1931. The organization included 5 civil service employees in Washington, D.C.; a field office with 26 employees in Denver; and 79 employees at four district offices or on projects within districts. The administration included a director and assistant director in Washington, D.C.; an assistant director with headquarters in the field office; 1 special engineer; 1 supervising engineer at large; 4 district or supervising engineers; 1 field cost accountant; 4 attorneys; 8 project engineers; and 75 assistant engineers. One of the Indian Office's chief objectives continued to be the defense of water rights. The specific objectives of the irrigation division were to evaluate and classify projects to recommend their continuation, abandonment or transfer to local districts and to make recommendations for clearing reimbursable charges.[41]

Both the Meriam report and the Preston-Engle report confirmed the failure of the government's Indian irrigation program. Interior Department and Indian Office administrators made no effort to enlist tribal support or to involve tribal members in the decision-making process, and Indians understandably resented being charged for projects that they had not asked for and could not use. Federal officials neglected to prepare the Indians for the construction of the projects or to develop adequate transportation facilities for marketing their products. Nor did they appropriate the money necessary to buy teams, tools, and other equipment, and the Indians lacked the credit available to white settlers living under similar conditions.[42] At the same time, the cost of irrigation raised the cost of the land, so it had to be used more efficiently to meet those higher costs. In other words, the Indians had to be better farmers than those on low cost land with adequate rainfall.

Policymakers failed to realize that Indian irrigation projects could not and should not be subject to the same financial standards as non-Indian projects. Indian landowners were not concerned with commercial operations; they used their irrigated land for subsistence farming. Thus while Indian irrigation projects might not have been economically feasible according to normal standards, they could still be justified on the basis of their "subsistence" value. In addition, unenlightened administrators failed to take into consideration the cultural differences which affected irrigation farming. Irrigated farming required steady attention and a fairly sophisticated knowledge of when and how much water should be applied. It also required consistent maintenance work. Many Natives had little interest in farming in general, much less in meeting the special demands of irrigated farming.

The Indian Office successfully brought hundreds of thousands of acres of arid land into productive use, but this irrigated land almost invariably fell into the hands of non-Indians. Thus, given its stated objective of promoting Indian self-sufficiency, the irrigation program was an embarrassing failure; it did little to increase the number of Indians who were able to support themselves by farming and often actually discouraged self-support. The program led directly to the sale and leasing of Indian land and to greater outside control of Indian resources. Indians who could or would not use all of their irrigated land or pay the ever-rising irrigation charges usually lost their land to whites. Instead of devising and administering a policy to protect Indians in their use and ownership of their land and providing the training and tools that they needed to succeed with irrigated farming, federal officials allowed and indeed sometimes encouraged Indians to part with that land. Clearly, to them the goal of making the land productive was more important than promoting Indian self-sufficiency.

7.

Fee Patents and Competency Commissions

Under the government's policy, each Indian would first receive an allotment and then learn to use the land productively. When he reached the point where he could support himself, he would receive unrestricted title to the land. Thus, issuing fee patents or deeds of ownership to the Indians for their land was the last step in "freeing" the Indians from government control. The goal of progressive policymakers in the early twentieth century was to make individuals "stand on their own two feet" by giving them unrestricted control over their land. This policy posed a dilemma because some Indians once released would become productive members of society, while others would become homeless paupers. Faced with this dilemma, policymakers ultimately decided that the anticipated benefits to the Indian race and to society as a whole outweighed the suffering of individuals. Thus a policy designed to promote Indian progress ultimately left thousands homeless and impoverished.

The Dawes Act stipulated that the government hold the title to each allotment in trust for twenty-five years. Non-Indians soon pressured federal officials to release Indians from guardianship before the end of the trust period in order to promote self-support. One of the early Indian commissioners responsible for implementing the Dawes Act, William A. Jones, enthusiastically endorsed the goal of self-sufficiency but favored a gradual end to guardianship because not all Indians were ready to be released from government control before the trust period expired. Jones believed that the government should protect the Indian's property and his person but after that it should throw him on his own resources to become a useful member of society. "He must remember," said Jones, "that in the sweat of his face he shall eat his bread." When Francis E. Leupp replaced Jones as commissioner in 1905, he too adopted a policy aimed at releasing Indians from government control and promoting Indian self-support and citizenship. "In short," he wrote, "our aim ought to be to keep him moving steadily down the path which leads from his close domain of artificial protection toward the broad area of individual liberty enjoyed by the ordinary citizen." He believed that if the number of dependent Indians declined, the final solution to the "Indian problem" would be near at hand. But the "solution" would not come easily. Both Jones and

Leupp conceded that there would be many failures and much suffering, that some Indians would "fall by the wayside and be trodden underfoot," but through the sacrifice and suffering, the Indian race as a whole would advance toward the height of civilization.[1]

Federal policymakers, while anxious to release Indians quickly from government supervision, assumed that under the Dawes Act Indians would receive citizenship and fee patents for their trust allotments simultaneously when the trust period expired. On April 10, 1905, however, the Supreme Court ruled in the *Matter of Heff* that an Indian became a citizen at the beginning of the trust period when he accepted his allotment.[2] Although the Heff ruling did not prevail very long, it created the complex situation in which the Indians remained under the jurisdiction of the state or territory in which they resided even though the federal government still retained control over their land through the trust patents. Congressmen who had mistakenly believed that the federal government had the authority over both the Indian and his land now had to formulate new legislation to insure that the government retained this authority until the allottee received the fee patent to his allotment.[3]

South Dakota Representative Charles Burke, who later became commissioner of Indian affairs, was concerned about this split jurisdiction; in 1906 he introduced an amendment to the Dawes Act that would postpone the granting of citizenship until the end of the twenty-five-year trust period, thus postponing the time when the Indians would be subject to the laws of the individual states.[4] It also directed the secretary of the interior to issue fee patents to competent allottees who were capable of managing their own affairs, thus removing all of the federal restrictions over them and their land. No longer would Congress have to enact special legislation to grant fee patents to competent Indians before their trust period expired. The bill placed the responsibility for determining competency on the secretary of the interior and the Indian Office.[5]

During the House debates, defenders of the bill argued that they wanted to keep Indians under federal supervision only until they received fee patents. The bill's supporters apparently believed that control of an allotment alone would prepare the allottee for citizenship, and they advocated no other organized efforts to promote citizenship. Under Burke's bill, allottees would be subject to the federal liquor laws, remain outside the jurisdiction of a state or territory, and not receive the right to vote. Burke pointed out that Indians in South Dakota were getting citizenship with their trust allotment when they had fulfilled none of the requirements. The Burke Act became law on May 8, 1906. Its purpose was clearly to protect the Indian allottee from the vices of non-Indian society by keeping him under federal supervision for as long as necessary. Only in those narrow and specific cases where the secretary believed the Indians were capable of managing their own affairs would he be allowed to issue fee patents to them before the end of the twenty-five-year trust period.[6] If the Burke Act did not expressly require study or investigation of competency, it did so by implication.

Commissioner Leupp enthusiastically endorsed the law because of the power it gave the Interior Department. "Any Indian," he wrote, "who is earning a livelihood at any honorable occupation, if he wishes to own his own land in fee, should have the privilege at once because a man who has worked for his own support for any length of time will generally have some idea of the value of his land." Leupp opposed using blood quantum and degree of education as the criteria for determining whether an Indian was competent because there were full bloods who could not speak or write English but who were successful farmers, freighters, and boatmen. Rather, Leupp would make industry the criterion for competency. "The Burke law, wisely administered, will accomplish more in this direction," he concluded, "than any other single factor developed in a generation of progress."[7]

The procedure for issuing fee patents was a simple one: the Indian first applied to the local superintendent and then completed a questionnaire to demonstrate his competency. The superintendent posted notice of the application in "conspicuous places" on the allottee's reservation for thirty days and then submitted the application to the commissioner of Indian affairs with a full report on the applicant's competency, giving detailed reasons for his recommendations. If the commissioner approved the application, he forwarded it to the secretary of the interior for final approval, and the secretary sent it on to the General Land Office. With hundreds of applications pouring in from the field, neither the commissioner nor the secretary had time to evaluate each one personally, so they established general guidelines that their subordinates could use for approving individual applications. When the government issued the fee patent, its trust responsibility for the Indian ended.[8]

During the first two years that the Burke Act was in effect, the Washington staff relied on the recommendations of superintendents for certifying competency. Leupp acknowledged that this method was ineffective because each superintendent colored his recommendations and reports with his own bias. "Doubtless mistakes have been made in its execution, but most of these will be found to have grown out of misinformation received by the office from other sources than its own agents." Surveys in 1908 revealed that with this procedure over 60 percent of the Indians who received fee patents quickly lost their land and squandered the proceeds. Moreover, on many reservations where land speculation was rampant, non-Indians had persuaded Indian allottees to apply for fee patents and cheated them out of the full value of their lands.[9]

Disturbed by such reports, Leupp moved to tighten the controls on the issuance of fee patents, directing superintendents to report any land sales made under duress at their agencies. As an added precaution, he suggested that the reports which the superintendents submitted with the fee patent applications provide the following information: age of applicant, degree of Indian blood, marital status, number in family, and whether the applicant was self-supporting, was industrious, attended school, or cultivated his land. The report should also note if the Indian had made a contract to sell his land, had been pressured by speculators to dispose of his lands, was physically qualified to work, was a man of good character and reputation, or was an alcoholic. The Indian Office did not expect the superintendents to answer all of these questions in each report but it did expect them to consider the questions when reviewing each application. Leupp warned the superintendents that the Indian Office would require more solid evidence that the applicant for the fee patent was able to take care of himself than it had in the past.[10]

The order apparently did not solve the problem, for in January 1909 Leupp again outlined procedures for reporting on fee patent applications. This time he presented a list of thirty-one questions for the superintendents to address in their reports, including the age of the applicant, estimated value of his land, degree of Indian blood, level of education, health, business experience, and reasons for wanting restrictions removed. With the introduction of these detailed guidelines, the number of applications approved by the Indian Office dropped from 1,787 in 1908 to 1,166 in 1909, and the number of applications rejected rose from 68 to 836 during the same period.[11]

In 1909 Leupp was replaced as commissioner by Robert G. Valentine, who also was cautious about issuing fee patents to Indian allottees. From 1907 to 1908, the Indian Office had approved 93 percent of the applications it had received, but from 1909 to 1912, under Valentine, the office approved only 62 percent.[12] Valentine looked for a more efficient procedure for determining competency and issuing fee patents. He argued that reservation superintendents could not be objective when it came to making competency recommendations and that they did not have the time to devote to this matter. Rather than wait for the Indian to apply for a fee patent or for the superintendent to recommend him, Valentine decided to use special commissions that would visit the Indians personally to determine competency. He created the first commission on the Omaha reservation in the rolling hills of eastern Nebraska, where local whites were pressuring the Indian Office to release the rich farmland from trust status so that they could purchase the land and so that it would become taxable. The commission consisted of a traveling inspector, the local superintendent, and a prominent citizen of that state.[13]

The commissioners worked feverishly on the Omaha reservation, and in February 1909 submitted the names of 230 Indians considered competent to receive fee patents. Even before all of the fee patents had been issued, the Indian Office had to send inspectors to the reservation to investigate charges that land grafters were already swindling the Indians. Later investigations revealed that less than 50 percent of the allottees who received fee patents from the competency commission used their patents wisely, and 95 percent lost their land.[14] The Indian Office established similar commissions on the Umatilla, Santee, and Seneca reservations, but the results from the Omaha reservation were so devastating that Valentine decided to ignore the reports of these commissions.[15]

After the Omaha disaster, Valentine began to have serious doubts about the effectiveness of the fee patenting policy. In late 1910 he conceded, "I am not at all satisfied that our competency commissions are doing the kind of work I had in mind in appointing them." To make matters worse, he had heard that the commissions relied solely on affidavits as to the character of the Indians instead of visiting them in their homes. The use of affidavits, he warned, "had better be eliminated as pretty useless."[16]

Alarmed by the "evil" effects of fee patenting, in January 1910 Commissioner Valentine ordered the superintendents to encourage the Indians to sell their land under government supervision rather than apply for fee patents so that they could sell the land themselves. He also changed the procedure for fee patent cases by directing that the applicants fill out their own applications whenever possible, sign them, and swear to their veracity before the superintendent or some other designated person.[17] Commissioner Valentine clearly opposed granting fee patents "unless circumstances clearly show that a title in fee will be of undoubted advantage to the applicant." "In the face of existing evidence of carelessness and incompetence any liberal policy of giving patents in fee," he added, "would be utterly at cross purposes with the other efforts of the government to encourage industry, thrift, and independence."[18]

In 1913 Cato Sells replaced Valentine as commissioner of Indian affairs. Both he and Secretary Lane enthusiastically endorsed a more liberal fee patenting policy because they believed that independent land ownership offered the only solution to the "Indian problem." They were also responding to pressure from non-Indians who were anxious to acquire Indian land and could not do so while the land was in trust status. Determined to release Indians from restriction whether they applied for fee patents or not, in 1913 Sells ordered the superintendents to submit the name of each Indian who was capable of managing his own affairs, along with a letter showing in detail how advanced the Indian was, how much property he had accumulated, the value of his allotment, and whether he had any dependents, so that the Interior Department could determine if the Indian was competent.[19]

Initially Lane included only twenty reservations in his scheme, reservations on the Northern Plains and in the Pacific Northwest where the Indians were considered the most advanced.[20] Although Lane's plan was not extensive, it stirred opposition from some officials in the Indian Office who questioned the legality and morality of foisting fee patents on allottees without their application or consent. Assistant Commissioner Edgar Meritt argued that under the laws of 1887, 1906, and 1910, the government broke up tribal holdings and gave allotted Indians trust patents with at least the implied promise that they could hold on to their land without paying taxes on it for twenty-five years. It therefore had a moral obligation to protect their property during that period. Meritt feared that few patentees would hold on to their land very long. For the government to issue fee patents to allottees before the trust period expired without their application or consent, he warned, would be immoral and illegal.[21]

Lane and Sells, however, were so determined to release competent Indians from restriction as soon as possible that they conveniently ignored the moral objections. "The way out," Lane explained, "is gradually and wisely to put the Indian out. Our goal is the free Indian. The orphan-asylum idea must be killed in the mind of the Indian and the white man." After carefully studying the Indian's nature and needs, Lane had concluded that the Indian Office should make a systematic effort to cast the full burden of independence and self-support on the Indians. He expected nothing short of a revolution, "the substitution of a new standpoint for one long taught by fathers and grandfathers," a revolution which would come about not through money or bayonets, but through education and experience. Even Lane admitted that the government could not assimilate Indians on a wholesale basis, though he would later try to do this. It should use one's ability to handle his own affairs, he said, not blood quantum, as the criterion for competency. If the government did not release the many thousands of Indians who were competent, he argued, it would be neglecting its trust responsibility.[22]

Commissioner Sells, who remained as enthusiastic as Lane about fee patenting, decided to use the Omaha reservation where fee patenting had been especially liberal as a test case to determine whether he should expand that policy. In late 1914, he ordered Superintendent Axel Johnson to survey the conditions on his reservation and to cite particular cases where the fee patent recipients used their land or the proceeds from its sale wisely and cases where they did not. In his response, Johnson described a pattern that would be repeated on many other reservations. Before 1890 the Omahas had lived communally in small villages. Each family had farmed approximately ten acres with potatoes, corn, pumpkins, melons, and other crops. They were a self-sufficient people, deriving their sustenance from the land.

In the late 1880s and early 1890s large pastures were fenced and thousands of cattle grazed on the reservation. In the mid 1890s these large pastures were broken up and used to raise cereal crops, as the pastoral stage of economic development gave way to the agricultural stage. A barter or money economy worked well during the pastoral and agricultural stages. The Natives had not advanced enough to understand a credit economy, Johnson observed, and were unprepared to use it. They would "sign any paper to get credit." An Indian would mortgage his teams, implements, and crops in order to throw a feast or visit another reservation, then sink helplessly into debt without having any idea how to pull himself out. Eventually his only recourse would be to sell part or all of his land. One of the chief forces dragging the Indian into debt was the prospect of obtaining land in the near future that he could sell because this prompted whites to extend credit before the Indian warranted it or could use it.

Johnson reported that only a pitiful 13 percent of the Indians who had received fee patents used their land productively; 7.1 percent of those who sold their land spent the proceeds wisely; and 80 percent had little or nothing to show for their land. He also noted that the liberal issuance of fee patents had demoralized whites as well as Indians by giving them a rich opportunity for graft. Unscrupulous whites had infested the Omaha reservation, plied the

Indians with liquor, made false promises, and given them worthless securities in return for their land. "A liberal policy," Johnson warned, "no matter what way it may be pursued is bound to lead to the Indian's losing his land."[23]

Perhaps dissatisfied with the results from his test case, Sells requested similar reports from the superintendents at the Winnebago, Santee, Sisseton, Yankton, and Potawatomi reservations. These reservations were prime targets and had been for some time because of the high annual rainfall, fertile soil, and other factors in contrast with the reservations further West which had only marginal value for farming. White settlement had been more aggressive around these reservations in the Middle West than it had been in other regions so Sells believed the Indians had more of an opportunity to come into close contact with white civilization.[24] The replies of these superintendents confirmed that the practice of issuing fee patents had failed tragically. On the Yankton reservation, 75 percent of the Indians with fee patents sold their land and squandered the proceeds, while on the Winnebago reservation 93 percent lost their land. Neighboring whites seized the opportunity for graft and sometimes induced the Indians to break the law by mortgaging their land repeatedly. "Grafting," said one superintendent, "has become in a measure respectable." The most astute Indians, realizing that the indiscriminate issuance of fee patents led to poverty, opposed that policy.[25]

Although reports from the reservations provided overwhelming evidence that Indians who received fee patents became homeless and impoverished, Lane and Sells forged ahead with plans for a more liberal policy because they believed that policy was necessary and proper and because they were pressured by whites who wanted to control Indian lands. The government, Sells concluded, needed to relieve itself of its trust responsibility at any cost. Under the 1906 and 1910 acts the Interior Department had no authority to issue fee patents without the application of the allottee, but Sells believed many Indians who were able to assume the duties of citizenship and pay taxes did not apply for fee patents, even with pressure from their superintendents.[26] The commissioner conceded that fee patents did not always benefit the Indians and sometimes had "disastrous" effects, as in the case of the Omaha reservation Indians. Yet, reflecting the optimism and materialism of the progressive era, he hoped that by owning and working their lands they would eventually be brought into "industrial efficiency."[27]

Secretary Lane's determined search for a more efficient and effective way to issue fee patents resulted in the appointment of competency commissions. Instead of relying upon the reports and recommendations of the superintendents, the Interior Department now turned to special officers whose sole work would be to determine which Indians were competent to receive full control of their land. The idea of using commissions to evaluate Indians in their own surroundings was good in theory, but the policy had disastrous effects on the Indians. As a result of the commissions' work the government removed many Indians from its care before they could successfully manage their land and support themselves.

When Lane first informed Sells of his plan to create a competency commission in 1914, he won Sells's enthusiastic support because Sells believed the only practical solution to the "Indian Problem" was to separate the competent Indians from the incompetent ones and release them from guardianship. Lane's plan, he said, "will at least go a long way toward curing the most vital evil which many years of administrative efforts have brought about in an honest attempt to settle the Indian's future and qualify him for real citizenship."[28]

Sells and Lane were not alone in perceiving the need for a competency commission; influential reform groups enthusiastically applauded their plan. The Indian Rights Association had earlier suggested that Congress authorize a commission to determine the Indians' fitness for citizenship—a permanent nonpartisan body, with coordinate branches all over the field to prevent needless delay.[29] The Board of Indian Commissioners believed the creation of the commission demonstrated that Lane intended to fulfill his 1914 pledge to free all competent Indians from restrictions. The board noted that this idea had been the basis for the allotment policy twenty-five years earlier, but the numerous restrictions and regulations had prevented superintendents from recommending competent Indians for fee patents.[30]

In April 1915, Lane informed several superintendents of the creation of the first competency commission, consisting of Major James McLaughlin, then an Interior Department inspector, and Frank A. Thackery, superintendent of the Pima reservation, to determine which Indians were competent to handle their own affairs.[31] Both men were well qualified and experienced. McLaughlin, of Scotch-Irish descent, was married to a Sioux mixed blood and had been involved in Indian affairs since 1871, first as an agent in the Indian Service in the Dakotas and then as an inspector in the Interior Department. The white-haired seventy-three-year-old "king" of inspectors was paternalistic, resourceful, and strong-willed. His partner Thackery had taught for many years in Indian schools in South Dakota, Nebraska, and Oklahoma, and since 1912 this honest, unselfish man had served as superintendent of the Pima and Maricopa agency. Soon after his appointment, however, the former superintendent began to question the legality and morality of forcing citizenship on a competent Indian who did not want it because he would have to pay taxes.[32]

Lane expanded competency work in January 1916 by giving McLaughlin a separate commission and a new partner, Orlando M. McPherson, a former Post Office inspector and special Indian agent.[33] Each commission consisted of two experienced men who, with the local superintendent, studied a list of the Indians living on that reservation, questioned the Indians, visited their homes, and determined whether they were capable of handling their own affairs and receiving fee patents. The commissioners used age, self-sufficiency, and knowledge of English as the general criteria for competency. After evaluating the Indians' qualifications, they submitted the names of the ones deemed competent to the secretary, along with a report and a fee patent application for each. The commissioners usually required the potential paten-tee to sign an application but if he refused the patent was issued anyway. The superintendent submitted a report along with that of the commissioners, but it carried less weight.[34]

In the spring of 1916 Lane appointed McPherson to head a third commission and assigned the superintendent of Seger agency, Walter Small, as McLaughlin's new partner. Eventually the Indian Office created new commis-sions to work among tribes in the Northwest and the Dakotas. Lane's expan-sion of competency work proved effective, for by June 1, 1916, the Interior Department had issued 576 fee patents on the recommendation of the compe-tency commissions. With their rigorous schedules, by September 1916 the competency commissions had reported on the Cheyenne River, Coeur d'Alene, Crow, Flathead, Fort Hall, Fort Peck, Fort Totten, Santee, Sac and Fox, Shawnee, Shoshone, Sisseton, Standing Rock, Umatilla, Yankton, and Fort Berthold reservations and had delivered fee patents on seven of these reser-vations.[35]

To the commissions fell the responsibility for recommending Indians for fee patents as well as delivering those patents after they were issued. In 1916 Lane decided to make the delivery of the patents a special event. With McLaughlin's help, he devised a colorful outdoor ceremony to impress upon the Indians the importance of citizenship and to dramatize the change occurring in their lives.[36]

During the ritual, each Indian who was to receive a fee patent and citizen-ship solemnly stepped from a tepee and shot an arrow to signify that he was leaving behind his Indian way of life. Moving forward slowly he placed his hands on a plow to demonstrate that he had chosen to live the farming life of a white man, with sweat and hard work. The secretary of the interior or other presiding official then handed the Indian a purse to remind him to save what he earned. Then with the secretary and the Indian holding the American flag, the Indian repeated these words: "Forasmuch as the President has said that I am worthy to be a citizen of the United States, I now promise this flag that I will give my hands, my head, and my heart to the doing of all that will make me a true American citizen." To conclude the ceremony, the secretary pinned on the recipient a badge decorated with the American eagle and the national colors—the emblem of citizenship, which would remind the Indian always to act in a way that would make the flag proud.[37]

The first citizenship ceremony was scheduled for 9:00 A.M. on May 13, 1916, at Greenwood on the Yankton reservation in eastern South Dakota. The Indian Office had carefully chosen this agency because many more Indians were reportedly ready for citizenship there than at other reservations and, more pragmatically, because it would be convenient for the secretary. Several very proud Yankton Indians invited Lane to attend so he could see firsthand the progress they had made and assure himself that releasing them from govern-ment supervision was not a mistake. Thirty years ago they had lived in wigwams, they told him, but they had since transformed the wild prairie into wavy fields of corn and wheat so the government no longer owed them a living.[38]

Upon arriving at Greenwood, McLaughlin and Lane were embarrassed to find that many of the patentees had already arranged to sell their land. After long hours of investigation, Lane scratched the names of twenty-five Indians who were to receive patents off the list, and the ceremony proceeded as planned. Although both men were disappointed that so many Indians had sold their land, they were not totally discouraged because they believed these Indians would be forced to hustle for a living and would become stronger than if kept under federal guardianship.[39]

The carefully orchestrated three-hour ceremony took place on the agency lawn where a tepee had been erected near the speaker's platform. Despite bad weather, two thousand people, a motion picture outfit, and three reporters looked on as the secretary handed patents to approximately two hundred Indians. Lane noted with satisfaction that the Indians took the ceremony very seriously. So pleased was he with the results that he suggested a similar ceremony be used in granting citizenship to foreigners. "Surely," he remarked, "it tends to instill patriotism and presents the duties of citizenship in a manner that leaves a lasting impression."[40]

More festive ceremonies soon followed on other reservations where they attracted neighboring whites and local officials. At Timberlake on the Cheyenne River reservation schools and businesses were closed so that the townspeople could attend. Various types of music ranging from a "cowboy band" to a seventeen-piece Indian band added to the festivity of the occasion. On the Crow reservation the ceremony took the form of a holiday.[41]

Despite the careful planning, the work of the competency commissions did not run as smoothly as Lane might have liked. With the Indians so widely scattered, weary commissioners had to travel long distances, often over rough terrain, to reach even a small number of them. McPherson, for example, spent an entire week in the field in one Oklahoma county with only three applications to show for his efforts, and Thackery traveled about seven hundred miles in one week. Poor weather often aggravated the transportation problem. In one instance, rain and the resulting washouts along the railroad tracks kept McLaughlin from traveling by train from Trail City to Faith on the Cheyenne River reservation and muddy roads and high water in many creek beds prevented travel by team conveyance. Many Indians could not reach either of the points on the reservation where he was delivering patents.[42]

Competency work also suffered because the commissioners were sloppy in performing their duties and sometimes abused their power. They recommended individuals for fee patents who were not competent and did not want the patents. Critics, for example, charged that the commission made full citizens of many Indians in the Dakotas who immediately afterward sold their land, squandered the proceeds, and became destitute.[43] When McLaughlin declared that one full blood Santee woman was competent, the local superintendent who had been a close friend and admirer of McLaughlin strenuously objected. "The Major was after all only human and therefore not infallible," he conceded. "In this case he and the competency commission made an indefensible error." The woman's record clearly indicated that she was not competent; intelligent Indians of her own tribe and the agency farmer considered her incompetent. In another instance, McLaughlin declared competent an Indian on the Cheyenne River reservation who was illiterate and could not speak or write English. "Is it any wonder," the agency farmer complained, "that he is now having trouble?"[44]

That such mistakes were made is understandable given the unseemly speed with which the commissions conducted their work. Rarely did they spend enough time with each prospective patentee to determine competency accurately and fairly. On some of the larger, more remote reservations such as Pine Ridge and Cheyenne River it should have taken months to visit each allottee, evaluate him carefully, and check his references. Yet, in only one week, the competency commission stormed across the Eagle Butte, Dupree, and Cherry Creek districts on the Cheyenne River reservation, met with all of the Indians living there, and induced thirty-four of them to sign applications for fee patents. From January 31 to February 12, 1916, it toured the entire Yankton reservation, and by March 4 it had conferred with 439 Indians there and secured 180 signatures on applications. Competency commissioner John R. Wise told a stunned congressional committee that he heard ordinary competency cases in fifteen to thirty minutes and on rare occasions heard twenty to twenty-five cases a day. He did not require that Indians have any education to qualify for competency.[45]

Although guidelines stipulated that the commissioners were to visit each Indian in his home, they declared Indians competent and recommended them for fee patents without seeing them.[46] When McLaughlin discovered that 90 percent of the Creeks he visited in Oklahoma were incompetent and incapable of managing their own business affairs, he concluded that it was a waste of time and money to visit the home of every Indian whose lands were held in trust, every restricted Indian, as the Indian Office had instructed. To do so he would have to travel long distances over very bad roads, sometimes on foot, to reach Indians who could not read, write, or speak English. He argued that it was not necessary to visit Indians whom the field clerks knew were incompetent. Despite McLaughlin's protest, Lane ordered him to visit every restricted Indian, no matter how long it took.[47] To make competency decisions without actually visiting the Indians was unfair and dangerous.

Angry Oklahomans charged that McPherson investigated only those Indians whom the field clerk suggested were competent rather than visiting all of them. Despite an order from Lane to investigate every allottee, McPherson chose to investigate closely only those with a "reasonable degree" of competency. He gave allottees who spoke no English and seemed to be backward only a cursory examination at a central location but examined seemingly competent Indians at length and visited them in their homes.[48]

Not all the Indians whom the commissions declared competent were willing to apply for or to accept fee patents, but Lane was determined that they receive them. He instructed the commissioners to submit the names of those Indians they considered competent but who refused to apply for a fee patent because these Indians were "the very ones we should be sure to get." McPherson carefully scrutinized such recalcitrant Indians as instructed, but he warned Lane that the list of those who refused to sign applications would be much longer than the list of those who consented. Often, then, the Indian Office issued patents to Indians who did not want them and had not signed applications. The determined McLaughlin simply informed allottees that they had no choice but to accept them.[49]

Under pressure to "free" the Indians quickly, the commissioners forced patents on unqualified Indians. Chief Rush Roberts, the president of the Pawnee Tribal Council, who had told the competency commission through an interpreter that he could not read, write, or speak English and that he did not want a fee patent, received one anyway. When Roberts protested that the Pawnees were not ready for fee patents, the commission ignored him. Few of these Indians would be able to hold on to their land after the commission finished its work. An Iowa Indian from Perkins, Oklahoma, described a similar encounter with a competency commission. "Well there was a party of people like you people came here," he told a Senate investigating committee, "and just picked me out and said I was a competent Indian and I know I was not but they just said I had to take the medicine with the rest of the boys that was picked out and I took it." He said the competency commission selected the names of prospective patentees from the office records rather than examining them individually for competency. When a competency commission came through Delaware county in Oklahoma in 1916, it removed restrictions despite the protests of the Indians. Only one of the ten to twelve Indians involved was actually competent, and all of the patentees quickly sold or mortgaged their land.[50]

Competency commissioner Wise, who readily pushed patents on resistant Indians in other parts of the country, had qualms of conscience when it came to treating the Five Civilized Tribes of Oklahoma this way because he believed the government had promised to hold the land in trust, tax free, for a certain period. When Wise expressed his misgivings to the House Committee on Indian Affairs, the committee sternly reminded him that only by removing restrictions could the Indian Office refute the charge that it was keeping competent people under wardship in order to perpetuate its own existence. Committee chairman Homer Snyder reiterated that Congress and his committee wanted competent Indians to be declared so, no matter how they felt.[51]

Some Indians, such as those on the Klamath and Fort Berthold reservations, resisted fee patents because they could not afford or did not want to pay taxes on their land, while others sincerely feared the harmful effects of removing restrictions. Whatever their reason for resisting, Lane was determined that Indians who had been declared competent receive their fee patents. If any

Indian refused to accept his patent, the superintendent was to send it by registered mail and to inform the tax collector that it had been issued. Lane would not let a qualified Indian avoid the responsibilities of citizenship simply by refusing to accept his fee patent. If the Interior Department mailed the fee patents, the Indians had to take them, and the department did not have the burden of holding the patents until the allottees acquiesced.[52]

Two Umatilla full bloods, Leo Sampson and Allen Patawa, who had been determined competent, pleaded with Lane not to issue their fee patents. Patawa loved his land and did not believe he would be happy anywhere else, but he was afraid that if he were forced to accept a fee patent, he would sell his land and squander the proceeds. Sampson, who was also worried about holding on to his allotment in the face of white land hunger, had no hopes for living peacefully among whites. They would try to grab his land, he explained, and if he had a fee patent, he would surely sell it. Sampson and Patawa were among the most competent Indians on the reservation and others envied their privileges. Yet, Sampson noted, "since the competency commission visited here they see that I am in danger, by reason of my competency, to be turned loose, and they say that if this is the result of competency they would rather be incompetent Indians."[53] The commission's report indicated that Sampson, age thirty-one, worked as an official interpreter for the government at $500 per year, was "well-educated, industrious and frugal," with enough experience to justify a fee patent, and Patawa, age thirty-six, owned one of the best farms on the reservation. On the basis of this report, Lane decided not to intervene on behalf of the Indians.[54]

As the competency work progressed, strong arguments both for and against the practice of issuing fee patents came from the field. Superintendents and inspectors who favored a liberal policy of issuing fee patents maintained that most mixed bloods could take care of themselves and should be given fee patents whether they wanted them or not. They believed the government should force competent Indians to accept fee patents so that they could no longer avoid paying taxes, and, more important, so that their land could be seized for debt. "It seems no more right," explained one superintendent, "for the Government to protect so-called Indians of this class than it would be to protect white men from defrauding their creditors."[55] These superintendents argued that only through the removal of restrictions could the Indians advance and learn to become good citizens. With their fee patents in hand, they could sell part of their land and use the proceeds to establish farms or raise cattle on the remainder.[56]

Some field officials supported the policy because they naively believed that even if the Indians sold their land and became impoverished, they gained valuable experience and learned to become more responsible and self-reliant. With a strange kind of illogic, superintendents carried this idea even further, arguing that the sooner an Indian sold his land and squandered his money, the better off he would be. Patentees on the Yankton reservation sold or mortgaged their land, but the superintendent calmly noted that the situation would be no different in ten years. The Indians had difficulty appreciating something they got for nothing, he explained; they lacked the incentive to earn a living because the government had always managed their affairs and provided them with food and clothing. If they received fee patents and sold their land, they would at least be forced to work and might learn to appreciate what they had. One group of Yankton Indians agreed with their superintendent, writing, "While it looks hard to see them throw their means away yet perhaps in the end they will be better off because afterwards they will have to get out and make a living for themselves." The competent Indians lacked only industry and incentive to succeed, the Indians charged, and if by mistake some incompetents were turned loose, they would be no worse off than they would be in ten years' time.[57]

Such positive support for foisting fee patents on reluctant Indians by no means reflected the attitude of all field officials. Some diligent superintendents opposed the practice, and they provided some staggering statistics. In 1915, for example, 95 percent of the Cheyenne River patentees sold or mortgaged their land. By 1916, Natives had sold 90 percent of the fee patent land on the Crow reservation and 70 percent of the fee patented land on the Fort Peck reservation. Approximately 90 percent of the Turtle Mountain reservation patentees sold or mortgaged their land at the first opportunity and then drifted back to the reservation to live off friends and relatives. On the Umatilla reservation roughly 75 percent of the patentees sold their land, and 10 percent of these families became destitute.[58]

These critics rejected the Indian Office's claim that the Indians advanced under fee patenting. The Crow superintendent complained that the patentees became agitators and troublemakers. On Crow Creek the issuance of fee patents reportedly created discontent and jealousy among the Indians who did not receive them, and incompetent Indians used underhanded methods to acquire fee patents. An Indian Office inspector found that fee patenting had failed on the Cheyenne River and Pine Ridge reservations because the Indians quickly lost their land, which was "all they have between them and poverty."[59]

Whether they supported the Indian Office's policy or not, most field officials at least claimed that they were implementing that policy faithfully. Some superintendents reported that they scrutinized each application carefully and made the Indian prove some degree of competency before submitting his or her application.[60] Others recommended a fee patent for only part of an Indian's land, thus putting him on probation. To give the Indian a chance with a small part of his land seemed wiser than waiting until the trust period expired and removing restrictions on all the land at once. Even if he sold the fee patented land and wasted the proceeds, he would still have some land left and might have learned a valuable lesson. Meanwhile, the Indian Office accumulated evidence showing whether the Indian was capable of supporting himself when given the chance.[61]

Despite their adamant claims of conservatism, many field officials implemented the policy poorly and violated the rights of the Indians by failing to protect them from unscrupulous whites. Land speculators in violation of the 1910 law frequently took mortgages on Indian land or bought it before the Indian owners received their fee patents. In other instances, when local whites heard that Indians were to receive fee patents, they encouraged them to run up debts so that they would be forced to sell the land to pay. On Pine Ridge, for example, crafty traders extended credit to the Indians and then took mortgages on their allotments to settle ordinary merchandise accounts, although the government had promised to turn the land over to the allottees without encumbrance and had declared that debts incurred before fee patenting could not be held against the allottees' land after the patents were issued.[62] To settle debts by taking mortgages was not only immoral, it was illegal.

Sells did little to remedy the situation except to order the superintendents to post notices that fee patent applications had been approved in "conspicuous" places on their reservations as soon as they were notified. If someone had persuaded the Indian to convey his land before the government issued the fee patent, the superintendents were to inform the Indian Office immediately so it could prosecute the land speculators and revoke its approval of the application. Rather than ending the abuses, at least on the Shoshone reservation this order might have encouraged them, for the public notice gave speculators a chance to begin negotiating for the purchase of Indian land before the owners received their fee patents.[63]

Greedy land speculators waited impatiently for the delivery of the patents. An Indian on the Rosebud reservation who received a fee patent was "dogged by land sharks" and pressured until he reluctantly agreed to sell.[64] For two or three weeks after the Indian Service delivered fee patents on the Yankton reservation, the superintendent complained, "land buyers, automobile agents and fakers of all kinds were busy almost day and night. The most susceptible were given the most attention. Smooth tongues [sic] mixed bloods were employed and given a bonus for each deal made." These land sharks bullied or tricked the Indians into selling or mortgaging their land. Although he urged the Indians to hold on to their land, they found it hard to resist the temptation to own a car when they saw their neighbors riding in them and when whites used high pressure sales tactics.[65]

Sometimes speculators had the benefit of advance knowledge. A leak apparently existed somewhere in the Indian Service through which land dealers in Montana received advance information about fee patents to be issued on the Flathead reservation. As a result, the rules were later changed to prevent Indian Office clerks from revealing any information, oral or written, regarding fee patents, until ten days after they had been mailed to the superintendent.[66]

Sells and Lane, dismissing the reports of abuses, continued to issue patents as quickly as possible because they believed releasing Indians from restrictions was more important than promoting their welfare. In 1916, the Indian Office approved 949 of the 1,298 applications it received, covering 132,647 acres, and Sells optimistically predicted that if the Indians continued to advance at the same rapid rate, within ten years they would be practically self-supporting.[67]

Ironically, some factions in Congress were complaining that the process of determining competency and issuing fee patents was too slow. When called before a congressional committee, Sells denied the charge. To issue patents without carefully considering the applicants' qualifications, he cautioned, would lead to their "utter destruction and poverty." Indians sometimes applied for fee patents, he admitted, under pressure from whites who wanted to buy their land. When congressional critics suggested that the Indian Office give superintendents the authority to determine competency by themselves, Sells candidly replied that some superintendents could not be trusted to determine competency because they lacked quality, integrity, and vision. Although the commissioner denied that the Indian Office had been removing restrictions and making Indians citizens against their will, his agency was issuing fee patents on the basis of competency commission recommendations without the application or the consent of the allottees.[68]

The competency commissions which Valentine, Lane, and Sells created to promote self-support ultimately led to poverty and dependency. Indians who were clearly not competent received fee patents on the basis of competency commission recommendations. Moreover, the commissions were inherently coercive in that an Indian deemed competent would receive a fee patent whether he wanted it or not. Sells and Lane recognized the tragic effects of all this, but they persevered because of pressure from non-Indian communities and from Congress to "free" the Indians quickly and also because they sincerely believed that they had discovered the solution to the "Indian problem."

8.
Declaration of Policy

As the Indian Office pushed fee patenting, the call for the forced removal of restrictions on Indian land grew louder. Policymakers such as Franklin Lane and Cato Sells were so anxious to satisfy white land hunger and so convinced that the progressive policy was the only solution that they began issuing fee patents on a massive scale. The actions of these men and their staffs in forcing fee patents on Indians were in most cases arbitrary, capricious, and illegal.

In 1917 the Indian Office came under pressure from Western congressmen, particularly Democratic ones, who wanted to accelerate the process of removing restrictions. Increased demand for agricultural produce to support the war effort made it more imperative that unproductive Indian land be made available. The competency commissions and fee patenting policies were in part a response to Westerners who were voting as a cohesive bloc in Congress. When the Indian appropriation bill went to the Senate in 1917, congressional critics condemned the Indian Office's fee patenting policy for being too expensive, inefficient, and slow. Senator Wesley Jones from Washington suggested that unless the Indian Office acted more aggressively to issue fee patents to competent Indians, Congress should direct the secretary of the interior to take over the job. Another Westerner, Senator Henry Myers of Montana, defended the Indian Office by arguing that it was doing the best it could, but to transform the basic nature of an entire race was a hard task. Therefore, Congress should support the Indians until they could defend themselves against unscrupulous whites. Like Jones, however, Myers looked forward to the eventual destruction of tribal life and the settlement of the reservations by whites.[1]

Commissioner Sells was attacked not only by politicians but also by reformers who were disappointed with the progress of the fee patenting policy. Early in 1917 the secretary of the Indian Rights Association, Herbert Welsh, warned Sells that there was formidable opposition to the present policy from people who believed the Indian Office was moving too slowly. Although most of this opposition was prompted by selfish motives, he conceded, certain flaws in the administration of Indian affairs made the Indian Office a good target. Welsh warned Sells not to lose sight of the goal of releasing Indians from government control and urged him to prepare the Indians to accept the full responsibilities of citizenship.[2]

This pressure made Sells even more determined to accelerate the process of issuing fee patents. He quickly seized the initiative. Rather than wait for formal legislation, on April 17, 1917, he issued his "declaration of policy," which would arbitrarily release thousands of Indians from guardianship and contribute greatly to the destruction of the Indian estate. "Broadly speaking," Sells wrote, "a new policy of greater liberalism will henceforth prevail in Indian administration to the end that every Indian, as soon as he has been determined to be as competent as the average white man, shall be given full control of his property and have all his lands and money turned over to him, after which he will no longer be a ward of the Government."[3]

Under this policy, all Indians with less than one-half Indian blood would receive complete control of all their property, as would Indians with one-half or more Indian blood who after careful examination were found competent, and Indian students twenty-one or older who had completed course work at a government school, received a diploma, and demonstrated competency. The new declaration of policy, Sells observed, "means the dawn of a new era in Indian administration. It means the competent Indian will no longer be treated as a half ward and half citizen. It means reduced appropriations by the Government and more self-respect and independence for the Indian. It means the ultimate absorption of the Indian race into the body politic of the Nation. It means, in short, the beginning of the end of the Indian problem."[4]

The rigid new policy was firmly rooted in the principle that Indians who were as competent as "ordinary" whites to manage their own affairs should be given complete control of their property and be assured all their personal property rights so that they could shape their own destinies. Sells, the pragmatist, noted that this practice would not only release Indians from restrictions, but also would cut government expenditures and allow the government to devote more attention to the Indians who still needed its protection.[5]

In his policy statement, the commissioner firmly linked percentage of white blood to competency and fee patents, believing that the most intelligent Indians had some white blood in them. Yet even Sells later conceded that this did not always mean the more white blood, the better.[6] The degree of Indian blood had no rational relation to the degree of competency, and even if blood quantum had some bearing on competency, the evidence was inconclusive. Other factors such as education, employment, and age were also important. After 1917, however, the government had the authority to force fee patents on Indians in two ways: on the basis of a competency commission recommendation, or by arbitrary issuance to an allottee with less than one-half Indian blood who was able-bodied and mentally competent. The 1906 Burke Act had given the Indian Office the authority to issue fee patents before the end of the trust period only when Indian landholders applied for them. Sells and Lane, however, misconstrued the Burke Act. Without any legislative authority, in 1917 they began forcing fee patents on all Indians with a certain blood quantum whether they wanted them or not.

Public support for the new policy was strong. The *Baltimore Star* called this "new deal" for the American Indian "one of the most important turnings in the entire history of relations between Uncle Sam and his redskin wards." The popular *Outlook* magazine welcomed the declaration, arguing that it would give the Indians more rights and responsibilities. Although the new policy would, it said, "ultimately result in poverty and moral decay for some Indians, there is no hope for the Indians as a race if they are forever kept in tutelage as wards of the Nation; and it is better that some Indians should be lost as the result of a courageous policy than that the whole Indian race should be denied the opportunity for that kind of human development which comes only in the atmosphere of freedom and in its bearing the burdens of responsibility which freedom entails." Another major paper, the *Boston Transcript*, heralded Sells's declaration as a radical and important change in policy.[7]

Reform groups supported the new policy as enthusiastically as the journalists. The Indian Rights Association praised it as evidence that Sells was determined to fulfill his stated objectives. The association promised to cooperate with Sells in implementing the new policy. "We want to help you and support you all the time," wrote one association member, "and we will if you let us."[8] A member of the Presbyterian Board of Home Missions, after characterizing the commissioner as a kind, sympathetic, and fearless man with a deep concern for Indian welfare, called the policy an important first step toward promoting Indian independence and self-sufficiency.[9]

Even the cautious Board of Indian Commissioners, which had previously favored a conservative approach, wholeheartedly endorsed the new policy because they believed it was consistent with the policy of gradual assimilation that they had been advocating for over twenty-five years. When successfully implemented, the board predicted, the policy would bring an end to the government's administration of Indian affairs.[10]

To implement his much-praised plan, Sells quickly ordered the superintendents to submit the names of all those under their jurisdiction who had less than one-half Indian blood, with their age, sex, blood quantum, and descriptions of their land, because the Indian Office intended to "turn loose" these Indians unless it had conclusive reasons for not doing so. If, however, the superintendent believed someone on the list should not receive a fee patent, he was to submit a special report stating the reason.[11]

As Sells received the lists he sent them on to the secretary of the interior's office for approval, after which the secretary's office instructed the General Land Office to issue the patents. This greatly reduced the work of the competency commissions because submission was automatic for Indians with one-half or less Indian blood.[12] Six weeks after the declaration, when Lane asked Sells how far along he was "in getting out the half breeds," Sells boasted that 211 fee patents had been issued. "I am confident," he added, "that within sixty days we shall have worked out a program of substantial progress in the accomplishment of our efforts to eliminate the white Indians."[13]

The Indian Office was so anxious to "free" the Indians that it sometimes violated its own regulations, issuing fee patents to new allottees before they had even received their trust patents, or to Indians who were under twenty-one and thus ineligible.[14] In recommending Indians who could not support themselves, field officials violated the spirit if not the actual provisions of the declaration. The Blackfeet reservation superintendent recommended twenty-one-year-old Flora McKelvey Brown for a fee patent because she was only one-eighth Indian and "reasonably intelligent," although Brown showed no sign of being able to support herself. He also recommended John Cobell, even though this thirty-one-year-old quarter blood was completing his second term in a federal penitentiary for stealing cattle and was considered "one of the boldest and most accomplished rustlers in that part of the country." A frustrated superintendent at Seger agency complained that his predecessors had issued patents that no "intelligent, fair-minded man" would have done.[15]

Field reports clearly indicated that wholesale fee patenting led to widespread poverty and suffering, especially on reservations in the Northwest and the upper Midwest where patentees almost invariably sold their land or mortgaged it and went into debt. On the Crow reservation, for example, Indians sold 90 to 95 percent of the patented land and mortgaged the rest at 10 to 12 percent interest, a rate high enough to swamp any white. In 80 to 85 percent of the cases fee patents led to extravagance, poverty, debauchery, and even death. Most of the money from land sales went for cars, which was perhaps to be expected, for many whites were mortgaging their homes to buy cars. At Fort Peck as well, fee patenting had devastating effects, with 90 percent of the fee patented land sold or mortgaged and 90 percent of the proceeds wasted. The superintendent of the Winnebago reservation in northeastern Nebraska observed simply that the most noticeable effect of issuing fee patents was "the enrichment of white land speculators."[16]

The situation was even more tragic on Pine Ridge reservation where most of the Natives were full bloods, unable to read, write, or speak English, who could in no way be classified as competent. Yet they received fee patents and soon sold their land. The proceeds most often went for provisions and "worthless trinkets." Many patentees quickly got a loan or mortgage on their land, and without any business experience or understanding of the need to pay taxes and interest on loans, they were often swindled out of it when the white lenders foreclosed.[17]

In 1920 the patentees at the White Earth reservation in Minnesota disposed of 90 percent of their allotments. Since the passage of the 1906 Clapp Act, which like Sells's declaration authorized fee patents for adult mixed bloods but applied only to White Earth, they had disposed of land worth roughly $3,250,000. Most of the proceeds from the land and timber sales went for food, clothing, liquor, and home improvements. The government turned loose nearly five thousand White Earth Indians who, during the process, lost their lands, spent their money, and either worked for white men who bought their lands, or drifted off the reservation.[18]

Despite the staggering number of Indians who lost their land, the superintendents generally supported Sells's policy. These field officials apparently agreed with the Indian Office's frightening premise that "freeing" the Indians was more important than protecting their land title. The Cheyenne River superintendent argued that the Indians who sold or mortgaged their land usually had that in mind when they applied for fee patents. Although 75 percent of the patentees sold their land and 40 percent squandered the proceeds, the superintendent believed the "free spenders" would eventually realize that work was their only salvation and accept the inevitable.[19]

Many superintendents believed, as Lane and Sells did, that the Indians had to learn to support themselves at any cost. An Indian who went broke, they reasoned, was no worse off than one who remained dependent on someone else. As long as the Indians could fall back on the government and avoid paying taxes, they would never accept any responsibility or become citizens. Only by being hungry, the superintendents argued, would the Indians come to appreciate the value of money. The Standing Rock superintendent proposed that it was better to place those who spoke and understood English on their own resources immediately than to wait fifteen years until their trust period expired, better for them to lose their land while they were young and healthy and could find a job than when they were old and feeble.[20]

As the superintendents debated, the government continued to foist thousands of fee patents on resistant Indians, some competent, some not. Under the declaration of policy, during an eighteen-month period it issued fee patents for approximately one million acres, which was more than it had issued during the previous ten years. Although some of the Indians who received fee patents could not support themselves, Sells conceded, the policy was justified, for, through the declaration of policy, the government had released the "white Indians" and given more attention to those who really needed its care and protection.[21]

Despite the vast amount of Indian land released from federal control, in 1918 congressional critics condemned the Indian Office for its paternalism and demanded that it release even more Indians from guardianship. The government's policy, complained Democratic Senator Edwin S. Johnson of South Dakota, had the effect of "destroying the usefulness of those people by taking from them the law of necessity for their own maintenance and substituting a law that compels them to be a nation of beggars." Another Westerner, Representative Charles Carter of Oklahoma, introduced a bill to remove restrictions automatically on all Indians with one-half or less Indian blood. Carter believed that, notwithstanding the declaration, Sells's fee patenting policy was too conservative to please the House Indian Affairs Committee, which had heard the testimony of many Indians who seemed perfectly competent but whose land remained under restriction.[22]

To quiet these critics, Commissioner Sells liberalized his policy even further. On March 7, 1919, he ordered the superintendents to submit to the Indian Office as soon as possible lists of all able-bodied and mentally competent Indians of one-half or less Indian blood who were twenty-one or older, with descriptions of their allotments, so that the Indian Office could issue fee patents to such Indians. Thus the lists now included the names of individuals with exactly one-half Indian blood.[23]

The commissioner continued to fight criticism that he was not moving fast enough. Thousands of full bloods and near full bloods were capable of supporting themselves, he noted, but they would not be able to withstand the competition after the federal government removed its trust restrictions. Yet, with enough funding for competency inquiries and with faithful adherence to the new policy, Sells claimed, the government would quickly separate the Indians who could stand on their own merits, pay taxes, and exercise citizenship from those who would continue to need government protection for a long time. "I shall not be outdone," he pledged, "by anyone who would hasten Indian progress by the extension of freedom and obligation to those who are ready for this status, nor shall I be swerved from what I believe to be a course of just aid and protection to the less fortunate and less progressive Indian." Indeed, between 1917 and 1919 the government issued 10,956 patents, most of them on the Northern Plains, which was 1,062 more than it had issued between 1907 and 1916.[24]

The same year Congress again evaluated Sells's fee patenting policy. When Lane heard congressmen charge that the government had 300,000 Indians under its jurisdiction and that "the greatest opponent of their being freed is the Indian Bureau," his temper flared. He assured the chairman of the House Indian Affairs Committee, Representative Homer Snyder, that the Indian Office was releasing competent Indians at a "reasonable" pace.[25] Throughout 1919 and 1920 the House Committee on Indian Affairs conducted a major investigation on the various reservations. When the committee called upon Sells to defend his policy, he assured them that he was working toward the eventual abolishment of the Indian Bureau, but the committee remained convinced that many competent Indians were still under restriction.[26]

Sells and Lane, who had pushed the fee patenting policy further than any of their predecessors, now adamantly opposed any further liberalization. Although they were anxious to please Congress, they also realized that a more liberal policy would cause tremendous suffering. Lane believed the government was already moving as rapidly as possible toward the goal of independence for the Indian. It had, after all, released 17,241 Indians from restriction during the Wilson administration and many Indians could not as yet protect themselves from their predatory white neighbors. Sells too argued that a more liberal fee patenting policy could be dangerous. "There would be no wisdom," he said, "in the withdrawal of federal supervision over all Indians at this time" because many old and incompetent Indians would soon be "fleeced" of their property and become dependent on the state governments.[27]

While Congress complained that the Indian Bureau issued too few fee patents, the Indians complained that it issued too many. Full blood and mixed blood Indians on the Umatilla, Yakima, and Flathead reservations refused to accept fee patents issued under the declaration of policy because they believed the government had no right to issue such patents unless they applied for them. They were not swayed by the argument that Congress had given the secretary of the interior the authority to issue fee patents to all competent

Indians.[28] The Indians became increasingly skeptical of the advantages of receiving fee patents, and cases such as John Elm's appeared more frequently. Elm, a Wisconsin Oneida Indian, observed that his fellow tribesmen who had received fee patents around 1908 sold their land and became homeless. Like many other Oneidas, Elm did not want a fee patent because his land would become taxable, and he argued that the government had no right to force him to accept one.[29]

By 1920 the tide of popular support for Sells's liberal policy was beginning to turn as supporters became alarmed by its devastating effects. Even the loyal Board of Indian Commissioners, no longer willing to follow Sells blindly, warned the government to be very careful in removing restrictions on individuals with more than one-half Indian blood. In freeing this class of Indians, it observed, "the government may be handing an unprotected incompetent over to an unscrupulous exploiter who had made his plans to rob the Indian even before the latter had received his certificate of independence." It reported that 73 percent of the Indians, excluding the Five Civilized Tribes, would need government supervision for many years, and only 55 percent, again excluding the Five Civilized Tribes, spoke English.[30] The Indian Rights Association also became more disillusioned with the administration of Indian affairs. One member angrily charged that those responsible for safeguarding Indian rights had failed to do so, and he condemned Sells for allowing whites to exploit the Indians. By 1920 the association's relations with Sells and Lane had clearly become strained.[31]

Secretary Lane resigned early in 1920, disillusioned and disturbed and no longer convinced that his Social Darwinist philosophy would make the world a better place. With his departure, reformers received a glimmer of hope, for President Wilson refused to replace Lane with a holdover from his own administration. Instead the president appointed John Barton Payne, a former Chicago lawyer and judge who had been on the Shipping Board of the Emergency Fleet Corporation in 1917 and had served as legal counsel to the Railroad Administration since 1918. Payne, who did not have Lane's Western sympathies, faced the difficult task of resisting political pressures and the demands of business interests. A well-intentioned man, he tried to follow a cautious and conservative policy.[32]

Payne stood firmly against the wholesale removal of restrictions, much to the displeasure of the House Indian Affairs Committee. The new secretary warned that the dangerous policy of issuing fee patents to the Indians and enabling them to sell the land would eventually pauperize thousands. Although he believed that every Indian family should own a home and learn through education to deal with whites on equal terms, he also recognized that patentees usually sold their lands quickly for a "woefully inadequate" sum and then squandered the proceeds. Those who forced Indians to deal with whites before they were ready did them great harm. Rather, Indians should gradually be made citizens, educated with whites, and encouraged to become part of white society.[33]

As reports continued to pour in of Indians selling their allotments and squandering the proceeds on luxuries, the secretary became increasingly alarmed. Payne evaluated every application carefully and rejected many of those that the competency commissions had approved, or he approved a fee patent for only part of the land mentioned in the application, so that an Indian might receive a patent for only 160 of his 320 acres or 320 out of 640 acres.[34] Late in 1920 Payne abolished the competency commissions altogether and ordered the superintendents to take over the work of recommending allottees for fee patents, using great caution. The Indians had to demonstrate that they could handle their own affairs, regardless of blood quantum. Under Payne, then, the Indian Office returned to its former practice of requiring applications and evaluating each applicant for competency before issuing a fee patent. Superintendents were again required to submit a full report on each applicant demonstrating that he was fully capable of handling his own affairs.[35]

The policy of arbitrarily issuing fee patents to certain Indians without their consent was immoral and illegal. It violated both the provisions and the intent of the Dawes Act. Moreover, that policy was racist in that it directly linked percentage of white blood to competency. Yet there was strong sentiment in the country to free the Indians from restriction. Sells and Lane had been responding to pressure from the influential Western bloc in Congress and from reformers who initially supported the fee patenting until its effects became apparent. Convinced that their policy would promote Indian assimilation they stubbornly clung to it until 1920. Thus, between 1917 and 1920 the government issued 17,176 fee patents, twice the number that it had issued from 1906 to 1916.[36] As a result, valuable farming and grazing land fell to non-Indians through sales, mortgages, or tax deeds. Payne's policy change in 1920 did little to alleviate the suffering of the thousands who had already lost their homes.

9.
Making Amends
Fee Patents, 1921–1934

Like his predecessor, Cato Sells, Charles Burke firmly believed that issuing fee patents was a proper and necessary last step toward independence, so he made it an essential element in his plan to promote Indian progress. But by the time he took office the policy's disastrous effects had become apparent. States and counties sagged under the heavy weight of responsibility for indigent Indians who had received fee patents. Realizing now that the Indian Office's liberal policy had caused much suffering, Burke adopted a more conservative approach and became the first commissioner to cancel a fee patent. Although the number of fee patents issued declined markedly during the Burke years, Indians who had already received them continued to suffer. The Indian Office could not effectively combat the strong pressure on patentees to mortgage or sell their lands.

Commissioner Burke found support for a conservative policy in Secretary of the Interior Hubert Work. Work believed that the removal of restrictions on Indian allotments was a wise policy, but only when the Indian owner was ready. He cautioned that the removal of restrictions was apt to prove overwhelming to impoverished Indians. Since they had never earned money, they could not be expected to spend it wisely or to realize the importance of saving a dollar. Never having been in business, they could not be expected to cope with the tactics of unscrupulous people. The government's fundamental responsibility, Work argued, was to encourage individual industry, thrift, and responsibility.

Burke also found support among the reform groups that had become so disenchanted with the policies of the previous administration. The Board of Indian Commissioners realized that policymakers were in the midst of a heated debate on whether the government should issue fee patents to all Indians immediately or keep them under government supervision, and it was anxious to provide Congress and the Indian Office with definite information so that those bodies could settle on a proper policy. To obtain such information, in 1921 the board asked numerous superintendents, field clerks, and reservation farmers—people who were in daily contact with the Indians—to report how many Indians in their jurisdiction received fee patents and when, what the size and character of their allotments were, how many sold or leased their land, what they did with the proceeds, what they did for a living, their general condition as compared to before fee patenting, and whether they were happy with their new freedom. The board began sending Burke scattered replies as they came in from the field until he finally asked it to prepare a summary of its findings.[1]

The board's report represented a devastating indictment of Sells's liberal policy. None of the respondents criticized the general proposition of freeing the Indians as soon as possible, and none opposed fee patenting so long as Indians were able to assume the responsibilities of citizenship. Most writers opposed allowing blood quantum or length of school attendance to determine competency, instead favoring examinations into the Indians' ability to support themselves.[2]

The survey clearly indicated that liberal fee patenting was extremely damaging to the Indians. Of the eighty-seven field men who replied, seventy-one (81.5 percent) indicated that most or all of the patentees either sold their land or lost it because they failed to pay the interest on their mortgages. This category no doubt included the large number of patentees who lost their land because they did not pay taxes on it. In many cases, the board noted "the issuance of patents in fee seems to be a shortcut to the separation of the freed Indians from their land and cash." Of these seventy-one field men, forty-six believed the current liberal fee patenting policy was flawed. Yet there was still some support for the policy among twenty-five of the writers (28.5 percent) who maintained that although the Indians lost their land, they would ultimately be better off for having to depend on themselves. Most Indians, the board explained, sold their land and used the proceeds to buy new cars, and when after use on poor reservation roads the cars broke down, the owners were left with nothing to show for their land but a junk heap.[3]

The Board of Indian Commissioners provided the new administration with the powerful ammunition needed to push through major policy changes. Burke also had the support of the secretary of the interior, Albert Fall. "The Indian is no more capable of handling his own affairs than the average white man," he argued, "and when restrictions upon alienation are removed, in very many cases he soon finds himself without property or resources." Henceforth, the government would consider each applicant's actual accomplishments on his land or in some productive occupation before recognizing his competency.[4]

In 1921 the Indian Office formally rejected the practice of issuing blanket fee patents to all Indians with one-half or less Indian blood and emphasized instead Payne's earlier policy of requiring a formal application and proof of competency. In defense of that new policy, Burke argued that few Indians could prudently manage their own business and land. Many of the Indians least competent to manage their own affairs applied for fee patents, he charged, while many truly competent Indians still held their lands in trust to avoid paying taxes.[5] Some change was necessary, he said, to check the unscrupulous whites who covertly pushed fee patenting for selfish reasons, to prevent incompetent Indians from disposing of their land, and to encourage competent ones to manage their own estates. The Indian Office, Burke urged, should evaluate competency by looking at applicants' accomplishments and at what they had actually done to support themselves and their families over a period of years.[6]

As part of its efforts to implement a stricter policy, the Indian Office revised the 1910 regulations for issuing fee patents and competency certificates to bring its practices more in line with transactions between whites.[7] In October 1922, the Indian Office ordered that all deeds to incompetent Indians include the clause: "subject to the condition that the land herein described shall not be alienated or encumbered without the consent of the Secretary of the Interior."[8]

Despite the more cautious policy, reports from the field clearly indicated that too many patents were still being issued too quickly, with devastating results. A staggering number of Indians lost their land and became paupers, as many as 75 to 100 percent of the patentees on most reservations.[9] Often these Indians had no choice but to sell their land because they could not make enough money off it to meet their taxes. Some Indians had no experience farming, or their lands were too poor to farm profitably. After the patentees sold their land, they spent the money on luxuries, especially cars. On Cheyenne River, for example, almost every Indian who received a fee patent bought a car if he made enough from selling his land to cover the purchase price. The practice became so common that when one of the reservation's most competent Indians was asked if he wanted to become a citizen, after a long pause he carefully replied that he did not know how to drive a car. After the Indians squandered the proceeds from the sale of their land, they had difficulty finding work; the big stock interests in the Northwest hired few Indians, and white homesteaders had little use for them.

Winnebago Superintendent F. T. Mann reported that on his reservation fee patents invariably led to the sale or mortgage of the Indians' allotments. There had been only three exceptions to this pattern. Yet, he observed, businessmen and land speculators in the region complained that the fee patenting policy was too conservative. Mann warned Commissioner Burke that these men were using their political influence to force the government to lift restrictions on trust land in order to throw that land on the market and stimulate business conditions. Burke, however, was convinced that the government had already opened up enough reservation land. "Our idea has not been to widen the field of the speculator at the expense of the Indian," he reminded Mann, "but to conserve his property either in land or funds and to obtain as good prices as possible." Burke conceded that some Indians had quickly lost their land to speculators because the speculators had "connived" with them, but it was hard to ascertain beforehand the influences behind a fee patent application. The problem continued as Indians who lost their land and money fled the reservation. Many headed for Sioux City, Iowa, where they appealed to the Welfare Bureau for help.[10]

Stripped of his land, the Indian was thrust into the competitive world of the whites, a world for which he was ill-prepared. "Land is the basic wealth in any community," explained the Pine Ridge superintendent, "and it is very clear that when an Indian squanders his land he is absolutely without a place of refuge." Reverting to a dependent state, the landless Indian either moved in with friends and relatives or relied on the state and county governments for food, clothing, and shelter. Clearly the issuance of fee patents discouraged rather than encouraged self-support, the professed goal of the Indian Office. "The effect of making the Indian landless," said one superintendent, "has been to make him more dissatisfied, less respected, and decreased his opportunity to be independent."[11]

Some superintendents, however, tended to gloss over the negative effects of fee patents. They offered the same feeble arguments in their support that had been popular during the Wilson administration. On the Flathead reservation, for example, although 75 percent of the patentees sold their land, the superintendent insisted that the policy was a good one because some Indians used the proceeds to buy better land or to improve the land they had. Others who wasted the proceeds were forced to go to work. The superintendent coolly observed that it was better to issue fee patents to Indians while they were young, vigorous, and healthy enough to earn a living than to wait until the trust period expired. The Fort Peck superintendent contended that fee patenting benefited the Indians because although they lost their land, some of them became more independent. The Crow superintendent was not disheartened by the fact that almost all the fee patented land was sold or mortgaged, and that 80 percent of the proceeds went to purchase cars or other luxuries or to pay off debts, because he believed that the removal of restrictions would ultimately force the Indians to work.[12]

Despite these optimistic predictions, the practice of issuing fee patents continued to arouse opposition, especially among state and county officials, who charged that the federal government used the fee patenting policy to relieve itself of its responsibility for the welfare of the Indians. After the Indians were released from restriction, states and counties were saddled with the heavy financial burden of providing for their education, health care, and other needs. To make matters worse, fee patents were issued to individuals who could not possibly support themselves and became completely dependent on the state.[13]

In response to growing criticism several congressional committees asked Burke to defend his policy. As the committees grilled him with questions, the commissioner clung steadfastly to his belief that the government should remove restrictions on all Indians competent enough to handle their own affairs and should reimburse the Indian for the cash value of his interest in tribal property so that he would no longer have any link with his tribe. Burke defined a competent Indian as one who understood the value of money and could make a living even if he squandered what he had. "The best evidence that an Indian is not competent," he told the committee, "is for him to ask for a fee patent, because he is better off without it if he means to keep his land."[14]

It is doubtful that either Burke or the committee recognized that this blunt statement was in effect an admission that the policy was fundamentally flawed and a miserable failure.

As his testimony continued, Burke also condemned the previous administration for implementing a liberal fee patenting policy that was illegal. Looking back, he now sadly conceded that the legislation bearing his name had been twisted; previous administrations had misconstrued the Burke Act. When Congress passed the Burke Act in 1906, he observed, it had not intended for a fee patent to be issued unless an Indian applied for it, but Lane had concluded that the issuance of a fee patent was entirely within his discretion. To quiet criticism that the Indian Office kept competent Indians in bondage, Sells and Lane had issued fee patents to thousands of Indians who were not competent, and Burke's administration had to clean up the mess they had left. Many of the current complaints about starvation and other problems, Burke explained, came from Indians who were freed too soon.[15]

Although Burke abhorred the harmful excesses of liberal fee patenting, he did not completely reject the practice of issuing fee patents. This commissioner who was one of the last advocates of rugged individualism believed that if an Indian was competent, the government must make him understand that after he wasted what he had, he could not expect the government to support him. In a statement reminiscent of the Social Darwinist philosophy of his predecessor, Burke coldly concluded, "If the man has any good in him disaster will make him succeed."[16]

Charles Burke was, however, a more effective and more humane administrator than the outspoken John Collier, executive secretary of the American Indian Defense Association (AIDA), and his other critics would admit. Under the commissioner's guidance, the government continued its more conservative policy, scrutinizing each fee patent application. In the last years of the Burke administration the Indian Office approved only 40 percent of the applications that it received, but the record still showed that most patentees lost their land by sale, unredeemed mortgages, and tax deeds. The government's protective policy did not prevent land sales, under government supervision and after competitive bidding, to provide funds in emergency cases.[17]

After 1921, the Indian Office not only issued fee patents more carefully but also helped Indians hold on to the land that had already been fee patented by restoring it to trust status. The restoration of land to trust status marked the beginning of a policy that would culminate in the Indian Reorganization Act of 1934 as the government attempted to reverse the pattern of dispossession established during the previous three decades.

As part of this effort Secretary Work pushed for legislation which would permit the secretary to cancel fee patents made to Indians who had not wanted or applied for them. Work presented strong arguments in favor of such legislation, including Burke's allegation that the Burke Act had been violated. Under Lane, he said, the government had issued patents to many adult allottees of less than one-half Indian blood without application. Many of these Indians had refused to accept the fee patents when issued, and some later accepted them unwillingly because they believed they would lose their land if they did not. Another class, principally of old and ignorant Indians, accepted the patents because they did not understand the effects of their actions. Almost all of their lands had since been placed on the tax rolls and some had been sold for nonpayment of assessments.[18]

The legislation to cancel fee patents that Secretary Work now proposed had a strong legal precedent. The Interior Department had recently canceled the fee patents issued to two Coeur d'Alene Indians who had refused to accept them or to pay taxes and had filed suit to cancel the assessments. In *United States v. Benewah County*, Idaho, and *United States v. Kootenai County*, Idaho, the U.S. circuit court of appeals, ninth district, held that the secretary of the interior had no authority under the 1906 Burke Act to issue a fee patent during the trust period without the application or consent of the allottee. Such patents, having been refused, did not confer title, so the land was not taxable. Thus, the court upheld the cancellation of the two patents.[19]

Other undelivered patents issued without application had also been canceled. There remained, however, a large group of Indians who had not applied for fee patents but accepted them believing they had no choice, and the courts had not decided whether these patents were valid and passed title. Nor was it clear that physical delivery of the patent in itself signified acceptance. The Interior Department wanted legislative authority to cancel these forced patents where the Indian had not yet sold or encumbered the land. Appealing to the current sentiment for fiscal conservatism, Work argued that the Interior Department could save state and federal governments money by doing so. Such cancellation would prevent Indians, especially the old and the disabled, from losing their homes and becoming burdens on the state.[20] Finally, Interior Department officials and congressional leaders probably favored the legislation because it would protect the interests of non-Indian third parties. These non-Indians would not have to worry about losing title to fee patented land that they had purchased. Under the court decision in *Benewah County* and *Kootenai County*, a third party who had purchased an Indian's land in good faith might now find that the original fee patent was illegal and the sale invalid. The proposed legislation, however, prevented the cancellation of a fee patent if the allottee or his heirs had sold or encumbered any part of the land.

The House Committee on Indian Affairs enthusiastically endorsed the Interior Department's legislation. During 1919 and 1920, the government had issued approximately ten thousand fee patents, often over the protest of Indians who received them. If the allottee had voluntarily encumbered or sold his fee patented land, the committee reasoned, this must be considered acceptance of the fee patent and a waiver of the tax-exempt privilege of a trust patent, but if he had not done so the fee patent should be canceled on application to the secretary. Many Indians had accepted patents under protest, because they did not understand their rights, and this should not prevent cancellation. Finally, the committee noted, the legislation would not only protect third parties who had acquired Indian land, but would also "remedy a great injustice to a considerable number of Indians."[21]

An act was approved on February 26, 1927, authorizing the cancellation of fee patents issued without the application or consent of the patentee, provided that the Indian owner had not sold or mortgaged any part of the land described in the patent.[22] The cancellation act had significant weaknesses. It did not deal with fee patent cases where the individual gave some evidence of consent and did not affect land that had already been surrendered to a third party. Moreover, the requirements for cancellation were rigid. The Indian could not have sold or mortgaged any of his land; he had to prove that he had not applied for or willingly accepted the patent, which was no easy task; and he had to make a written application to have the patent canceled. Because of the weaknesses in the law and the rigid requirements, few Indians benefited from it. For example, of the 647 forced patents issued to the Flathead Indians under the 1917 declaration, only thirty-two, or 5 percent, were canceled. By May 1928 the government had canceled roughly two hundred patents on the basis of the court decisions and the 1927 act, a pitifully small number when compared to the thousands illegally issued between 1917 and 1920.[23]

Although the Interior Department canceled a small percentage of forced fee patents, some congressmen, not satisfied that it was doing enough to implement the 1927 law, introduced a bill in the Senate on April 2, 1928, to create a commission to investigate the issuance of forced fee patents. Anxious to avoid such an investigation and to retain its authority and initiative in Indian affairs, the Interior Department pleaded with Congress to let it compile information and work on the problem without any outside interference. The bill was later scrapped.[24]

To quiet congressional critics, in June 1928 Burke ordered the superintendents to submit detailed information on Indians in their jurisdiction to whom a fee patent had been issued before 1921 without application or consent during the trust period so the Indian Office could devise a plan to give relief if possible, through legislation or otherwise, to those who had lost their lands.[25] Most superintendents reported that the overwhelming majority of patentees were destitute and living off relatives. Other superintendents had trouble following Burke's instructions. The Fort Berthold superintendent, for one, had difficulty collecting the required information because the records did not clearly indicate which patents were issued without application. He often found applications typed by clerks and marked by thumbprint or not signed at all, or he found correspondence concerning the application but not the application itself. The Shawnee superintendent found thirty-six allottees who had received patents without applying for them, but he could not submit detailed reports on each of them because they were scattered and some of them had not been heard from for years. The Ponca superintendent sent out circulars to locate the Indians who had received fee patents without applying for them, but the government did not pursue the issue and apparently canceled no patents in his region.[26]

The reports clearly indicated that many patentees had lost their land in mortgage foreclosures and tax sales or had sold it for inadequate consideration, but in some cases patentees had sold or mortgaged only part of the land. In 1931 at the request of the Interior Department, Congress passed another cancellation bill, which authorized the secretary to cancel the fee patent on any portion of an Indian's land that had not been sold and was not presently encumbered by a mortgage.[27] The 1931 law gave the secretary more authority to cancel the partial remaining forced patents, but fewer than 200 fee patents were canceled. In all, under both the 1927 and 1931 acts, the government canceled approximately 470 forced fee patents out of the original ten thousand unapplied-for patents.[28] Neither act dealt with fee patents where individuals gave some evidence of consent; nor did they offer any relief for destitute patentees who had already lost their land.

To critics of the government's fee patenting policy, the flaws in the 1927 and 1931 legislation were readily apparent. John Collier observed that the 1927 cancellation act was no solution. "The fee-patent Indians," he wrote, "are frightfully victimized; being held in a limbo where they are nobody's responsibility." The present policy and the circumstances surrounding it, he charged, "is unconsciously designed as an instrument of destruction or torture." Collier's AIDA demanded that the government resume responsibility for the fee patented Indians. The government, it said, had brought the bewildered Indians to "the final dumping-off place" without preparing them in any way for what they would face. These Indians should receive the same benefits as Indians in trust status, and those states which were ready for the responsibility should plan comprehensive education, health, and welfare services for both classes of Indians to be financed with federal funds. Unless federal and state governments developed some kind of procedure along those lines, the association warned, thousands of landless, uneducated, unorganized Indians would have to rely on local authorities or private charities for help.[29] The AIDA apparently realized the massive problem that thousands of impoverished Indians posed for the various state governments. Ironically, at the same time Collier and his followers attacked the government for abandoning its trust responsibility, Congress was working to restore Indian land to trust status through the cancellation acts.

Criticism of the government's policy became louder and more insistent during the late 1920s because, despite attempts by the Indian Office to improve the practice of issuing fee patents, most patentees continued to sell their land and squander the proceeds. The pressure from unscrupulous whites and the lure of quick, easy money were simply too compelling. A growing number of critics maintained that the Indian Office had been too liberal in allotting and leasing Indian land and in issuing fee patents. They demanded a more enlightened policy under which the Indian Service would keep the reservations intact, preserve Indian culture, and give Indians the same rights as other citizens. Their views provided the basis for the Indian New Deal.

By the 1920s some intellectuals and reformers had repudiated the emphasis on assimilation in favor of cultural pluralism, one of the new themes of Indian reform that arose after World War I. Rather than uphold the ideal of the melting pot, they sought to preserve the diverse cultures and traditions of this country. To these reformers Indians had virtues and a humanity that mainstream society seemed to have lost. The spokesman for this group, John Collier, viewed Indian culture as an alternative to the fragmentation of American life. He represented a different philosophical outlook than virtually any of the previous reform critics.

The Pueblo lands controversy in the early 1920s had given Collier national attention and had prompted the formation of his AIDA. The AIDA called for basic reforms such as Indian citizenship, termination of allotment, improved health and education, and the reestablishment of tribal government. It stressed cultural pluralism and sought to apply social science methodology to Indian problems. In 1926 Collier concluded, "The granting of unrestricted fee simple patents to individual Indians has been generally disastrous, both during the period before the Dawes Act and in the period since the Dawes Act when competency certificates have been granted." On the basis of past experience, he charged, to advocate fee patenting was to "preach a counsel of despair."[30]

Collier pointed out that the government issued fee patents to Indians who had not received individual or group training in modern business life or citizenship, did not have enough land to live on, had no experience in getting or using credit, and were heavily indebted to the government for reimbursable funds. Rather than issue the competency certificates with due notice to the tribe as a whole so that it could organize for mutual aid, he said, it issued them "hit-and-miss" to individuals. This prevented the Indians from uniting in credit enterprises or in making joint contracts for buying goods or selling crops and thus made it impossible for them to succeed as farmers and stockmen.[31]

Collier was not the only critic of the fee patent process. The Meriam report recommended that the government use "extreme conservatism" in issuing fee patents. The Indian Office, it said, should keep better records of the Indians' accomplishments in the field so that it could base competency decisions more on definite achievements than opinion, and it should require Indians who wanted fee patents to serve probationary periods in which they demonstrated their self-sufficiency. The report conceded that the government's failure to protect Indian rights had usually been the result of poor judgment rather than malice. Nonetheless, it charged, "through government action, many really incompetent Indians have been permitted to lose possession of their individually owned property before they were ready to maintain themselves in the presence of the civilization which confronts them."[32]

By 1928 Congress had lost patience with the current policy and in frustration called Assistant Commissioner Meritt to testify. This faithful bureaucrat who for years had steadfastly supported the policies of Lane and Sells now seemed to experience a change of heart, claiming that he personally opposed liberal fee patenting because 90 percent of the patentees lost their land. Bitter and disillusioned, he now condemned the policy that he had helped implement a few years earlier. To turn the Indians loose before they were ready, as Lane had done, he sadly conceded, was "a great crime." Lane's intentions had been good, but his Indian policy had been wrong. Meritt warned that freeing the Indians would not solve the Indian problem and that such a policy was impractical. Without government protection, the Indians would not retain one percent of the land they then owned. On a more encouraging note, however, he observed that the Indians had progressed as rapidly as any dependent people in the past fifty years. In two or more generations, or in one more generation of educated Indians, he predicted, there would be a "wonderful showing" in the country if the government continued its protection.[33]

The Rhoads-Scattergood administration scaled down the fee patenting policy significantly. In 1930, the Indian Office issued only 113 fee patents covering 13,441 acres and 166 fee patents covering 24,447 acres the following year. The Indian Office approved fewer than 50 percent of the fee patent applications that it received, and it continued to cancel fee patents under the authority of the 1927 act.[34]

Despite the efforts of Work and Burke to repair some of the damage done by the ruthless removal of restrictions under their predecessors, for most Indians who had received fee patents and subsequently lost their land, there was little help. Burke and Rhodes continued to issue fee patents, though on a drastically reduced scale, and patentees continued to alienate their land. Not until 1933 would the Indian Office under its new commissioner, John Collier, reverse the policy and refuse to accept any more applications for fee patents or competency certificates except in special cases.[35] In taking steps to reverse the disastrous effects of issuing fee patents, policy makers of the 1920s had at least laid the foundation for the Indian New Deal of the 1930s.

Conclusion

By 1934, the grim picture of a shriveling land base and an economically deprived people was clearly drawn. Two-thirds of the Indians were either completely landless or did not own enough land to make a subsistence living. The Indian estate had shrunk from 138 million acres in 1887 to 52 million acres. This 86-million-acre land loss came in four ways: 38 million acres of surplus land ceded after allotment, 22 million acres of surplus land opened to white settlement, 23 million acres of fee patented land lost, and 3.4 million acres of original and heirship allotments sold. By 1934, federal officials had carved 246,569 allotments out of 40,848,172 acres on roughly 100 reservations. Many tribes were left with land assets that were not usable because of "checkerboarding" and complicated land titles, overgrazing and erosion, or lack of irrigation.[1]

The government's policy had been to break up reservations, give Indians title to individual tracts of land, and allow them to sell or lease that land. This policy, an Interior Department study noted, created "a race of petty landlords" and of small capitalists who were conditioned to continue their idleness by the unearned income they derived from the sale or lease of capital assets.[2]

Allotment forced many Indians to lease their lands and made them dependent on rental income. It caused 100,000 Indians to lose their land because they alienated it after receiving fee patents. Heirship policies so subdivided Indian lands among multiple owners that they were no longer economically viable units and the only way to get a return was to lease it. One 160-acre allotment made in 1887 would by 1985 pass to 312 heirs. The largest holding was four acres and the smallest was .0009 acres (the yearly income for the owner of this plot was less than one cent). In a scathing indictment of federal policy, a 1934 Interior Department study concluded, "The Indian Service, under the allotment and heirship system, has been irresistibly driven to the adoption of a policy of liquidation."[3]

As Indians disposed of their allotments they were replaced by whites moving onto the reservation so that by 1934 a checkerboard pattern dominated maps of allotted reservations. While whites steadily consolidated their holdings into viable farming and grazing units by purchasing or leasing allotments, Indian lands became more divided. The Indian Reorganization Act of 1934 would try to reverse the checkerboard pattern and consolidate what was left of the Indian estate.

The pattern of land loss established during the period 1887–1934 continues to this day. A survey of the four largest reservations in Montana illustrates the scope of this loss. The Crow reservation had 2,400,174 acres in 1891. The government allotted 2,200,000 acres, leaving 200,000 acres of rough mountainous land in tribal ownership. Today whites own over 1,000,000 acres, and land ownership on the reservation is fragmented. Fort Peck reservation had 622,000 acres of which 470,000 acres were allotted, and 100,000 acres of this are white owned. The Flathead reservation had 1,248,000 acres and 720,000 allotted acres, 640,000 of which are white owned. The Blackfeet reservation had 1,520,000 acres and 721,000 allotted acres, 600,000 of which are white owned. Tribes in Montana lost 5,332,317 of their original 11,631,407 acres. Over 80 percent of the best allotted land in Montana ended up in the hands of non-Indians. On the Crow reservation whites owned 44 percent of the 2,000,000 acres of allotted land and leased most of the rest. Whites leased 53 percent of the land on the Blackfeet reservation, 36 percent on Fort Peck reservation, and 48 percent at Fort Belknap reservation.[4]

The decline of the Indian estate was not the only significant effect of federal Indian land policy during the period 1887–1934. Ironically, a land policy initiated to "free" the Indians from federal supervision promoted the growth of an administrative bureaucracy that worked to keep Indians dependent. The bureaucratic structure of the Indian Office became more complex and specialized, and administrative tasks became more time consuming. Amendments to the Dawes Act resulted in an increase in administrative authority over Indians that contradicted the Dawes Act concept of self-support.

Under the allotment system the Indian Office dealt directly with thousands of individual landowners rather than with tribes. It assumed responsibility for supervising the sale and lease of Indian land and the issuance of fee patents for allotments, and it managed an increasingly complex fractionated estate. In addition, Indian Office staff created a field organization for irrigation complete with irrigation districts and supervising engineers along with an even more extensive organization for promoting and supervising Indian farming and stockraising. As historian Vine Deloria explains, the amendments to the Dawes Act "shifted the theoretical base of allotment from an educative process whereby Indians could learn how to manage private property to an administrative problem in which the federal government was assumed to be the supervisor of how Indian property was used."[5]

Management of this unwieldy bureaucracy often became more important than safeguarding Indian rights and land title. The Indian Office staff devoted more of its time and manpower to monitoring lease arrangements and fractionated estates and determining competency than it did to instructing Indians in irrigation techniques and methods of land use. Even the most well intentioned officials and field agents found their efforts thwarted by this bureaucratic mass. At the same time that Secretary of the Interior Wilbur testified before a congressional committee in 1932 that the goal of the Indian Service was to "work itself out of a job in 25 years," field service employees found themselves spending more and more time on paperwork and less in the field.[6] As the allotment era ended, the administrative bureaucracy reached an all-time high and the Indian Office underwent one of the most significant reorganizations in its history.

Federal Indian land policy not only promoted land loss and increased the Indian Service's administrative responsibilities, but it also had devastating effects on Indian social and economic life. Allotment broke up the tribal organization which had been a crucial cohesive force in Indian culture. Moreover, allotment divided families as effectively as it divided tribes because allotments were made to individuals, not to family units. The divisions were emotional as well as physical. In addition, the policies that evolved in conjunction with allotment such as leasing and fee patenting also tended to divide tribal members, separating those who accepted the policies from those who resisted, those who succeeded financially from those who did not.

On the Cheyenne River reservation, for example, as historian Frederick Hoxie demonstrates, allotment changed the Indian environment dramatically, dispersing the population across the reservation. The Indians no longer settled together in bands but rather moved out on their own. They lived near their land and began to think of themselves as members of the Cheyenne River Sioux tribe rather than as Sans Arc, Minneconjou, Blackfeet, or Two Kettle bands.

It is important to note, however, that not all reservations responded to the allotment policy in the same way. Another historian, Donald Berthrong, shows that allotment did not eliminate tribalism among the Cheyenne and Arapahos. Indians continued to live together in extended families and small villages and resisted white education, Christianity, and the concept of private property. Although the cultural effects might not have been as great as on other reservations, the pattern of land loss remained constant. Marginal soil fertility and rainfall, minimal capacity to operate farm machinery, and a deep aversion to farm labor prevented them from becoming farmers. Eight years after allotment, only 15–18 percent of the adult males were occupying and farming their land.[7]

Berthrong's account touches on some of the basic reasons for the failure of federal Indian land policy. Significant obstacles prevented Indians from using their allotments productively. First, the Indians lacked the capital and credit that they needed to purchase seeds, equipment, and stock. Their allotments could not be used for credit while the government held the titles in trust. Second, environmental factors were a deterrent. Most of the reservations were located in arid regions with marginal agricultural potential, and it was unreasonable for Congress and the Indian Office to expect anyone to farm this land successfully. With water in short supply, much of the land could not be farmed without irrigation. The poor soil was often more suitable for stockraising than farming. In addition, many reservations on the Northern Plains and in the Pacific Northwest were in a climate zone with a short growing season, and farmers risked early crop-killing frosts and freezes.

Third, many Indians resisted cultural change. It was sociologically unsound to expect the rapid transition of Indians from a hunting to a farming economy. Traditionally farming was regarded as "women's work" in many Indian communities so male and female labor roles had to be transformed. Native Americans often had neither the aptitude nor the desire to replace a diversified subsistence farming system with more materialistic commercial farming.

Although the reasons for the failure are complex, much of the blame rests with policymakers and administrators. Clearly none of the Indian commissioners serving from 1887 to 1934 implemented the government's policy successfully given their stated objectives, for they failed to transform the Indians into independent citizens or to protect them from white exploitation and greed. Instead of promoting Indian self-support and the productive use of Indian land, the liberal progressive solution of freeing Indians from government control led to the loss of land and the pauperization of the Indians. Gone was the Dawes idea of protecting Indians in their landownership. Lane, Burke, and other policymakers were ultimately more concerned with putting Indian land in use than promoting Indian self-support or protecting Indian rights. Thus what was proposed as being in the best interest of the Indians turned out instead to benefit the whites. Each step proposed along the white man's road to self-support and assimilation actually hastened the disintegration of the Indian estate.

Policymakers and administrators simply did not understand the magnitude and complexity of the "Indian problem." As a result, they relied too heavily on the effect of individual ownership and did little to educate the Indians in the use of the land. They failed to provide them with the training, experience, and financial support they needed to function effectively in an industrial society and forced the responsibilities of individual landownership and citizenship on them without preparing them to meet these responsibilities. Shortsighted officials subverted their own goals of independence and self-support by encouraging leasing and land sales and by issuing fee patents to unqualified Indians. The progressive doctrine of self-support became a tool to justify dispossession. In an age obsessed with economic and industrial progress, policymakers and administrators concluded that the Indians had to use their land according to white standards of productivity or surrender it.

Indian land policy also failed because policymakers never fully recognized the fundamental cultural differences involved and made no effort to understand and appreciate the culture they were dealing with. Moreover, they failed to recognize the cultural differences among the Indians themselves. Reservations had scores of tribal communities with different lifestyles and languages. They demanded that the Indians adopt white ways and move into the twentieth century along with the rest of American society, even though the Indians already had their own highly developed culture and value system. The Indians had no concept of permanent ownership and title to land and did not place the same importance on money, hard work, and self-support as did Secretary Lane and other whites. White Americans defined progress as efficiency, order, prosperity, technological advances, and industrialization. Their middle class values were simply incompatible with traditional Indian values and the Indian emphasis on community. While government officials successfully shattered the Indians' tribal culture and forced many natives to accept "independence," they could not force them to accept the materialistic culture and values of the dominant white society.

Commissioners Sells and Burke were among the last believers in allotment. By the late 1920s concerned individuals realized that the current policies had fallen short of the goals set forth in the Dawes Act. No longer optimistic about the prospects of assimilation, they began to emphasize instead cultural pluralism and Indian self-determination, ideas which would become the core of the Indian New Deal of the 1930s. Indian policy in the 1930s would be shaped not by the progressive goal of self-support but by the need to maintain social stability and provide social security through government action.

NOTES

Introduction

1. Francis E. Leupp, *The Indian and His Problem* (New York: Charles Scribner's Sons, 1910; reprint ed., New York: Arno Press, 1971), p. 93.

2. D. S. Otis, *The Dawes Act and the Allotment of Indian Lands*, ed. Francis Paul Prucha (Norman: University of Oklahoma Press, 1973), pp. 8, 9, 13, 19; J. P. Kinney, *A Continent Lost—A Civilization Won: Indian Land Tenure in America* (Baltimore: Johns Hopkins University Press, 1937; reprint ed., New York: Arno Press, 1975), p. ix.

3. Otis, *Dawes Act*, pp. 82–83.

4. Frederick E. Hoxie, *A Final Promise: The Campaign to Assimilate Indians, 1880–1920* (Lincoln: University of Nebraska Press, 1984).

5. William T. Hagan, "Justifying the Dispossession of the Indian: Land Utilization Argument," in *American Indian Environments: Ecological Issues in Native American History*, ed. Christopher Vecsey and Robert W. Venables (Syracuse University Press, 1980), pp. 65–80.

6. For information on public land policy, see Benjamin H. Hibbard, *A History of Public Land Policies* (New York: Peter Smith, 1939); E. Louise Peffer, *The Closing of the Public Domain: Disposal and Reservation Policies, 1900–1950* (Stanford, Calif.: Stanford University Press, 1951); Roy M. Robbins, *Our Landed Heritage: The Public Domain, 1776–1936* (Princeton: Princeton University Press, 1942; reprint ed., Gloucester, Mass.: Peter Smith, 1960); and William K. Wyant, *Westward in Eden: The Public Lands and the Conservation Movement* (Berkeley: University of California Press, 1982).

1. Allotment: The Land Divided

1. Francis Paul Prucha, "Thomas Jefferson Morgan," in *The Commissioners of Indian Affairs, 1824–1977*, ed. Robert M. Kvasnicka and Herman J. Viola (Lincoln: University of Nebraska Press, 1979), pp. 193–203; Thomas G. Alexander, *A Clash of Interests: The Interior Department and the Mountain West, 1863–1896* (Provo, Utah: Brigham Young University Press, 1977), p. 158; ARCIA, 1900, pp. 12, 639.

2. Donald Parman, "Francis Ellington Leupp," *Commissioners of Indian Affairs*, pp. 221–22; Brian W. Dippie, *The Vanishing American: White Attitudes and United States Indian Policy* (Middletown, Conn.: Wesleyan University Press, 1982), pp. 181–82.

3. ARCIA, 1905, pp. 3–44.

4. *Report of the Twenty-Seventh Annual Lake Mohonk Conference of the Friends of the Indians, 1909*, p. 19; Diane Putney, "Robert Valentine (1909–1912)," *Commissioners of Indian Affairs*, p. 233; ARCIA, 1911, p. 20.

5. ARCIA, 1913, p. 2.

6. Laurence F. Schmeckebier, *The Office of Indian Affairs: Its History, Activities, and Organization* (Baltimore: Johns Hopkins University Press, 1927), pp. 143–44, 146; *U.S. Statutes at Large*, vol. 24, p. 388; Burton M. Smith, "The Politics of Allotment: The Flathead Indian Reservation as a Test Case," *Pacific Northwest Quarterly* 70 (July 1979):139.

7. Ibid.

8. Paul Stuart, *The Indian Office: Growth and Development of an American Institution, 1865–1900* (Ann Arbor: UMI Research Press, 1978), p. 122; Cato Sells to John Baum, October 17, 1913, SI-CCF, 5–1, Indian Agencies, Pima, Allotments; Sells to E. L. Swartzlander, May 2, 1917, SI-CCF, 5–1, Indian Agencies, Umatilla, Allotments; C. F.

Hauke to William Kohlenberg, April 23, 1914, SI-CCF, 5–1, Indian Agencies, Crow Creek, Allotments.

9.   Klara B. Kelley, *Economic Development in American Indian Reservations* (University of New Mexico, Native American Studies, Development Series, No. 1, 1979), p. 32; ARCIA, 1900, p. 54; ibid., 1890, p. 38; ibid., 1891, pp. 43–44; ibid., 1916, pp. 93–99; Alexander, *Clash of Interests*, pp. 159–60.

10.   ARCIA, 1911, pp. 21–22; ibid., 1912, pp. 131–34; ibid., 1915, pp. 35–36; ibid., 1916, pp. 93–99; ibid., 1920, p. 168.

11.   Ibid., 1913, pp. 2, 7, 41; U.S. House, Committee on Indian Affairs, *Indians of the United States*, Hearings, vol. I: *On the Condition of Various Tribes of Indians*, 66th Cong., 1st sess., 1919, pp. 23, 43–44, 46.

12.   Fred L. Isreal, *The State of the Union Messages of the Presidents* (New York: Chelsea House, 1966), 3:2625; Roy M. Robbins, *Our Landed Heritage: The Public Domain, 1776–1936* (Princeton: Princeton University Press, 1942; reprint ed., Gloucester, Mass.: Peter Smith, 1960), pp. 398–402; John Ise, *The United States Oil Policy* (New Haven: Yale University Press, 1926), pp. 356–87; Donald C. Swain, *Federal Conservation Policy, 1921–1933* (Berkeley: University of California Press, 1963), p. 160.

13.   Herbert Corey, "He Carries the White Man's Burden," *Collier's* 71 (May 12, 1923):13; *Biographical Directory of the American Congress, 1774–1971* (Washington: Government Printing Office, 1971), p. 669; Charles Carter to Albert Fall, March 11, 1921, SI-CCF, 22–33, Presidential Appointments, Commissioner of Indian Affairs; Richard Pratt to Fall, April 4, 1921, ibid.; IRA Report, 1921, pp. 3–4.

14.   Charles Burke to William Williamson, September 16, 1921, William Williamson Papers, Box 2, File—Indian Matters, Miscellaneous, I. D. Weeks Library, University of South Dakota, Vermillion, South Dakota.

15.   SANR, Crow, 1919, p. 19 (Reel 30); act of June 4, 1920, *U.S. Statutes at Large*, vol. 41, p. 751; SANR, Crow, 1921, p. 16 (Reel 30); F. E. Brandon, Report on the Crow Reservation, June 23, 1922, BIA, Inspection Reports; U.S. House, Committee on Appropriations, *Interior Department Appropriation Bill, 1931*, Hearings, 71st Cong., 2d sess., 1929, p. 127; U.S. House, Committee on Appropriations, *Interior Department Appropriation Bill, 1930*, Hearings on H.R. 15089, 70th Cong., 2d sess., 1928, p. 693.

16.   Lawrence C. Kelly, "Charles James Rhoads," *Commissioners of Indian Affairs*, p. 266; U.S. Department of Interior, Natural Resources Board, *Indian Land Tenure, Economic Status, and Population Trends*, Part X of *The Report on Planning* (Washington: Government Printing Office, 1935), pp. 5, 7.

17.   Act of May 30, 1908, *U.S. Statutes at Large*, vol. 35, p. 558; Sells to Lane, September 28, 1914, SI-CCF, 5–1, Indian Agencies, Fort Peck, Allotments; Bo Sweeney to Cato Sells and Clay Tallman, July 1, 1915, ibid.; act of August 1, 1914, *U.S. Statutes at Large*, vol. 38, p. 593; S. M. Brosius to Herbert Welsh, August 20, 1917, IRA Papers (Reel 32).

18.   Sells to Lane, September 28, 1914; *U.S. Statutes at Large*, vol. 38, pp. 593, 681; proclamation of April 28, 1917, ibid., vol. 40, p. 1660; act of February 14, 1920, ibid., vol. 41, pp. 408–21; Burke to A. W. Simington, April 15, 1922, SI-CCF, 5–1, Indian Agencies, Fort Peck, Allotment; U.S. House, Committee on Indian Affairs, *Indian Appropriation Bill, 1920*, Hearings on H.R. 14746, 65th Cong., 3d sess., 1919, pp. 305–306. A 1909 bill provided that a person who settled on public domain land classified as agricultural prior to the discovery of coal would get the patent on his land if he let the government reserve the subsurface coal rights. For more information, see Roy M. Robbins, *Our Landed Heritage*, p. 371.

19.   Burke to Simington, March 22, 1923, BIA, Letters Sent Relating to Land Allotment, 817; Burke to Simington, April 15, 1922, SI-CCF, 5–1, Indian Agencies, Fort Peck, Allotments; Burke to P. H. Moller, September 16, 1926, ibid.

20.   Act of March 1, 1907, *U.S. Statutes at Large*, vol. 34, p. 1035; Sells to Lane, March 31, 1917, SI-CCF, 5–1, Indian Agencies, Blackfeet, Allotments; James Mahaffie to Lane,

July 11, 1917, ibid.; Sells to Lane, July 24, 1917, ibid.; U.S. House, Committee on Indian Affairs, *Indian Appropriation Bill, 1919*, Hearings on H.R. 8696, 65th Cong., 2d sess., 1918, p. 198.

21.   Assistant Commissioner of Indian Affairs to the Secretary of the Interior, January 19, 1921, BIA, Letters Sent Relating to Land Allotment, 611.

22.   Meritt to Charles Roblin, April 1, 1925, CI-CCF, 5–1, Indian Agencies, Taholah, Allotments; Burke to Fall, March 3, 1922, ibid.; Burke to Fall, March 9, 1922, ibid.; ARCIA, 1925, p. 11; U.S. House, Committee on Appropriations, *Interior Department Appropriation Bill, 1929*, Hearings on H.R. 9136, 70th Cong., 1st sess., 1928, p. 148.

23.   SANR, Klamath, 1919 (Reel 73); ibid., 1920; ibid., 1923.

24.   Albert Fall to Homer P. Snyder, May 26, 1922, BIA, Letters Sent Relating to Land Allotment, 1308; Work to Thomas Lang, April 8, 1924, SI-CCF, 5–1, Indian Agencies, Klamath, Allotment; J. P. Kinney, *A Continent Lost—A Civilization Won: Indian Land Tenure in America* (Baltimore: Johns Hopkins University Press, 1937; reprint ed., New York: Arno Press, 1975), p. 338; Theodore Stern, *The Klamath Tribe: A People and Their Reservation* (Seattle: University of Washington Press, 1965), p. 155.

25.   Act of February 25, 1920, *U.S. Statutes at Large*, vol. 41, p. 452; Hugh L. Scott, "Flathead Agency, Montana," September 26, 1929, BIC, *Special Reports*, VIII.

26.   *U.S. Statutes at Large*, vol. 18, p. 420; ibid., vol. 23, p. 96; ibid., vol. 26, p. 795; Schmeckebier, *Office of Indian Affairs*, p. 146; Hauke to L. J. Bolster, October 2, 1913, BIA-CCF, General Services, 12701–13–313.

27.   *U.S. Statutes at Large*, vol. 23, p. 96; ibid., vol. 36, p. 855.

28.   Sells to Lane, November 12, 1913, SI-CCF, 5–6, Indian Office, General, Allotment, Public Domain.

29.   Jones to Sells, March 3, 1915, ibid.

30.   U.S. Office of Indian Affairs, *Regulations Governing Indian Allotments on the Public Domain under Section Four of the Act of February 8, 1887 as Amended by the Act of February 28, 1891 and as Further Amended by the Act of June 25, 1910*, April 15, 1918 (Washington: Government Printing Office, 1918); ARCIA, 1915, pp. 90–93; ibid., 1920, p. 82.

31.   U.S. Senate, Committee on Indian Affairs, *Indian Appropriation Bill, 1914*, S. Rept. 63 to accompany H.R. 1917, 63d Cong., 1st sess., 1913, serial 6510.

32.   U.S. Senate, Committee on Indian Affairs, *Indian Appropriation Bill, 1914*, Hearings on H.R. 1917, 63d Cong., 1st sess., 1913, pp. 502–507; *U.S. Statutes at Large*, vol. 38, p. 78.

33.   Brosius to Sells, October 29, 1913, BIA-CCF, General Services, 135801–13–313.

34.   Brosius to Sells, November 7, 1913, ibid.; Sells to Brosius, December 3, 1913, ibid.

35.   U.S. Senate, Committee on Indian Affairs, *Indian Appropriation Bill, 1915*, Hearings on H.R. 12579, 63d Cong., 2d sess., 1914, pp. 292–97, 464–65; *U.S. Statutes at Large*, vol. 38, p. 582.

36.   Lawrence C. Kelly, *The Navajo Indians and Federal Indian Policy* (Tucson: University of Arizona Press, 1968), p. 34.

37.   Joint report, H. J. McQuigg and Frank A. Thackery to Cato Sells, February 6, 1914, BIA-CCF, General Services, 61842–13–313.

38.   James A. Record to Matthew K. Sniffen, August 1, 1914, IRA Papers (Reel 29).

39.   Petition, Papago delegation to Sells, February 2, 1915, BIA-CCF, General Services, 61842–13–313; Sells to Lane, n.d., ibid.; Sells to Thackery, February 23, 1915, ibid.

40.   McQuigg to Sells, February 15, 1915, ibid.

41.   Board of Indian Commissioners, "Board Recommendations, 1912–1916," Memoranda and Correspondence Concerning Board Recommendations, BIC; U.S. House, Committee on Indian Affairs, *Investigation of Indian Affairs*, Hearings of a Joint Commission to Investigate Indian Affairs, 2 vols., 63d Cong., 1–2d sess., 1914, p. 66.

42.   *Report of the Thirty-Third Annual Lake Mohonk Conference of the Friends of the Indians, 1915*, p. 66.

43. Charles J. Kappler, comp., *Indian Affairs: Laws and Treaties*, 5 vols. (Washington: Government Printing Office, 1904–1941), 4:1005, 1008; IRA Report, 1916, pp. 43–44.

44. IRA Report, 1917, p. 8.

45. Kinney, *Continent Lost*, p. 293; Kelly, *Navajo Indians*, p. 33; *U.S. Statutes at Large*, vol. 40, pp. 561, 570; ibid., vol. 41, pp. 3, 34.

46. U.S. Office of Indian Affairs, *Regulations Government Indian Allotments on the Public Domain Under Section Four of the Act of February 8, 1887 as Amended by the Act of June 25, 1910*, February 1, 1928 (Washington: Government Printing Office, 1928).

47. Hugh L. Scott, "Report on the Navajo Indians of Arizona and New Mexico," October 11, 1921, BIC, *Special Reports*, IV.

48. Samuel F. Stracher to Burke, December 23, 1921, Hugh Lenox Scott Papers, Box 49, Manuscripts Division, Library of Congress; Rev. Marcellus Troester to Scott, January 14, 1922, ibid.

49. ARCIA, 1931, p. 36; U.S. House, Committee on Appropriations, *Interior Department Appropriation Bill, 1931*, Hearings, 1929, pp. 124, 127, 183.

2. Allotment: Policy Implementation

1. George W. Cross to Burke, April 12, 1922, BIA-CCF, Fond du Lac, 35116–15–313; Burke to Matthew K. Sniffen, November 8, 1922, IRA Papers (Reel 38); SANR, Fort Hall, 1924 (Reel 50); ibid., Colorado River, 1926 (Reel 23); Sells to John Baum, October 17, 1913, SI-CCF, 5–1, Indian Agencies, Pima, Allotments; John F. Armstrong to the Commissioner of Indian Affairs, June 13, 1913, BIA-CCF, Yakima, 57132–13–313; SANR, Pine Ridge, 1914 (Reel 106); Sally Jean Laidlaw, *Federal Indian Land Policy and the Fort Hall Indians*, Occasional Papers of the Idaho State College Museum, No. 3 (Pocatello, Idaho, 1960), p. 12.

2. Malcolm McDowell, "Report on the Needs of Some California Indians," pp. 3–4, January 15, 1920, BIC, *Special Reports*, vol. II; Frank Knox, "Report on the Ute Indians of Utah and Colorado," pp. 4–5, October 15, 1915, ibid., vol. I; *Carlisle Arrow*, October 12, 1915, BIA, Newspaper Clippings.

3. SANR, Salt River, 1922, section 5 (Reel 125); ibid., Colorado River, 1923 (Reel 23); ibid., 1924.

4. A. A. Jones to Cates and Robinson, Attorneys, June 11, 1914, SI-CCF, Indian Agencies, Pima, Allotments; W. W. McConihee, "Report on the Pine Ridge reservation," April 5, 1913, p.5, BIA-CCF, 150, Pine Ridge; SANR, Taholah, 1919 (Reel 145).

5. James E. Hatchett to the Commissioner of Indian Affairs, March 29, 1890, BIA, Letters Received, 1881–1907, 9611/1890; E. W. Foster to Thomas J. Morgan, September 11, 1890, ibid., 28625/1890; Medicine Crow et al. to the Commissioner of Indian Affairs, December 1, 1891, ibid., 43669/1891.

6. Robert Valentine to Hiram F. White, January 15, 1910, Klamath, BIA-CCF, General Services, 103186–09–313; C. F. Hauke to Charles H. Bates, March 17, 1910, BIA-CCF, General Services, 19577–10–313; Charles L. Davis, Inspection Report, August 17, 1909, BIA-CCF, Klamath, 68958–10–313.

7. Don M. Carr to the Commissioner of Indian Affairs, February 13, 1913, BIA-CCF, Yakima, 57123–13–312; Hauke to Armstrong, May 6, 1913, ibid.; Armstrong to the Commissioner of Indian Affairs, June 13, 1913, ibid.; Hauke to M. F. Nourse, July 18, 1913, ibid.; Nourse to Sells, August 22, 1913, ibid.; Sells to Nourse, September 8, 1913, ibid.; Hauke to Carr, December 9, 1913, ibid.

8. Sells to Lane, April 6, 1914, SI-CCF, 22–1, Presidential Appointments, Allotting Agents, Finch R. Archer; Armstrong to H. F. Nielsen, December 16, 1913, ibid., John Armstrong; John Hurley to the Commissioner of the General Land Office, December 29, 1913, ibid.; M. L. Dorr to Lane, January 13, 1914, ibid.; Armstrong to Sells, January

30, 1914, ibid.; Sells to Armstrong, March 16, 1914, ibid.; Sells to Lane, April 10, 1914, ibid.; Armstrong to Sells, April 1, 1914, ibid.

9. U.S. House, Committee on Indian Affairs, *Indian Appropriation Bill, 1914*, Hearings on H.R. 1917, 63d Cong., 1st sess., 1913, pp. 23–24.

10. U.S. Senate, Committee on Indian Affairs, *Indian Appropriation Bill, 1915*, Hearings on H.R. 12579, 63d Cong., 2d sess., 1914, pp. 178–79.

11. SANR, Pine Ridge, 1915, section 7 (Reel 106); ibid., Salt River, 1915, section 7 (Reel 124); ibid., 1916, section 6; Board of Indian Commissioners, "Minutes of Board Meetings, 1869–1915," 1914, pp. 410–11, BIC; Wilson and a Yuma delegation to Work, May 11, 1923, IRA Papers (Reel 39); James E. Hatchett to the Commissioner of Indian Affairs, March 29, 1890, BIA, Letters Received, 1881–1907, 9611/1890.

12. ARCIA, 1904, p. 37; Charles H. Bates to the Commissioner of Indian Affairs, December 18, 1907, BIA-CCF, Pine Ridge, 99203–07–313; Bates to Commissioner of Indian Affairs, September 25, 1909, BIA-CCF, Pine Ridge, 77570–09–313.

13. SANR, Mission, 1922, section 5, (Reel 83); telegram, Burke to Phil D. Swing, May 3, 1923, BIA, Letters Sent Relating to Land Allotment, 1375; Burke to Adam Costillo, May 4, 1923, ibid.; Burke to Stella Atwood, May 11, 1923, ibid.; Burke to William Spry, May 24, 1923, ibid.; Burke to Charles Ellis, June 15, 1923, BIA-CCF, Mission, 94531–21–313.

14. Elizabeth Green, "The Indians of Southern California and Land Allotment," June 1923, IRA Papers (Reel 126, Frame 191).

15. John Collier, "The Accursed System," *Sunset* 52 (June 1924):16.

16. Hubert Work to Herbert K. Stockton, August 30, 1923, BIA-CCF, Mission, 94531–20–313; Work to E. J. Reynolds, October 25, 1925, Box 1, Hubert Work Office Files, Record Group 48, National Archives; Fall left office on March 4, 1923. He was unhappy over his declining influence in Harding's cabinet and probably concerned that his dealings with oil interests in the Teapot Dome scandal would be made public. For biographical information on Work, see Eugene P. Trani, *The Secretaries of the Department of the Interior, 1849–1969* (Washington: National Anthropological Archives, 1975).

17. Acting Commissioner of Indian Affairs to Phil D. Swing, September 29, 1923, BIA-CCF, 94531–20–313.

18. SANR, Mission, 1924 (Reel 83); Burke to Adam Costillo, February 14, 1924, BIA-CCF, Mission, 94531–20–313; SANR, Mission, 1924 (Reel 83).

19. Work to Juan Diego Lachappa, November 24, 1923, SI-CCF, 5–1, Indian Agencies, Mission, Allotments; Samuel Blair, "Report of the Meeting Held with the Palm Springs Indians at Palm Springs Reservation," April 9, 1924, BIA-CCF, 45742–24–150; Blair, "Report of the Meeting Held at the Torres-Martinez Indian Agency," April 15, 1924, ibid.; memorandum for Charles Burke, February 17, 1925, ibid.

20. Burke to Work, December 22, 1926, SI-CCF, 5–1, Indian Agencies, Mission, Allotment; Board of Indian Commissioners, "Review of Recommendations, Annual Meeting, 1928," Memoranda and Correspondence Concerning Board Recommendations, BIC; Sells to Lane, October 18, 1913, Woodrow Wilson Papers, Library of Congress (Reel 179); John Collier, "Record of Assistant Commissioner of Indian Affairs E. B. Meritt in Its Bearing on the Future," March 15, 1929, John Collier Papers, Part 1, Series 3, Box 19, File 50.

21. John Collier to James Frear, January 23, 1926, John Collier Papers, Part 1, Series 1, Box 3, File 66, Sterling Memorial Library, Yale University, New Haven, Connecticut; Collier, "The Allotment Law: Considerations about Its Amendment," ibid.

22. IRA Report, 1926, p. 11.

23. U.S. House, Committee on Appropriations, *Interior Department Appropriation Bill, 1930*, Hearings on H.R. 15089, 70th Cong., 2d sess., 1928, pp. 692–93.

24. Lewis Meriam and others, *The Problem of Indian Administration* (Baltimore: Johns Hopkins University Press, 1928), pp. 460–61.

3. Putting the Land to Work

1. U.S. Department of Interior, Natural Resources Board, *Indians Land Tenure, Economic Status, and Population Trends*, Part X of *The Report on Land Planning* (Washington: Government Printing Office, 1935), p. 8.
2. Indian Office Memorandum, November 1910, BIA-CCF, General Services, 52360–11–1910; Laurence F. Schmeckebier, *The Office of Indian Affairs: Its History, Activities, and Organization* (Baltimore: Johns Hopkins University Press, 1927), pp. 248–50; ARCIA, 1910, p. 506.
3. Charles Davis, "Memorandum for the Commissioner," BIA-CCF, General Services, 108554–12–1916; Department of Interior, Indian Office, "Handbook Relating to the Duties of Farming, Stockmen, and Industrial Employees on Indian Reservations," 1914, ibid.
4. Indian Service Bulletin, No. 2, March 5, 1910, BIA-CCF, General Services, 52360–11–916.
5. Indian Service Bulletin, No. 3, January 16, 1911, ibid.
6. J. R. Eddy to the Commissioner of Indian Affairs, April 18, 1912, BIA-CCF, General Services, 59812–12–916; Charles Davis to the Commissioner of Indian Affairs, April 18, 1912, ibid.; Indian Office Memorandum, November 1910, BIA-CCF, General Services, 52360–11–916; SANR, Crow Creek, 1910.
7. SANR, Crow Creek, 1912; Indian Service Bulletin, No. 3, January 16, 1911, BIA-CCF, General Services 52360–11–916; BIA-CCF, Omaha, 6116–12–056; Stephen Jones to Commissioner of Indian Affairs, April 24, 1912, BIA-CCF, General Services, 59812–12–916.
8. Franklin K. Lane, "From the Warpath to the Plow," *National Geographic*, 27 (January 1915):87.
9. Eugene P. Trani, *The Secretaries of the Department of the Interior, 1849–1969* (Washington: National Anthropological Archives, 1975), pp. 204–205; see also Keith Olson, *Biography of a Progressive: Franklin K. Lane, 1864–1921* (Westport, Conn.: Greenwood Press, 1979).
10. Franklin Lane to John Wigmore, March 9, 1913, *The Letters of Franklin Lane*, ed. Anne W. Lane and Louise H. Wall (Boston: Houghton Mifflin Co., 1922), pp. 131–32.
11. ARSI, 1913, pp. 3, 5.
12. E. Louise Peffer, *The Closing of the Public Domain: Disposal and Reservation Policies: 1900–1950* (Stanford, Calif.: Stanford University Press, 1951), pp. 15, 136; Donald C. Swain, *Federal Conservation Policy, 1921–1933* (Berkeley: University of California Press, 1963), p. 54.
13. Arthur Link, *Wilson*, vol. II: *New Freedom* (Princeton: Princeton University Press, 1956), p. 126; John Ise, *The United States Oil Policy* (New Haven: Yale University Press, 1926), pp. 335–37; J. Leonard Bates, *The Origins of Teapot Dome: Progressives, Parties, and Petroleum, 1909–1921* (Urbana: University of Illinois Press, 1963), p. 202.
14. Ise, *Oil Policy*, p. 336. Link disagrees with Ise's charge that Lane was dangerous. He contends that Lane made a sizable contribution to conservation in devising policies for Alaska, water power, and western resources. See *New Freedom*, p. 135.
15. Peffer, *Public Domain*, p 174.
16. E. Marshall Young, "Leaders of Men," *Investors* (November 1919):5–6.
17. Address by Lane, September 5, 1913, *Transactions of the Commonwealth Club of California*, vol. 8, no. 10, p. 529, Franklin Lane Papers, Bancroft Library, University of California, Berkeley, California.
18. *Cleburne (Texas) Daily Enterprise*, September 25, 1914; Matthew K. Sniffen, "A Man and His Opportunity," May 1, 1914, Indian Rights Association Publications, second series, no. 95. For an excellent brief account of Sells's background and term as

commissioner, see *The Commissioners of Indian Affairs, 1824–1977*, ed. Robert Kvasnicka and Herman Viola (Lincoln: University of Nebraska Press, 1979), pp. 243–50.

19.   Link, *New Freedom*, pp. 20, 57, 80.

20.   Circular 892, Sells to All Superintendents, August 10, 1914, BIA, Circulars.

21.   IRA Report, 1913, p. 53; Warren K. Moorehead, *The American Indian in the United States* (Andover, Mass.: Andover Press, 1914; reprint ed., Freeport, New York: Books for Libraries Press, 1969), pp. 359, 366.

22.   ARCIA, 1913, p. 9.

23.   Sells, "Land Tenure and the Organization of Agriculture," *International Review of Agricultural Economics* 77 (May 1917):63; circular 857, Sells to All Superintendents, April 5, 1914, BIA, Circulars, copy in Hugh Lenox Scott Papers, Manuscripts Division, Library of Congress; ARCIA, 1914, p. 21; circular 892, Sells to All Superintendents, August 10, 1914, BIA, Circulars.

24.   Schmeckebier, *Office of Indian Affairs*, p. 88. The appropriations acts of 1921 and after prohibited the use of gratuity appropriations to buy herds.

25.   SANR, Crow Creek, 1913 (Reel 30); ibid., Standing Rock, 1914 (Reel 144); U.S. House, Committee on Indian Affairs, *Investigation of Indian Affairs*, Report of the Joint Commission to Investigate Indian Affairs, S. Doc. 984, 63d Cong., 3d sess., March 3, 1915, serial 6784.

26.   SANR, Cheyenne River, 1914 (Reel 16); ibid., Crow, 1915, section 4 (Reel 30); ibid., Standing Rock, 1916 (Reel 144); ARCIA, 1916, p. 27; Sells, "Land Tenure," p. 74; ARCIA, 1920, p. 10.

27.   Sells to Lane, May 18, 1917, BIA, Special Agents Files, William Thackery, 49371–17–160.2; U.S. Department of the Interior, *Report on the Cultivation of the Public Domain and Indian Lands*, S. Doc. 127, 65th Cong., 2d sess., 1917, serial 7329.

28.   U.S. Senate, Committee on Indian Affairs, *Indian Appropriation Bill, 1919*, Hearings on H.R. 8696, 65th Cong., 2d sess., 1918, pp. 292, 295.

29.   Circular 1241, Sells to All Superintendents, January 1, 1917, BIA, Circulars; Eugene Tandy to Sells, January 22, 1917, BIA, Replies to Circulars, 1241; W. E. McCouihe to Sells, January 19, 1917, ibid.; S.A.M. Young to Sells, January 29, 1917, ibid.; E. A. Hutchison to Sells, January 22, 1917, ibid.; A. R. Snyder to Sells, April 3, 1917, ibid.; C. E. Faris to Sells, April 4, 1917, ibid.; W. M. Peterson to Sells, January 18, 1917, ibid.

30.   Circular 1268, Sells to All Superintendents, March 2, 1917, BIA, Circulars; Sells to T. P. Martin, Jr., April 27, 1917, BIA-CCF, General Services, 39042–17–916.

31.   ARCIA, 1917, p. 25; Robert Daniel to Sells, April 16, 1917, BIA-CCF, General Services, 36361–17–916.

32.   ARCIA, 1916, pp. 25–26.

33.   John J. Terrell to Sells, April 27, 1917, BIA-CCF, General Services, 36361–17–916; Terrell to Sells, May 17, 1917, ibid.; telegram, Horace Wilson to Sells, May 26, 1917, ibid.

34.   ARCIA, 1917, pp. 28–29.

35.   Fred C. Morgan to Sells, March 18, 1918, BIA, Replies to Circulars, 1399; James W. Balmer to Sells, March 12, 1918, ibid.; Theodore Sharp to Sells, March 13, 1918, ibid.; O.J. Green to Sells, March 14, 1918, ibid.; George Cross to Sells, May 29, 1918, ibid.; R. C. Craige to Sells, April 5, 1918, ibid.; Byron A. Sharp to Sells, April 1, 1918, ibid.

36.   ARSI, 1918, p. 72; ARCIA, 1918, p. 15; Sells, "The 'First Americans' as Loyal Citizens," *Review of Reviews* 57 (May 1918):523–24.

37.   Circular 1507, Sells to All Superintendents, January 25, 1919, BIA, Circulars.

38.   U.S. House, Committee on Appropriations, *Interior Department Appropriation Bill, 1925*, Hearings on H.R. 5078, 68th Cong., 1st sess., 1924, p. 135.

39.   ARCIA, 1921, pp. 11, 20; ibid., 1928, p. 17; ARSI, 1927, p. 17.

40.   For more information on farming conditions during the postwar period, see Elliot Brownlee, *The Dynamics of Ascent: A History of the American Economy* (New York:

Alfred Knopf, 1974); Murray R. Benedict, *Farm Policies of the United States, 1790–1950* (New York: Twentieth Century Fund, 1953); James H. Shidler, *Farm Crisis, 1919–1923* (Berkeley: University of California Press, 1957); Theodore Saloutos and John D. Hicks, *Agricultural Discontent in the Middle West, 1900–1939* (Madison: University of Wisconsin Press, 1951).

41. Circular 1701, Burke to All Superintendents, August 1, 1921, BIA, Circulars.

42. Circular 1774, Burke to All Superintendents, March 23, 1922, ibid.; ARCIA, 1924, p. 16; ibid., 1925, p.20.

43. U.S. House, Committee on Indian Appropriations, *Interior Department Appropriation Bill, 1923*, Hearings on H. R. 10329, 67th Cong., 2d sess., 1921, p. 151; see also John Collier, *Indians of the Americas* (New York: W. W. Norton and Co., 1947), p. 246.

44. Gordon Macgregor, *Warriors without Weapons* (Chicago: University of Chicago Press, 1946), pp. 39–40; Harold Fey and D'Arcy McNickle, *Indians and Other Americans* (New York: Harper and Bros., 1959), pp. 76–77; Roy W. Meyer, *The Village Indians of the Upper Missouri* (Lincoln: University of Nebraska Press, 1977), pp. 170–71; SANR, Pine Ridge, 1922, section 4 (Reel 106); ibid., Standing Rock, 1920 (Reel 144); ibid., Fort Hall, 1921 (Reel 49).

45. ARCIA, 1921, p. 12; John C. Ewers, *The Blackfeet: Raiders on the Northwestern Plains* (Norman: University of Oklahoma Press, 1958), p. 319; SANR, Blackfeet, 1920, section 4 (Reel 5); ibid., Crow, 1920 (Reel 30); ibid., Crow, 1922, section 4.

46. ARCIA, 1921, p. 12.

47. Circular 1818, Burke to All Superintendents, October 9, 1922, BIA, Circulars; SANR, Blackfeet, 1923 (Reel 5); ARCIA, 1923, p. 12; circular 1819, Burke to All Superintendents, October 10, 1922, BIA, Circulars.

48. ARCIA, 1923, p. 11; ibid., 1924, p. 12.

49. SANR, Pine Ridge, 1922, section 4 (Reel 106); ibid., 1923; ibid., 1925; ibid., Standing Rock, 1922 (Reel 144); ARCIA, 1923, p. 11; ibid., 1924, p. 12; ibid., 1927, p. 16; U.S. House, Committee on Appropriations, *Interior Department Appropriation Bill, 1928*, Hearing on H.R. 14827, 69th Cong., 2d sess., 1926, p. 81.

50. SANR, Cheyenne River, 1928 (Reel 17); ibid., Crow, 1928 (Reel 30); U.S. Senate, Committee on Indian Affairs, *Survey of Conditions of the Indians in the United States*, Hearings pursuant to S. Res. 341, 69th Cong., 2d sess., February 23, 1927, pp. 22–23, 81.

51. ARCIA, 1928, p. 18.

52. Circular 2305, Burke to All Superintendents, April 1, 1927, BIA, Circulars; circular 2361, Meritt to All Superintendents, September 6, 1927, ibid.

53. Circular 2522, Burke to All Superintendents, December 26, 1928, ibid.

54. U.S. House, Committee on Appropriations, *Interior Department Appropriation Bill, 1931*, Hearings, 71st Cong., 3d sess., 1929, pp. 243–44.

55. ARCIA, 1931, p. 16; ibid., 1932, p. 12; U.S. House, Committee on Appropriations, *Interior Department Appropration Bill, 1933*, Hearings, 72d Cong., 1st sess., 1932, pp. 290–91.

4. Leasing: A Policy Unfolds

1. U.S. Department of the Interior, Natural Resource Board, *Indian Land Tenure, Economic Status, and Population Trends*, Part X of *The Report on Land Planning* (Washington: Government Printing Office, 1935), p. 7; Laurence F. Schmeckebier, *The Office of Indian Affairs: Its History, Activities, and Organization* (Baltimore: Johns Hopkins University Press, 1927), p. 178; J. P. Kinney, *A Continent Lost—A Civilization Won: Indian Land Tenure in America* (Baltimore: Johns Hopkins University Press, 1937; reprint ed., New York: Arno Press, 1975), pp. 221–22; act of February 28, 1891, *U.S. Statutes at Large*, vol. 26, p. 794; act of August 15, 1894, ibid., vol. 28, p. 305; act of June 7, 1897, ibid., vol. 30,

p. 85; ARCIA, 1894, pp. 32–34; ibid., 1900, p. 75; quoted in Brian W. Dippie, *The Vanishing American: White Attitudes and United States Indian Policy* (Middletown, Conn.: Wesleyan University Press, 1982), p. 179.

2. ARCIA, 1900, p. 13; U.S. Department of Interior, *Indian Land Tenure*, p. 7.

3. ARCIA, 1901, p. 793; ibid., 1900, pp. 648, 716.

4. Ibid., 1901, p. 6; ibid., 1902, pp. 4–5.

5. Ibid., 1900, p. 78; ibid., 1901, p. 72; *Rules and Regulations Governing the Department of the Interior and Its Various Branches*, S. Doc. 306, Part 4, 59th Cong., 2d sess., February 26, 1907, serial 5088.

6. Francis E. Leupp, *The Indian and His Problem* (New York: Charles Scribner's Sons, 1910; reprint ed., New York: Arno Press, 1971), pp. 39, 93; ARCIA, 1907, p. 74.

7. *Rules and Regulations Governing the Department of the Interior*, 1907, pp. 117, 123–30.

8. ARCIA, 1907, p. 74; C. H. Larrabee to Acting Secretary of Interior, June 18, 1907, BIA, Special Case 191, Crow Creek; circular 247, Larrabee to Agents and Bonded Superintendents, October 29, 1908, BIA, Circulars; circular 327, F. H. Abbott to Superintendents, August 13, 1909, ibid.

9. Robert G. Valentine, "Making Good Indians," *Sunset* 24 (1910):601; ARCIA, 1911, pp. 24–27; ibid., 1910, p. 34.

10. ARCIA, 1921, p. 24; ibid., 1911, pp. 26–27.

11. Circular 969, Edgar Meritt to All Superintendents, April 6, 1915, BIA, Circulars.

12. Meritt, "Memorandum for the Commissioner," December 1, 1913, pp. 7–8, BIA-CCF, General Services, 152466–13–312.

13. *U.S. Statutes at Large*, vol. 39, p. 128; ARCIA, 1916, p. 30; Kinney, *Continent Lost*, pp. 252, 296–97; circular 1402, Sells to All Superintendents, March 11, 1918, BIA, Circulars.

14. Circular 1402, March 11, 1918; C. Foggeshall to Sells, March 24, 1918, BIA, Replies to Circulars, 1402; L. Bonnin to Sells, April 1, 1918, ibid.; E. A. Hutchinson to Sells, May 2, 1918, ibid.

15. ARCIA, 1917, p. 29; ibid., 1920, pp. 22–23.

16. *U.S. Statutes at Large*, vol. 39, p. 128; ARCIA, 1916, p. 30; Kinney, *Continent Lost*, pp. 252, 296–97.

17. U.S. House, Committee on Indian Affairs, *Hearings on the Indian Appropriation Bill, 1919*, Hearings on H.R. 8696, 65th Cong., 2d sess., 1918, pp. 109–13.

18. ARCIA, 1919, pp. 38–39.

19. ARSI, 1920, p. 43.

20. ARCIA, 1921, p. 4.

21. U.S. House, Committee on Indian Affairs, *Interior Department Appropriation Bill, 1923*, Hearings on H.R. 10329, 67th Cong., 2d sess., 1921, pp. 162–63.

22. ARCIA, 1921, p. 4; *U.S. Statutes at Large*, vol. 41, p. 1232; circular 1663, Meritt to All Superintendents, March 24, 1921, BIA, Circulars; Kinney, *Continent Lost*, p. 297.

23. U.S. Office of Indian Affairs, *Regulations Concerning the Execution of Leases of Indian Allotted and Tribal Lands for Farming, Grazing, and Business Purposes*, July 20, 1923 (Washington: Government Printing Office, 1923), pp. 1, 7, 9.

24. Circular 2153, Burke to All Superintendents, October 24, 1925, BIA, Circulars.

25. Circular 2113, Meritt to All Superintendents, April 28, 1925, ibid.

26. Burke to Fred C. Campbell, December 14, 1928, SI-CCF, 5–1, Indian Agencies, Blackfeet, Leases; Burke to Evan Estep, December 5, 1927, ibid.

27. ARCIA, 1925, p. 11; circular 2209, Burke to All Superintendents, April 19, 1928, BIA, Circulars.

28. E. M. Sweet to Burke, April 27, 1921, BIA, Special Agents Files, E. M. Sweet, 36551–21–320.

29. Act of August 15, 1894, *U.S. Statutes at Large*, vol. 28, p. 305; Hubert Work to

Scott Leavitt, June 14, 1926, June 14, 1926, SI-CCF, 5–6, Indian Office, General, Leases-Legislation.

30.   *U.S. Statutes at Large*, vol. 44, p. 894; Kinney, *Continent Lost*, p. 297.

31.   Act of February 28, 1891, *U.S. Statutes at Large*, vol. 26, p. 794; act of June 7, 1897, ibid., vol. 30, p. 85; A. A. Jones to John Stephens, March 18, 1914, SI-CCF, 5–6, Indian Office, General, Leases, Legislation-63d Congress.

32.   *U.S. Statutes at Large*, vol. 21, p. 31; U.S. Senate, Committee on Indian Affairs, *Mining for Metalliferous Minerals in Indian Reservations*, S. Rept. 880 to accompany H.R. 12426, 64th Cong., 2d sess., 1916, p. 3, serial 7106; *Congressional Record*, 65th Cong., 2d sess., vol. 56, pp. 7477–83, 7894; Lawrence C. Kelly, *The Navajo Indians and Federal Indian Policy, 1900–1935*, (Tucson: University of Arizona Press, 1968), pp. 37–47.

33.   For information about the General Leasing Act of 1920, see E. Louise Peffer, *The Closing of the Public Domain: Disposal and Reservation Policies, 1900–1950* (Stanford, Calif.: Stanford University Press, 1951), pp. 129–32; John Ise, *The United States Oil Policy* (New Haven: Yale University Press, 1926), pp. 342–54; Benjamin H. Hibbard, *A History of the Public Land Policies* (York: Peter Smith, 1939), p. 524; Donald C. Swain, *Federal Conservation Policy, 1921–1933* (Berkeley: University of California Press, 1963), pp. 126–42; Roy M. Robbins, *Our Landed Heritage: The Public Domain, 1776–1936* (Princeton: Princeton University Press, 1942; reprint ed., Gloucester, Mass.: Peter Smith, 1960), pp. 387–98; J. Leonard Bates, *The Origins of Teapot Dome: Progressives, Parties, and Petroleum, 1909–1921* (Urbana: University of Illinois Press, 1963), pp. 189, 198.

34.   A. A. Jones to Sen. William Stone, December 13, 1913, SI-CCF, 5–6, Indian Office, General, Leases, Legislation-63d Cong.; U.S. House, Committee on Indian Affairs, *Indian Appropriation Bill, 1916*, Hearings on H.R. 20150, 63d Cong., 2d sess., 1915, pp. 141–42.

35.   U.S. House, Committee on Indian Affairs, *Indian Appropriation Bill, 1918*, Hearings on H.R. 18453, 64th Cong., 2d sess., 1917, p. 98.

36.   *U.S. Statutes at Large*, vol. 41, p. 437.

37.   For a detailed account of the controversy about leasing executive order reservation land, see Kelly, *Navajo Indians*, pp. 55–58, 76–81, 88–100.

38.   Ibid., pp. 57–58; U.S. House, Committee on Indian Affairs, *Leasing of Allotted Indian Lands*, Hearings on H.R. 8823, 69th Cong., 1st sess., April 10, 14, 16, 1926, p. 70; U.S. House, Committee on Indian Affairs, *Oil and Gas Mining Leases upon Unallotted Land*, H. Rept. 1791 to accompany H.R. 15021, 69th Cong., 2d sess., 1927, p. 11, serial 8688.

39.   IRA, "In re. Executive Order Indian Reservations," March 19, 1923, IRA Papers (Reel 39).

40.   U.S. House, Hearings on H.R. 8823, p. 70; U.S. Senate, Committee on Indian Affairs, *Development of Oil and Gas Mining Leases on Indian Reservations*, Hearings on S. 1722 and S. 3159, 69th Cong., 1st sess., February 27 and March 5, 9, 10, 1926, p. 54.

41.   Work to Sheldon Spencer, December 6, 1923, BIA-CCF, General Services, 93208–23–013; U.S. Senate, Committee on Indian Affairs, *To Provide for the Disposition of Bonuses, Rentals and Royalties from Unallotted Lands in Executive Order Reservations*, S. Rept. 669 to accompany S. 876, 68th Cong., 1st sess., 1924, serial 8221.

42.   U.S. Department of Interior, *Indian Policies, Comments on the Resolutions of the Advisory Council on Indian Affairs by Hubert Work* (Washington: Government Printing Office, 1924), p. 13; U.S. House, Hearings on H.R. 8823, pp. 15–16.

43.   U.S. Department of Interior, *Indian Policies*, p. 13; U.S. House, Hearings on H.R. 8823, pp. 15–16, 70; *Indian Truth*, 1 (June 1924):3; IRA Report, 1926, p. 16.

44.   U.S. Senate, Hearings on S. 1722 and S. 3159, p. 6; U.S. House, Hearings on H.R. 8823, p. 16; U.S. Senate, Committee on Indian Affairs, *To Authorize Oil and Gas Mining Leases upon Unallotted Lands within Executive Order Reservations*, S. Rept. 1240 to accompany S. 4893, 69th Cong., 2d sess., 1927, serial 8685.

45. *U.S. Statutes at Large*, vol. 43, p. 244; U.S. Senate, Hearings on S. 1722 and S. 3159, p. 9; Kelly, *Navajo Indians*, p. 78; *Congressional Record*, 68th Cong., 2d sess., vol. 66, pp. 998, 2117, 2233, 2342, 2765.

46. S. M. Brosius to the President, March 6, 1923, BIA-CCF, General Services, 93208–23–013, *Congressional Record*, 68th Cong., 2d sess., vol. 66, pp. 5433–34.

47. U.S. House, Hearings on H.R. 8823, p. 71.

48. U.S. House, Committee on Indian Affairs, *Leasing of Executive Order Reservations*, Hearings on H.R. 9133, 69th Cong., 1st sess., February 19, 1926, pp. 1–2.

49. U.S. House, Hearings on H.R. 9133, p. 23; U.S. House, Hearings on H.R. 8823, pp. 71–73; Kelly, *Navajo Indians*, pp. 78–80; U.S. Senate, Hearings on S. 1722 and S. 3159, pp. 57, 59–61.

50. U.S. Senate, Hearings on S. 1722 and S. 3159, p. 56.

51. *Congressional Record*, 69th Cong., 1st sess., vol. 67, p. 8081; U.S. House, Hearings on H.R. 9133, pp. 26–27.

52. *Congressional Record*, 69th Cong., 2d sess., vol. 67, pp. 5037, 6116; U.S. Senate, Hearings on S. 1722 and S. 3159, pp. 1–3, 53–61; Kelly, *Navajo Indians*, pp. 80, 88, 90.

53. *Congressional Record*, 69th Cong., 2d sess., vol. 67, pp. 10919–25; Kelly, *Navajo Indians*, pp. 90, 92; U.S. Senate, *Message from the President of the United States Returning without Approval the Bill (S. 4152) to Authorize Oil and Gas Mining Leases upon Unallotted Land within Executive Order Indian Reservations, and for Other Purposes*, Doc. 156, 69th Cong., 1st sess., 1926, pp. 1–2, serial 8558.

54. *Congressional Record*, 69th Cong., 2d sess., vol. 68, pp. 2793–95; H. Rept. 1791, *Oil and Gas Mining Leases upon Unallotted Lands*; U.S. House, Committee on Indian Affairs, *Leasing of Executive Order Indian Reservations*, Hearings on H.R. 15021, 69th Cong., 2d sess., January 6, 12, 13, 1927, p. 41.

55. *Congressional Record*, 69th Cong., 2d sess., vol. 68, p. 4575.

56. *U.S. Statutes at Large*, vol. 44, p. 1374; ARCIA, 1927, p. 15.

57. For a clear, concise account of the heirship problem, see David M. Holford, "The Subversion of the Indian Land Allotment System, 1887–1934," *Indian Historian* 8 (Spring 1975):14; see also Wilcomb Washburn, *Red Man's Land/White Man's Law* (New York: Charles Scribner's Sons, 1971), pp. 150–51; Stephen A. Lagone, "The Heirship Land Problem and Its Effect on the Indian, the Tribe, and Effective Utilization," in *Toward Economic Development for Native American Communities. A Compendium of Papers Submitted to the Subcommittee on Economy in Government of the Joint Economic Committee* (Washington: Government Printing Office, 1969), p. 532; Ward Shepard, "Land Problems of an Expanding Population," in *The Changing Indian*, ed. Oliver LaFarge (Norman: University of Oklahoma Press, 1942), pp. 78–79.

58. Act of May 27, 1902, *U.S. Statutes at Large*, vol. 32, pp. 245, 275; Frederick E. Hoxie, *A Final Promise: The Campaign to Assimilate Indians, 1880–1920* (Lincoln: University of Nebraska Press, 1984), p. 159; ARCIA, 1904, pp. 62–63; ibid., 1920, p. 169.

59. Act of March 1, 1901, *U.S. Statutes at Large*, vol. 34, pp. 1015, 1018; circular 181, Leupp to Agents and Superintendents, January 9, 1908, BIA, Circulars; C.F. Larrabee to U.S. Indian Agent, Sisseton, September 13, 1907, BIA-CCF, Sisseton, 71771–07–313; ARCIA, 1920, p. 169.

60. Valentine, "Making Good Indians," p. 601.

61. U.S. Office of Indian Affairs, *Rules and Regulations Relating to the Issuance of Patents in Fee and Certificates of Competency and the Sale of Allotted and Inherited Indian Lands*, October 12, 1910 (Washington: Government Printing Office, 1910), pp. 9–14.

62. Ibid.; circular 459, C. F. Hauke to Superintendents and Agents, August 10, 1910, BIA, Circulars; circular 462, Hauke to Superintendents, August 15, 1910, ibid.

63. Circular 1095, Sells to All Superintendents, March 11, 1916, BIA, Circulars; Evan Estep to Sells, April 6, 1916, BIA, Replies to Circulars, 1095; IRA Report, 1920, p. 44.

64. ARCIA, 1917, pp. 4–5.

65. Memorandum, Sells to Lane, April 14, 1917, SI-CCF, 5–6, Indian Office, General, Land Sales.

66. ARCIA, 1920, p. 49; W. S. Coleman, Report on the Flathead Reservation, May 22, 1917, BIA, Inspection Reports.

67. ARCIA, 1921, p. 23; ibid., 1926, p. 11; circular 2545, Burke to All Superintendents, January 28, 1929, BIA, Circulars.

68. C. H. Asbury to Burke, November 8, 1921, BIA, Replies to Circulars, 1717; F. E. Brandon, Report on the Crow reservation, May 23, 1922, BIA, Inspection Reports; SANR, Crow, 1924, section 6 (Reel 30); ibid., 1923, section 4; ibid., Fort Peck, 1926, section 5 (Reel 53); ibid., Fort Hall, 1924, section 6 (Reel 49), "Report on the Chippewa, Turtle Mountain, North Dakota," September 5, 1921, p. 7, BIC, *Special Reports*, II; SANR, Cheyenne River, 1921 (Reel 17).

69. ARCIA, 1923, p. 9; ibid., 1924, p. 9; ibid., 1928, p.24.

70. ARCIA, 1930, p. 25; ibid., 1931, p. 37.

71. Samuel Blair, Report on the Fort Peck reservation, March 31, 1926, BIA, Inspection Reports; Blair, Report on the Fort Peck reservation, August 31, 1926, BIA-CCF, Fort Peck, 42141–26–150.

72. U.S. Senate, Committee on Indian Affairs, *Survey of Conditions of Indians in the United States*, Hearings pursuant to S. Res. 341, 69th Cong., 2d sess., February 23, 1927, p. 74.

73. Circular 1855, Burke to All Superintendents, February 26, 1923, BIA, Circulars.

5. Leasing: Problems and Abuses

1. L. A. Dorrington, Report on the Umatilla reservation, July 26, 1915, section 3, pp. 1–2, BIA-CCF, 150, Umatilla; Frank A. Thackery to Lane, April 3, 1916, SI-CCF, 5–6, Indian Office, General, Competent Indians, General; *Annual Report of the Chief Engineer of Irrigation, 1914*, p. 5, BIA, hereafter cited as *Chief Irrigation Engineer's Report*; ibid., 1916, p. 6.

2. C. R. Trowbridge, Report on the Pine Ridge reservation, March 8, 1920, p. 14, BIA-CCF, Pine Ridge, 28114–20–150; Rudolph Johnson et al. to the President, February 4, 1920, SI-CCF, 5–1, Indian Agencies, Pima, Leases.

3. E. M. Sweet, Report on the Colorado River reservation, January 27, 1917, p. 46, BIA, Inspection Reports; SANR, Pine Ridge, 1920 (Reel 106).

4. Charles E. Coe, Report on the Flathead reservation, October 18, 1920, BIA, Inspection Reports; William Ketcham, "Report on the Flathead Reservation," January 1, 1919, BIC Report, 1919, p. 249.

5. Office of the Secretary of Interior, Statement for the Press, January 9, 1915, (copy) Franklin Knight Lane Papers, Bancroft Library, University of California, Berkeley, California; C. L. Davis, Report on the Cheyenne River reservation, August 14, 1913, BIA-CCF, 150, Cheyenne River; SANR, Cheyenne River, 1913, section 4 (Reel 16); ibid., Standing Rock, 1914 (Reel 144).

6. ARCIA, 1900, p. 697; Juan Grant and a Yuma delegation to Herbert Welsh, October 1, 1913, IRA Papers (Reel 39); John Armstrong to Sells, June 10, 1913, John Armstrong file, BIA, Special Agents Files; U.S. Indian Agent to the Commissioner of Indian Affairs, October 7, 1907, BIA-CCF, Sisseton, 82233–07–321; Alfred Gossitt and F. T. Bounot to S. M. Brosius, June 12, 1902, RG 279, Indian Claims Commission, Docket 332-D, Petitioners Exhibit H-1599.

7. Report of Inspector Duncan, May 15, 1901, Santee, Inspection Reports, 1900–1907, Santee Agency; Superintendent of the Sisseton reservation to the Commissioner of Indian Affairs, January 26, 1910, BIA-CCF, Sisseton, 95750–09–313.

8. Edgar Meritt to H. H. Miller, April 12, 1919, SI-CCF, 5–1, Indian Agencies, Fort Hall, Leases; telegram, Sells to E. A. Hutchison, January 7, 1918, SI-CCF, 5–1, Indian Agencies, Shoshone, Leases.

9. Herbert Welsh et al. to the President, February 14, 1920, SI-CCF, 5–1, Indian Agencies, Pima, Leases.

10. Sells to Homer P. Snyder, February 27, 1920, IRA Papers (Reel 34); Snyder to Sells, March 6, 1920, ibid.

11. IRA, "Threatened Exploitation of the Pima Indians," IRA Papers (Reel 102, B119); Meritt to W. R. Elliot, October 25, 1920, SI-CCF, 5–1, Indian Agencies, Pima, Leases; John B. Payne to Elliot, January 22, 1921, ibid.

12. U.S. House, Committee on Indian Affairs, *Indian Appropriation Bill, 1918*, Hearings on H.R. 18453, 64th Cong., 2d sess., 1917, pp. 93–94; Horace Wilson, Report on the Umatilla reservation, August 9, 1917, BIA, Inspection Reports; Sells to E. L. Swartzlander, February 1, 1918, SI-CCF, 5–1, Indian Agencies, Umatilla, Investigations.

13. U.S. House, Committee on Indian Affairs, *Indian Appropriation Bill, 1919*, Hearings on H.R. 8689, 65th Cong., 2d sess., 1918, pp. 16–19; Malcolm McDowell, "Report on the Crow Indians," December 17, 1917, pp. 17, 27, BIC, *Special Reports*, I; William Ketcham, "Report on the Crow Indian Reservation," November 1, 1918, p. 3, ibid., II.

14. IRA Report, 1919, pp. 13–15.

15. U.S. Senate, Committee on Indian Affairs, *Leasing of Crow Indian Lands*, Hearings on S. 2890, 66th Cong., 1st sess., 1919, pp. 16–19.

16. U.S. House, Committee on Indian Affairs, *Indian Appropriation Bill, 1920*, Hearings on H.R. 14746, 65th Cong., 3d sess., 1919, pp. 157–69.

17. E. B. Linnen, Report on the Pine Ridge reservation, September 29, 1929, p. 1, BIA, Inspection Reports; C. R. Trowbridge, Report on the Pine Ridge Reservation, March 8, 1920, p. 14; BIA-CCF, Pine Ridge, 28114–20–150; U.S. House, Committee on Indian Affairs, *Complaint of the Pine Ridge Sioux*, Hearings, 66th Cong., 2d sess., April 16, 1920, pp. 4–6, 28–29.

18. *Complaint of the Pine Ridge Sioux*, pp. 11, 33, 58.

19. Circular 1718, Burke to All Superintendents, October 17, 1921, BIA, Circulars; circular 1841, Burke to All Superintendents, December 16, 1922, ibid.

20. U.S. Senate, Committee on Indian Affairs, *Survey of Conditions of Indians in the United States*, Hearings pursuant to S. Res. 79. Part XV, Oklahoma, November 17–22, 1930, pp. 7343–44, 7374. Hereafter cited as *Senate Survey of Conditions*.

21. Ibid., Part I, pp. 25–28; ibid., Part IV, Washington, D.C., February 1–March 1, 1929, p. 1735.

22. F. E. Brandon, Report on the Crow reservation, June 23, 1922, BIA, Inspection Reports.

23. Burke to Fred C. Campbell, January 20, 1922, SI-CCF, 5–1, Indian Agencies, Blackfeet, Leases; Burke to Campbell, December 26, 1923, ibid.

24. Circular 2452, Meritt to All Superintendents, May 21, 1928, BIA, Circulars.

25. A. W. Leech to Burke, July 3, 1928, BIA, Replies to Circulars, 2452; James D. Hyde to Burke, June 28, 1928, ibid.; H. M. Tidwell to Burke, July 6, 1928, ibid.; Evan Estep to Burke, June 22, 1928, ibid.; C. H. Asbury to Burke, June 30, 1928, ibid.

26. *Senate Survey of Conditions*, Part IV, pp. 1736–37.

27. Ibid., Part IV, p. 1179; ibid., Part I, pp. 65, 90–93.

28. Louis Ballou to Matthew K. Sniffen, July 1, 1921, IRA Papers (Reel 37).

29. Ballou to Sniffen, July 5, 1921, ibid.

30. Captain Henry Wilson and other Yumas to Hubert Work, May 14, 1923, ibid. (Reel 39).

31. Patrick Miguel to E. P. Sanguinetti, October 8, 1925, ibid. (Reel 42); *Senate Survey of Conditions*, Part II, San Francisco, California, Riverside, California and Salt Lake City, Utah, November 19–26, 1928, pp. 657–58, 661–62.

32. Juan Grant to Work, October 1, 1923, IRA Papers (Reel 39); Burke to Sniffen

and Brosius, February 13, 1924, ibid. (Reel 40); telegram, Herbert Welsh to Calvin Coolidge, February 5, 1926, ibid. (Reel 42); Burke to Welsh, February 5, 1926, ibid. (Reel 42).

33. C. R. Trowbridge, Report on the Umatilla reservation, March 2, 1928, p. 15, BIA-CCF, Umatilla, 10622–28–150; George Vaux, "Report on the Sisseton Agency, S.D.," June 31, 1922, p. 11, BIC, *Special Reports*, IV; Lewis Meriam and others, *The Problem of Indian Administration* (Baltimore: Johns Hopkins University Press, 1928), pp. 29–30.

34. F. W. Seymour, "Report on the Devils Lake Reservation," September 15, 1927, pp. 11–14, BIC, *Special Reports*, V.

6. Land and Water

1. Harold E. Driver, *Indians of North America* (Chicago: University of Chicago Press, 1969), pp. 10, 71; William Reed, *Irrigation Work of the United States Indian Service* (Washington: Government Printing Office, 1919), pp. 1–2.

2. March 2, 1867 Act, *U.S. Statutes at Large*, vol. 14, p. 492; ibid., vol. 23, p. 94; Laurence F. Schmeckebier, *The Office of Indian Affairs: Its History, Activities, and Organization* (Baltimore: Johns Hopkins University Press, 1927), p. 238; Donald J. Pisani, "Irrigation, Water Rights, and the Betrayal of Indian Allotment," *Environmental Review*, v. 10, no. 3 (Fall 1986):158; Francis Paul Prucha, *The Great Father: The United States Government and the American Indians* (Lincoln: University of Nebraska Press, 1984), p. 891.

3. Pisani, "Irrigation, Water Rights," p. 159; Thomas G. Alexander, *A Clash of Interests: The Interior Department and the Mountain West, 1863–96* (Provo, Utah: Brigham Young University, 1977), p. 160.

4. Reed, *Irrigation Work*; ARCIA, 1916, pp. 41, 45; Irrigation Report, Pine Ridge Reservation, South Dakota, by C. R. Olberg, Superintendent of Irrigation, U.S. Indian Service, January 1910, RG 75, Irrigation Division: Reports and Related Records—Pine Ridge; ARCIA, 1900, p. 668; Pisani, "Irrigation, Water Rights," pp. 158–59.

5. Frederick E. Hoxie, *A Final Promise: The Campaign to Assimilate the Indians, 1880–1920* (Lincoln: University of Nebraska Press, 1984), pp. 170–71.

6. ARCIA, 1906, pp. 82–83.

7. Pisani, "Irrigation, Water Rights," p. 159; *Senate Survey of Conditions*, Part VI, p. 2259; ARCIA, 1907, pp. 50–51; Felix S. Cohen, *Handbook of Federal Indian Law* (Charlottesville, Va.: Bobbs-Merrill, 1982), p. 729; *U.S. Statutes at Large*, vol. 43, p. 402.

8. Pisani, "Irrigation, Water Rights," p. 163; Hoxie, *Final Promise*, p. 172; Daniel McCool, *Command of the Waters: Iron Triangles, Federal Water Development, and Indian Water* (Berkeley: University of California Press, 1987), pp. 113–14. See also Norris Hundley, "The Winters Decision and Indian Water Rights: A Mystery Reexamined," *The Plains Indians of the Twentieth Century*, ed. Peter Iverson (Norman: University of Oklahoma Press, 1985), pp. 77–99; Robert G. Dunbar, *Forging New Rights in Western Waters* (Lincoln: University of Nebraska Press, 1983).

9. McCool, pp. 115–19; Report of William H. Code, n.d., SI-CCF, General Irrigation.

10. ARCIA, 1900, p. 58; *U.S. Statutes at Large*, vol. 33, p. 1049; *Interior Department Appropriation Bill, 1933*, Hearings, 72d Cong., 1st sess., 1932, p. 31.

11. Reed, *Irrigation Work*.

12. Hoxie, *Final Promise*, pp. 169–70; *U.S. Statutes at Large*, vol. 34, pp. 375, 1035, 448–49, 558; Projects on the Crow, Blackfeet, Flathead, Fort Belknap, Fort Hall, and Yuma projects were authorized by special legislation, see *Senate Survey of Conditions*, Part VI, p. 2285; ARCIA, 1900, p. 58; ibid., 1909, p. 49.

13. ARCIA, 1910, pp. 21, 59; ibid., 1916, p. 42; U.S. Senate, Committee on Indian Affairs, *Indian Appropriation Bill*, Hearings on H.R. 12579, 63d Cong., 2d sess. 1914, pp. 194–95.

14. Cohen, *Handbook of Federal Indian Law*, p. 729, Hoxie, *Final Promise*, pp. 169–71.

15. ARCIA, 1913, p. 18; IRA Report, 1913, p. 52; F. H. Abbott, "Comments on Irrigation Law and Administration on Indian Reservations," pp. 1–9, BIC, Reference Material, Tray 117, Irrigation, RG 75; "Briefs on Indian Irrigation and Indian Forests," Letter from Frederick H. Abbott to the Chairman of the Senate Committee on Indian Affairs (Washington: Government Printing Office, 1914).

16. House, *Indian Appropriation Bill, 1915*, p. 190; *U.S. Statutes at Large*, vol. 38, p. 583; Schmeckebier, *Office of Indian Affairs*, p. 240; ARCIA, 1914, p. 37; *Chief Irrigation Engineer's Report*, 1915, p. 13.

17. U.S. House, Committee on Indian Affairs, *Indian Appropriation Bill, 1920*, Hearings on H.R. 14746, 65th Cong., 3d sess., 1919, pp. 34–35.

18. U.S. House, Committee on Indian Affairs, *Indians of the United States*, Hearings, vol. I: *On The Condition of Various Tribes of Indians*, 66th Cong., 2d sess., 1919, Part II, pp. 5, 18–21.

19. Ibid., p. 20; House, *Indian Appropriation Bill, 1920*, pp. 36, 172–74, 178; *Congressional Record*, 66th Cong., 2d sess., vol. 59, pp. 1111–13.

20. *U.S. Statutes at Large*, vol. 41, p. 408; ARCIA, 1920, p. 26; Meritt, "Regulations Governing Partial Payment of Construction Charges on Indian Irrigation Projects," BIC, Reference Material, Tray 117, Irrigation.

21. Circular 1594, Sells to All Superintendents, February 16, 1920, BIA, Circulars; R. J. Bauman to Sells, February 27, 1920, BIA, Replies to Circulars, 1594; T. T. McCormick to Sells, February 25, 1920, ibid.; Walter West to Sells, March 12, 1920, ibid.

22. Theodore Sharp to Sells, February 27, 1920, ibid.; J. D. Oliver to Sells, March 8, 1920, ibid.; E. Jenkins to Sells, March 1, 1920, ibid.

23. P. Hoffman to Sells, February 25, 1920, ibid; Don E. Carr to Sells, March 16, 1920, ibid.; Herbert V. Clotts to Sells, April 19, 1920, ibid.; H. R. Robinson to Sells, April 8, 1920, ibid.; H. W. Dietz to L. W. Aschemeier, April 30, 1920, ibid.

24. Donald C. Swain, *Federal Conservation Policy, 1921–1933* (Berkeley: University of California Press, 1963), p. 79; William K. Wyant, *Westward in Eden: The Public Lands and the Conservation Movement* (Berkeley: University of California Press, 1982), pp. 68–69.

25. ARSI, 1921, pp. 14–15; *Chief Irrigation Engineer's Report*, 1921, p. 10; ARCIA, 1921, p. 20; U.S., House, Committee on Appropriations, *Interior Department Appropriation Bill, 1922*, Hearings on H.R. 7848, 67th Cong., 1st sess., 1920, p. 20.

26. Frank E. Smith, *The Politics of Conservation* (New York: Pantheon Books, 1966), p. 167; ARSI, 1923, p. 2; see also Swain, *Federal Conservation Policy*, pp. 73–96; Roy M. Robbins, *Our Landed Heritage: The Public Domain, 1776–1936* (Princeton: Princeton University Press, 1942; reprint ed., Gloucester, Mass.: Peter Smith, 1960), pp. 402–404; Robert G. Dunbar, *Forging New Rights in Western Waters*, pp. 54–56.

27. ARCIA, 1924, p. 20; circular 2209, Burke to All Superintendents, April 19, 1926, BIA, Circulars.

28. ARCIA, 1926, pp. 24–25; circular 1624a, Burke to All Superintendents, July 23, 1927, BIA, Circulars.

29. ARCIA, 1927, p. 22; J. P. Kinney, *A Continent Lost—A Civilization Won: Indian Land Tenure in America* (Baltimore: Johns Hopkins University Press, 1937, reprint ed., New York: Arno Press, 1975), pp. 316, 379.

30. Leonard A. Carlson, *Indians, Bureaucrats, and Land: The Dawes Act and the Decline of Indian Farming* (Westport, Conn.: Greenwood Press, 1981), p. 140.

31. *Congressional Record*, 64th Cong., 1st sess., vol. 53, p. 4901; Carlson, *Indians, Bureaucrats and Land*, pp. 140–41; John C. Ewers, *The Blackfeet: Raiders on the Northwestern Plains* (Norman: University of Oklahoma Press, 1958), pp. 317–18.

32. Kirke Kickingbird and Karen Ducheneaux, *One Hundred Million Acres* (New York: Macmillan, 1973), pp. 96–98; Ronald Trosper, "The Economic Impact of the Allotment Policy on the Flathead Indian Reservation" (Ph.D. dissertation, Harvard University, 1975), pp. 188–96; Carlson, *Indians, Bureaucrats and Land*, p. 140; U.S. House,

On the Conditions of the Various Tribes of Indians, pp. 5, 18–21; *Senate Survey of Conditions*, VI, p. 2217.

33.   Theodore Stern, *The Klamath Tribe: A People and Their Reservation* (Seattle: University of Washington Press, 1966), pp. 148–51.

34.   *Senate Survey of Conditions*, Part VI, p. 2217.

35.   Lewis Meriam et al., *The Problem of Indian Administration* (Baltimore: Johns Hopkins University Press, 1928), pp. 508–11.

36.   *Senate Survey of Conditions*, Part VI, pp. 2217–18, 2237.

37.   ARCIA, 1931, p. 22; U.S. House, Committee on Appropriations, *Interior Department Appropriation Bill, 1931*, Hearings, 1929, p. 371.

38.   Memorandum, Charles Rhoads to the Secretary of Interior, January 15, 1930, in U.S. House, Committee on Indian Affairs, *Deferring Collection of Construction Costs Against Indian Land within Irrigation Projects*, H. Rept. 996 to accompany H.R. 5282, 71st Cong., 2d sess., 1930, serial 9191.

39.   U.S. Senate, Committee on Indian Affairs, *Authorizing the Secretary of the Interior to Adjust or Eliminate Reimbursable Debts of Indians*, Hearings on H.R. 8898 and H.R. 10884, 72d Cong., 1st sess., May 25, 1932; see also Lawrence C. Kelly, "Charles James Rhoads (1929–33)" in *The Commissioners of Indian Affairs, 1824–1977*, ed. Robert M. Kvasnicka and Herman Viola (Lincoln: University of Nebraska Press, 1979), p. 265.

40.   *U.S. Statutes at Large*, vol. 47, p. 564; John Collier to Superintendents, August 26, 1933; Prucha, *Great Father*, p. 927; ARCIA, 1932, p. 18.

41.   Kelly, "Charles James Rhoads," p. 265; ARCIA, 1931, pp. 18–19, 22; U.S. House, Committee on Appropriations, *Interior Department Appropriation Bill, 1933*, Hearings, 72d Cong., 1st sess., 1932, p. 310.

42.   Abbott, "Comments on Irrigation Law," pp. 1–9.

7. Fee Patents and Competency Commissions

1.   ARCIA, 1901, pp. 4–5; ibid., 1905, p. 5; Francis E. Leupp, *The Indian and His Problem* (New York: Charles Scribner's Sons, 1910; reprint ed., New York: Arno Press, 1971), p. 60.

2.   *Matter of Heff*, 197 U.S. 488; U.S. House, Committee on Indian Affairs, *Allotment of Lands in Severalty to Certain Indians*, H. Rept. 1558 to accompany H.R. 11946, 59th Cong., 1st sess., 1906, serial 4906.

3.   Ibid.

4.   Ibid.

5.   *Congressional Record*, vol. 40, pt. 4, pp. 3599–3600.

6.   Ibid.; see also Paul Stuart, *The Indian Office: Growth and Development of an American Institution, 1865–1900* (Ann Arbor: UMI Research Press, 1978), p. 123.

7.   ARCIA, 1906, p. 30.

8.   U.S. Office of Indian Affairs, *Rules and Regulations Relating to the Issuance of Patents in Fee and Certificates of Competency and the Sale of Allotted and Inherited Lands*, October 12, 1910 (Washington: Government Printing Office, 1910), pp. 5–7; Laurence F. Schmeckebier, *The Office of Indian Affairs: Its History, Activities, and Organization* (Baltimore: Johns Hopkins University Press, 1927), p. 155.

9.   ARCIA, 1907, p. 68; ibid., 1909, p. 63.

10.   Circular 254 1/2, Francis L. Leupp to All Superintendents, November 18, 1908, BIA, Circulars.

11.   Circular 261, Leupp to All Agents and Superintendents, January 9, 1909, ibid.

12.   ARCIA, 1909, p. 63.

13.   Ibid., 1910, p. 48; Robert Valentine, "Making Good Indians," *Sunset* 24 (1910):600–601, 611; *Pender (Nebraska) Times*, June 11, 1909; U.S. Senate, Committee on Indian Affairs, *Taxation of Omaha Indian Lands in Nebraska*, Rept. to accompany S. 4490,

61st Cong., 2d sess., 1910, serial 5583. For a more detailed discussion of the competency commission work on the Omaha reservation, see Janet A. McDonnell, "Land Policy on the Omaha Reservation: Competency Commissions and Fee Patents," *Nebraska History* 63 (Fall 1982):399–412.

14. Sells to Lane, May 19, 1915, BIA-CCF, General Services, 70942–10–312.
15. Ibid.
16. Robert Valentine to E. P. Holcombe, November 19, 1910, BIA-CCF, 349–09–127.
17. F. H. Abbott to H. G. Wilson, January 13, 1911, BIA-CCF, 70492–10–312.
18. ARCIA, 1911, p. 23.
19. Lane to Sells, November 10, 1913, BIA-CCF, General Services, 511501–14–127; Sells to the Superintendents, December 27, 1913, BIA-CCF, General Services, 152466–13–312.
20. Memorandum by Sells, November 11, 1913, BIA-CCF, General Services, 152466–13–312.
21. Memorandum, Meritt to Sells, December 1, 1913, ibid.
22. ARSI, pp. 6–9; see also James Hemphill, "Franklin Knight Lane," *North American Review* 206 (April 1917):251–60.
23. Sells to Axel Johnson, December 4, 1914, James McLaughlin Papers, Assumption Abbey Archives, Richardton, North Dakota (Reel 5, Frame 714); Report on the Omaha Reservation, Johnson to Sells, January 1, 1915, ibid. (Reel 6, Frame 9).
24. Sells to S.A.M. Young, December 4, 1914, James McLaughlin Papers (Reel 5, Frames 710–13, 716); Sells to Charles E. Burton, December 4, 1914, ibid.; Sells to E. D. Mossman, December 4, 1914, ibid.; Sells to A. W. Leech, December 4, 1914, ibid.; Sells to Arvel R. Snyder, December 4, 1914, ibid.; Sells to Lane, May 19, 1915, BIA-CCF, General Services, 55961–15–312.
25. Leech to Sells, December 15, 1914, James McLaughlin Papers (Reel 5, Frame 718); Mossman to Sells, December 28, 1914, ibid. (Reel 5, Frame 746).
26. Sells to Lane, May 19, 1915, BIA-CCF, General Services, 55961–15–312.
27. Ibid.
28. Lane to Sells, June 12, 1914, SI-CCF, 5–6, Indian Office, General, Competent Indians, General; Sells to Lane, May 19, 1915, BIA-CCF, General Services, 55961–15–312; Sells to Lane, December 14, 1914, BIA-CCF, Flathead, 132598–14–150.
29. IRA Report, 1914, pp. 18–19.
30. BIC Report, 1915, pp. 7–8.
31. Lane, "To Whom It May Concern," April 8, 1915, James McLaughlin Papers (Reel 6, Frame 71).
32. Indian Office Memorandum, "To Whom It May Concern," n.d., SI-CCF, 5–6, Indian Office, General, Competent Indians; Louis L. Pfaller, *James McLaughlin: The Man with an Indian Heart* (New York: Vantage Press, 1978), pp. 90, 191–92, 302; Carl E. Grammer to Lane, September 1915, IRA Papers (Reel 30); Frank A. Thackery to Matthew K. Sniffen, May 25, 1915, ibid.
33. Indian Office Memorandum, "To Whom It May Concern," n.d.; McLaughlin to Joseph H. Norris, March 25, 1916, James McLaughlin Papers (Reel 6, Frame 756).
34. U.S. House, Committee on Indian Affairs, *Indian Appropriation Bill, 1917*, Hearings on H.R. 10385, 64th Cong., 1st sess., 1916, pp. 27–28; Lane to Charles Curtis, February 2, 1920, BIA-CCF, General Services, 45100–19–013.
35. McLaughlin to Evan Estep, June 7, 1916, James McLaughlin Papers (Reel 7, Frames 110–11). For the names and schedules of the competency commissions, see BIA-CCF, General Services, 00–20–312. ARSI, 1916, p. 25; ARCIA, 1916, p. 49; McLaughlin to Lane, September 9, 1916, SI-CCF, 5–6, Indian Office, General, Competent Indians, General; McLaughlin to Lane, September 16, 1916, ibid.; McLaughlin to Lane, October 14, 1916, ibid.; memorandum, Indian Office to Mr. Schaffer, September 15, 1916, ibid.

36. F. A. Meyer to Joe Chapple, August 25, 1916, ibid.; Lane to McLaughlin, September 2, 1915, James McLaughlin Papers (Reel 6, Frame 225).

37. Lane to H. R. Brougham, May 20, 1916, in Franklin Lane, *The Letters of Franklin Lane*, ed. Anne W. Lane and Louise H. Wall (Boston and New York: Houghton Mifflin Co., 1922), pp. 208–10. Joseph T. Cook, from the Yankton reservation, was the first person to go through the ceremony. See McLaughlin to Meyer, May 15, 1916, McLaughlin Papers (Reel 7, Frame 60), and Frederick E. Hoxie, *A Final Promise: The Campaign to Assimilate Indians, 1880–1920* (Lincoln: University of Nebraska Press, 1984), pp. 180–81.

38. McLaughlin to Fred C. Morgan, May 2, 1916, James McLaughlin Papers (Reel 7, Frame 2); Meyer to Chapple, August 25, 1916.

39. McLaughlin to McPherson, June 9, 1916, James McLaughlin Papers (Reel 7, Frames 78–79).

40. Telegram, to James Keeley, n.d., SI-CCF, 5–6, Indian Office, General, Competent Indians, General; Lane to Brougham, May 20, 1916; McLaughlin to McPherson, June 9, 1916.

41. McLaughlin to Lane, June 10, 1916, SI-CCF, 5–6, Indian Office, General, Competent Indians, General; SANR, Crow, 1917,p. 70 (Reel 30); McPherson to Lane, December 8, 1916, SI-CCF, 5–6, Indian Office, General, Competent Indians, General; McLaughlin to Lane, May 29, 1916, ibid.

42. McPherson to Lane, July 9, 1916, SI-CCF, 5–6, Indian Office, General, Competent Indians, General; Thackery to Lane, July 15, 1916, ibid.; McLaughlin to Lane, May 29, 1916, ibid.; Lane to McPherson, February 23, 1917, ibid.; McLaughlin to Lane, March 20, 1916, James McLaughlin Papers (Reel 6, Frame 731).

43. Malcolm McDowell to Hugh Scott, May 16, 1919, Hugh Lenox Scott Papers, Box 49, Library of Congress.

44. R.E.L. Daniel to H. W. Sipe, October 2, 1924, Allotment and Estate File #126, Santee agency, Winnebago, Nebraska; Daniel to the Commissioner of Indian Affairs, October 10, 1924, ibid.; Michael Wolf to C. D. Munro, January 27, 1922, Allotment and Estate File #1211, Cheyenne River agency, Eagle Butte, South Dakota.

45. U.S. House, Committee on Indian Affairs, *Investigation of the Field Service*, Hearings, 66th Cong., 3d sess., 1920, pp. 62, 74; McLaughlin to Lane, September 13, 1919, BIA-CCF, Cheyenne River, 79850–19–127; C. M. Knight, Report on the Yankton agency, May 26, 1916, BIA-CCF, 150, Yankton; McLaughlin to Lane, February 2, 1916, SI-CCF, 5–6, Indian Office, General, Competent Indians.

46. A. F. Greene to Orpha Collins Trevillyan, November 1, 1917, Allotment and Estate File #3269, Cheyenne River agency, Eagle Butte, South Dakota; Greene to Trevillyan, October 12, 1917, ibid.; see Reports on Patent in Fee in BIA-CCF, Cheyenne River, 92414–17–312, 92401–17–312, 92407–17–312.

47. McLaughlin to Lane, October 19, 1918, James McLaughlin Papers (Reel 10, Frame 165); Lane to McLaughlin, November 1, 1918, ibid. (Reel 10, Frame 232).

48. McPherson to Lane, August 17, 1916, SI-CCF, Indian Office, General, Competent Indians, General; McPherson to Lane, June 1, 1917, ibid.

49. Lane to McPherson, June 2, 1916, ibid.; McPherson to Lane, June 6, 1916, ibid.; S. B. Mewhister to W. F. Dickens, July 9, 1932, Allotment and Estate File #1040, Cheyenne River agency; Luther A. Williams to the Commissioner of Indian Affairs, April 16, 1927, BIA-CCF, Cheyenne River, 82874–17–127; A. F. Greene to Orpha Collins Trevillyan, October 12, 1917.

50. *Senate Survey of Conditions*, Part XV, Oklahoma, November 17-March 22, 1930, pp. 7006, 7010, 7170–71, Part IV, Washington, D.C., February 1-March 1, 1929, pp. 5994–95.

51. U.S. House, *Investigation of the Field Service, 1920*, pp. 58–74.

52. U.S. House, Committee on Indian Affairs, *Indian Appropriation Bill, 1919*, Hear-

ings on H.R. 8696, 65th Cong., 2d sess., 1918, p. 442; McLaughlin to Lane, September 16, 1916, James McLaughlin Papers (Reel 7, Frame 463); Thackery to Lane, April 10, 1916, SI-CCF, 5–6, Indian Office, General, Competent Indians, General; memorandum, Indian Office to Mr. Schaffer, September 15, 1915, ibid.; H. A. Meyer to Lane, June 23, 1916, ibid.; Meyer to Meritt, June 17, 1916, ibid.; Meyer to McLaughlin, June 16, 1916, ibid.

53. Leo Sampson and Allen Patawa to Lane, April 17, 1916, SI-CCF, 5–1, Indian Agencies, Umatilla, Patents.

54. Lane to Sampson and Patawa, April 19, 1916, ibid.

55. Charles L. Davis, Report on the Turtle Mountain agency, June 14, 1913, BIA-CCF, 150, Turtle Mountain; SANR, Cheyenne River, 1914 (Reel 16); ibid., Colville, 1913 (Reel 25).

56. SANR, Cheyenne River, 1916 (Reel 16); ibid., Fort Peck, 1913 (Reel 52).

57. SANR, Cheyenne River, 1913; ibid., Standing Rock, 1916 (Reel 144); ibid., Lower Brule, 1919; ibid., Standing Rock, 1918; A. W. Leech to Lane, June 21, 1916, SI-CCF, 5–6, Indian Office, General, Competent Indians, General; Felix Brunot and others to Lane, July 27, 1916, ibid.

58. SANR, Cheyenne River, 1913 (Reel 16); ibid., 1914; ibid., 1915; ibid., Crow, 1916 (Reel 30); ibid., Fort Peck, 1916 (Reel 52); L. F. Michael, Report on the Turtle Montain reservation, November 17, 1915, BIA-CCF, 150, Turtle Mountain; Otis B. Goodall, Report on the Umatilla reservation, February 28, 1916, BIA-CCF, 150, Umatilla.

59. SANR, Crow, 1915 (Reel 30); ibid., Crow Creek, 1914, pp. 34–35 (Reel 31); Sells to Lane, May 19, 1915, BIA-CCF, General Services, 55961–15–312; S.A.M. Young, Report on the Cheyenne River reservation, June 14, 1913, BIA-CCF, 150, Cheyenne River.

60. SANR, Fort Berthold, 1916 (Reel 46); ibid., Crow Creek, 1916 (Reel 31); ibid., Klamath, 1915 (Reel 73); L. F. Michael, Report on Fond du Lac; L. A. Dorrington, Report on the Umatilla reservation, July 26, 1915, BIA-CCF, 150, Umatilla; Otis B. Goodall, Report on the Umatilla, February 28, 1916, ibid.; S.A.M. Young, Report on Crow Creek reservation, May 25, 1914, BIA-CCF, 150, Crow Creek.

61. SANR, Fort Peck, 1915 (Reel 52); ibid., Pine Ridge, 1913 (Reel 106).

62. Charles L. Davis, Report on Pine Ridge reservation, October 27, 1913, BIA-CCF, 150, Pine Ridge; SANR, Turtle Mountain, 1916 (Reel 16).

63. Circular 1070, Sells to All Superintendents, January 17, 1916, BIA, Circulars; E. Hutchinson to Sells, August 31, 1920, BIA, Replies to Circulars, 1070.

64. Hugh Scott, "Report on the Rosebud Agency, South Dakota," August 15, 1920, BIC Report, 1921, p. 29.

65. Leech to Lane, June 21, 1916, SI-CCF, 5–6, Indian Office, General, Competent Indians, General; Felix Brunot et al. to Lane, July 27, 1916, ibid.

66. Memorandum, E. M. Albright, June 9, 1914, BIA-CCF, Flathead, 132598–14–150; Sells to Lane, December 14, 1914, ibid.

67. ARCIA, 1916, p. 49; *New York Times*, October 29, 1916, section 5, p. 10.

68. U.S. House, Committee on Indian Affairs, *Indian Appropriation Bill, 1917*, Hearings on H.R. 10385, 64th Cong., 1st sess., 1916, pp. 29–32.

8. Declaration of Policy

1. *Congressional Record*, 64th Cong., 2d sess., vol. 54, pp. 2110–15.

2. Herbert Welsh to Sells, March 23, 1917, IRA Papers (Reel 32).

3. ARCIA, 1917, pp. 3–5.

4. Ibid.

5. Ibid.

6. U.S. House, Committee on Indian Affairs, *Indians of the United States*, Hearings, vol. I: *On the Condition of Various Indian Tribes*, 66th Cong., 1st sess., 1919, p. 46.

7. *Baltimore Star*, April 17, 1917, BIA, Newspaper Clippings; "A New Step in Our Indian Policy," *Outlook* 116 (May 23, 1917):136; *Boston Transcript*, April 17, 1917, BIA, Newspaper Clippings.

8. William Alexander Brown to Sells, July 3, 1917, IRA Papers (Reel 32); S. M. Brosius to Matthew K. Sniffen, April 17, 1917, ibid.; IRA Report, 1917, p. 38.

9. Thomas C. Moffett to Sniffen, January 31, 1918, IRA Papers (Reel 33).

10. BIC Report, 1917, p. 14.

11. C. F. Hauke to Thomas Ferris, July 26, 1917, BIA-CCF, Blackfeet, 89756–17–313.

12. Sells to Lane, August 13, 1917, SI-CCF, 5–1, Indian Agencies, Yakima, Patents; Sells to Lane, August 15, 1917, BIA-CCF, Blackfeet, 98756–17–313; Sells to Lane, August 15, 1917, SI-CCF, 5–1, Indian Agencies, Klamath, Patents; Sells to Lane, August 20, 1917, SI-CCF, 5–1, Indian Agencies, Flathead, Patents; Hauke to Lane, August 8, 1918, SI-CCF, 5–1, Indian Agencies, Shoshone, Patents; U.S. House, Committee on Indian Affairs, *Indian Appropriation Bill, 1920*, Hearings on H.R. 14746, 65th Cong., 3d sess., 1919, p. 111.

13. Sells to Lane, June 2, 1917, SI-CCF, 5–6, Indian Office, General, Competent Indians, General; Lane to Sells, June 1, 1917, ibid.

14. Hauke to Lane, January 31, 1918, SI-CCF, 5–1, Indian Agencies, Blackfeet, Patents; J. H. Dortch to Lane, June 19, 1918, SI-CCF, 5–1, Indian Agencies, Crow Creek, Patents.

15. Charles Ellis, Reports on Flora McKelvey Brown and John Cobell, March 20, 1917, BIA-CCF, Blackfeet, 89756–17–313; U.S. House, Committee on Indian Affairs, *Investigation of the Field Service*, 66th Cong., 3d sess., 1920, p. 579.

16. SANR, Crow, 1917 (Reel 30); ibid., 1918; ibid., Fort Peck, 1917 (Reel 52); ibid., 1919; ibid., Winnebago, 1919.

17. E. B. Linnen and C. M. Knight, Report on Pine Ridge reservation, May 28, 1917, BIA-CCF, Pine Ridge, 52157–17–150; W. S. Coleman, Report on Pine Ridge reservation, September 15, 1917, BIA, Inspection Report; SANR, Pine Ridge, 1919 (Reel 106).

18. SANR, White Earth, 1917, pp. 28–29 (Reel 169); Malcolm McDowell, "Report on the Chippewa Indians of Minnesota," November 30, 1920, BIC Report, 1921, p. 110.

19. SANR, Cheyenne River, 1917 (Reel 16); ibid., 1918.

20. SANR, Crow, 1918 (Reel 30); ibid., Crow Creek, 1917 (Reel 31); W.S. Coleman, Report on the Flathead reservation, May 22, 1917, BIA, Inspection Reports; SANR, Standing Rock, 1918 (Reel 144).

21. ARSI, 1918, p. 43; Sells, "The 'First Americans' as Loyal Citizens," *Review of Reviews*, 57 (May 1918):524.

22. *Congressional Record*, 65th Cong., 2d sess., vol. 56, p. 4212; ibid., 66th Cong., 1st sess., vol. 58, pp. 258–59; Lane to Charles Carter, March 1918, BIA-CCF, General Services, 18155–18–013.

23. Circular, Sells to All Superintendents, March 7, 1919, BIA-CCF, General Services, 21986–19–312; J. H. Dortch to Lane, June 23, 1919, SI-CCF, 5–1, Indian Agencies, Crow Creek, Patents; Dortch to Lane, June 23, 1919, SI-CCF, 5–1, Indian Agencies, Shoshone, Patents; Dortch to Lane, June 30, 1919, SI-CCF, 5–1, Indian Agencies, Yakima, Patents.

24. ARCIA, 1919, pp. 7–10.

25. Lane to Sells, May 24, 1919, SI-CCF, 5–6, Indian Office, General, Competent Indians, General; Lane to Homer P. Snyder, July 18, 1919, BIA-CCF, General Services, 45100–19–013.

26. U.S. House, *Condition of Various Indian Tribes*, p. 42; U.S. House, Committee on Indian Affairs, *Indians of the United States, Field Investigation*, H. Rept. 1133, 66th Cong., 3d sess., 1920, pp. 17–18, serial 7776; U.S. House, Committee on Indian Affairs, *Reorganizing the Indian Service*, H. Rept. 1189 to accompany H.R. 15663, 66th Cong., 3d sess., 1921, serial 7776.

27. Lane to Woodrow Wilson, February 28, 1920, SI-CCF, 22–44, Presidential Appointments, Secretary of Interior, Sells to Mrs. F. W. Harman, March 31, 1920, Woodrow Wilson Papers (Reel 179), Library of Congress; reprinted in ARCIA, 1920, p. 9.

28. SANR, Umatilla, 1917 (Reel 159); ibid., Yakima, 1921 (Reel 171); ibid., Flathead, 1920 (Reel 42).

29. John Elm to the Indian Rights Association, February 6, 1918, IRA Papers (Reel 33).

30. BIC Report, 1920, pp. 8–9.

31. Statement by William A. Brown, March 29, 1920, IRA Papers (Reel 35); IRA Report, 1920, pp. 4–5.

32. J. Leonard Bates, *The Origins of Teapot Dome: Progressives, Parties, and Petroleum, 1909–1921* (Urbana: University of Illinois Press, 1963), pp. 201, 203; Lane, *The Letters of Franklin K. Lane*, ed., Anne W. Lane and Louise H. Wall (Boston and New York: Houghton Mifflin Co., 1922), pp. 312–14, 323–26; Board of Indian Commissioners to Lane, February 5, 1920, BIC, General Correspondence, 1919–33, Tray 62, File 111.11; Lane to Malcolm McDowell, February 6, 1920, ibid.; Eugene P. Trani, *The Secretaries of the Department of the Interior, 1849–1969* (Washington: National Anthropological Archives, 1975), p. 214.

33. McDowell to George Vaux, January 13, 1921, BIC, General Correspondence, 010, Members, Vaux; ARSI, 1920, p. 9.

34. James McLaughlin to E. W. Jermark, March 13, 1922, James McLaughlin Papers, Assumption Abbey Archives, Richardton, North Dakota (Reel 13, Frames 626–27); McLaughlin to Agnes G. Fredette, March 5, 1921, ibid. (Reel 13, Frame 422); McLaughlin to Charles Ellis, January 24, 1921, ibid. (Reel 13, Frame 365); McLaughlin to Charles E. Coe, February 4, 1921, ibid. (Reel 13, Frame 375).

35. Circular 1649, Sells to All Superintendents, November 23, 1920, BIA, Circulars; Hubert Work to George Vaux, January 13, 1921, BIC, Reference Material, Tray 140, Allotment; McLaughlin to Jane Peterson, February 15, 1921, James McLaughlin Papers (Reel 13, Frame 630).

36. ARCIA, 1920, pp. 48–49.

9. Fee Patents, 1921–1934

1. Hubert Work, "Our American Indians," *Saturday Evening Post* 196 (May 31, 1924):27, 92; BIC Report, 1921, pp. 5–9; Burke to Malcolm McDowell, May 25, 1921, BIC, General Correspondence, 1919–1933, Tray 62, File 111.2; McDowell to Burke, May 3, 1921, BIA-CCF, General Services, 56074–21–312.

2. BIC Report, 1921, pp. 5–9.

3. Ibid.

4. ARSI, 1921, pp. 14–15, 54.

5. ARCIA, 1921, pp. 23–26; U.S. Office of Indian Affairs, *Rules and Regulations Relating to the Issuance of Patents in Fee and Certificates of Competency and the Sale of Allotted and Inherited Indian Lands*, May 1, 1922 (Washington: Government Printing Office, 1922), pp. 2–6.

6. Burke to F. T. Mann, March 4, 1926, BIA-CCF, Winnebago, 67144–25–127.

7. ARCIA, 1922, p. 15; Burke to the Secretary of Interior, March 28, 1922, SI-CCF, 5–6, Indian Office, General, Land Sales; ARCIA, 1922, p. 15.

8. Circular 1825, C. F. Hauke to All Superintendents, October 21, 1922, BIA, Circulars.

9. SANR, Fort Hall, 1921 (Reel 49); ibid., Crow, 1921 (Reel 30); ibid., Pine Ridge, 1921 (Reel 106); ibid., 1927; ibid., Cheyenne River, 1922 (Reel 16); ibid., 1923 (Reel 17); ibid., Fort Peck, 1922 (Reel 52); ibid., 1926 (Reel 53); ibid., Standing Rock, 1927 (Reel 144); F. E. Brandon, Report on the Crow reservation, June 23, 1922, BIA, Inspection

Reports; Hugh Scott, "Report on the Fort Peck Indian Agency, Montana," October 1, 1924, pp. 1–2, BIC, *Special Reports*, V; SANR, Winnebago, 1926 (Reel 170); F. T. Mann to Burke, February 5, 1926, BIA-CCF, Winnebago, 67144–25–127; Burke to Mann, March 4, 1926, ibid.; Mann to Burke, March 10, 1926, ibid.

10. Ibid.

11. Ibid.

12. SANR, Flathead, 1922 (Reel 42); ibid., Fort Peck, 1922 (Reel 52); ibid., Crow, 1924, p. 23 (Reel 32).

13. Peter Norbeck to John Barron, March 5, 1928, #0170, File 29, Taxation-Indian Lands, Peter M. Norbeck Papers, I. D. Weeks Library, University of South Dakota, Vermillion, South Dakota; Resolution of the County Commissioners, Zieback County, South Dakota, March 5, 1928, ibid.; F. T. Mann to Burke, March 10, 1926, BIA-CCF, Winnebago, 67144–25–127; W. W. Coon to Burke, March 19, 1925, BIA-CCF, General Services, 34722–31–312.

14. U.S. House, Committee on Appropriations, *Interior Department Appropriation Bill, 1923*, Hearings on H.R. 10329, 67th Cong., 2d sess., 1921, pp. 158–60; ibid., *Interior Department Appropriation Bill, 1924*, H.R. 13559, 67th Cong., 4th sess., 1922, p. 164.

15. Ibid., 1924, pp. 162–63; ibid., 1923, p. 158; U.S. House, Committee on Indian Affairs, *Leasing of Allotted Indian Lands*, Hearings on H.R. 8823, 69th Cong., 1st sess., April 10, 14, 16, 1926, p. 23.

16. U.S. House, *Interior Department Appropriation Bill, 1924*, p. 163; ibid., *Interior Department Appropriation Bill, 1923*, p. 168.

17. ARCIA, 1926, pp. 10–11; ibid., 1927, p. 12; ibid., 1928, p. 24.

18. Work to J. W. Harreld, January 18, 1926, SI-CCF, 5–6, Indian Office, Patents, Legislation.

19. Ibid.

20. Ibid.

21. U.S. House, Committee on Indian Affairs, *Cancellation of Patents in Fee Simple to Indians for Allotments Held in Trust by the United States*, H. Rept. 1896 to accompany S. 2714, 69th Cong., 2d sess., 1927, serial 8689.

22. ARCIA, 1927, p. 12; Burke to Frank Kirkpatrick, March 13, 1928, SI-CCF, 5–6, Indian Office, Patents; *U.S. Statutes at Large*, vol. 45, p. 1247.

23. Work to Scott Leavitt, May 21, 1928, SI-CCF, 5–6, Indian Office, Patents, Legislation; Ronald Trosper, "The Economic Impact of the Allotment Policy on the Flathead Reservation" (Ph.D. dissertation, Harvard University, 1975), pp. 38–39.

24. U.S. Senate, Committee on Indian Affairs, *Cancellation of Certain Patents in Fee Simple Issue Issued to Indians for Allotments without Their Consent*, S. Rept. 1595 to accompany H.R. 15267, 71st Cong., 3d sess., 1931, serial 9323.

25. Circular 2464, Burke to All Superintendents, June 18, 1928, BIA-CCF, General Services, 21986–19–312; ARCIA, 1928, p. 24; ARSI, 1928, p. 65.

26. *Senate Survey of Conditions*, Part XIV, Oklahoma, November 10–15, 1930, pp. 5403, 5415, 5560, 5968, 5994–95; ibid., Part XV, Oklahoma, November 17–22, 1930, pp. 7009, 7011; L. W. Page to Burke, November 11, 1928, BIA, Replies to Circulars, 2464; A. W. Leech to Burke, March 20, 1929, ibid.

27. *U.S. Statutes at Large*, vol. 46, p. 1205.

28. U.S. House, Committee on Indian Affairs, *Relief of Indians Who Have Paid Taxes on Allotted Lands*, H. Rept. 2673 to accompany H.R. 10644, 75th Cong., 3d sess., 1938, serial 10235.

29. American Indian Defense Association, 70th Cong., Bulletin No. 7, "Uncle Sam, the Patent Fee Indians and the States and Counties," December 29, 1927, IRA Papers (Reel 129, Item 307).

30. Collier, "The Allotment Law: Considerations About Its Amendment," John Collier Papers, Part I, Series I, Box 3, File 66, Sterling Memorial Library, Yale University, New Haven, Connecticut; for information on the reform movement of the 1920s, see

Lawrence C. Kelly, *The Assault on Assimilation: John Collier and the Origins of Indian Policy Reform* (Albuquerque: University of New Mexico Press, 1983), and Kenneth R. Philp, *John Collier's Crusade for Indian Reform, 1920–1954* (Tucson: University of Arizona Press, 1977).

31. Ibid.

32. Lewis Meriam et al., *The Problem of Indian Administration* (Baltimore: Johns Hopkins University Press, 1928), pp. 29–30, 100, 471–72.

33. U.S. Senate, Committee on Indian Affairs, *Survey of Conditions of Indians in the United States*, Hearings Pursuant to S. Res. 79, 70th Cong., 1st sess., January 10, 13, 1928, pp. 13–14, 34.

34. ARCIA, 1930, p. 25; ibid., 1931, pp. 37–38.

35. Order, Collier to All Superintendents, August 8, 1933, SI-CCF, 5–6, Indian Office, General, Land Sales.

Conclusion

1. J. E. Chamberlain, *The Harrowing of Eden: White Attitudes Toward American Natives* (New York: Seabury Press, 1975), p. 41; U.S. Department of the Interior, Natural Resource Board, *Indian Land Tenure, Economic Status, and Population Trends*, Part X of *The Report on Land Planning* (Washington: Government Printing Office, 1935), p. 1.

2. *Indian Land Tenure*, pp. 1–2.

3. Ibid., pp. 1–2, 10–11, 19.

4. *Land Ownership and Economic Development*, pp. 130–33.

5. Brian W. Dippie, *The Vanishing American: White Attitudes and United States Indian Policy* (Middletown, Conn.: Wesleyan University Press, 1982), p. 178; Paul Stuart, *The Indian Office: Growth and Development of an American Institution, 1865–1900* (Ann Arbor: UMI Research Press, 1978), pp. 122–23; Vine Deloria Jr., ed., *American Indian Policy in the Twentieth Century* (Norman: University of Oklahoma Press, 1985), p. 247.

6. U.S. House, Subcommittee, Committee on Appropriations, *Interior Department Appropriation Bill, 1933*, Hearings, 72d Cong., 1st sess., 1932, p. 5.

7. Frederick E. Hoxie, "From Prison to Homeland: The Cheyenne River Reservation Before World War I," in *The Plains Indians of the Twentieth Century*, ed. Peter Iverson (Norman: University of Oklahoma Press, 1985), p. 60; Donald J. Berthrong, "Legacies of the Dawes Act: Bureaucrats and Land Thieves at the Cheyenne-Arapaho Agencies of Omaha," ibid., pp. 34–35.

SELECTED BIBLIOGRAPHY

Records of the National Archives

Record Group 75. Records of the Bureau of Indian Affairs

Records of the Bureau of Indian Affairs
Central Classified Files
Circulars
Replies to Circulars
Orders
Special Cases

Records of the Inspection Division
Inspection Reports
Special Agents Files

Records of the Irrigation Division
Annual Reports of the Chief Engineer

Records of the Land Division
Notes Concerning Allotment on Reservation Letters Sent Relating to Land Allotment

Records of the Statistics Division
Superintendents' Annual Narrative Reports

Records of the Board of Indian Commissioners

Record Group 48. Records of the Office of the Secretary of the Interior

Central Classified Files
Records of Secretary of the Interior Hubert Work
Records Relating to Legislation

Record Group 200. National Archives Gift Collection

Herbert J. Hagerman Papers

Record Group 279. Indian Claims Commission

Manuscript Collections

John Collier Papers. Sterling Memorial Library. Yale University. New Haven, Connecticut.
Calvin Coolidge Papers. Library of Congress.
Indian Rights Association Papers. Historical Society of Pennsylvania. Philadelphia (Microfilm edition, Glen Rock, New Jersey: Microfilming Corporation of America).

Franklin Knight Lane Papers. Bancroft Library. University of California. Berkeley, California.

James McLaughlin Papers. Assumption Abbey Archives. Richardton, North Dakota (Microfilm edition, Richardton, North Dakota: Assumption Abbey College Archives Publications).

Peter M. Norbeck Papers. I. D. Weeks Library. University of South Dakota. Vermillion, South Dakota.

Hugh Lenox Scott Papers. Library of Congress.

William Williamson Papers. I. D. Weeks Library. University of South Dakota. Vermillion, South Dakota.

Woodrow Wilson Papers. Library of Congress.

Selected items have been used at the following depositories: Cheyenne River Agency, Eagle Butte, South Dakota; Santee Agency, Winnebago, Nebraska.

Government Documents

Serial Set Documents

House Committee on Indian Affairs. *Allotment of Land in Severalty to Certain Indians*. H. Rept. 1558 to accompany H.R. 11946, 59th Cong., 1st sess., 1906, serial 4906.

Rules and Regulations Governing the Department of the Interior and Its Various Branches. S. Doc. 306, Part 4, 59th Cong., 2d sess., February 26, 1907, serial 5088.

Senate Committee on Indian Affairs. *Taxation of Omaha Indian Lands in Nebraska*. S. Rept. to accompany S. 4490, 61st Cong., 2d sess., 1910, serial 5583.

Senate Committee on Indian Affairs. *Indian Appropriation Bill for 1914*. S. Rept. 63 to accompany H.R. 1917, 63d Cong., 1st sess., 1913, serial 6510.

House Committee on Indian Affairs. *Investigation of Indian Affairs*. Report of the Joint Commission to Investigate Indian Affairs. S. Doc. 984, 63d Cong., 3d sess., March 3, 1915, serial 6784.

Senate Committee on Indian Affairs. *Mining for Metalliferous Minerals on Indian Reservations*. S. Rept. 880 to accompany H.R. 12426, 64th Cong., 2d sess., 1916, serial 7106.

U.S. Department of Interior. *Report on the Cultivation of the Public Domain and Indian Lands*. S. Doc. 127, 65th Cong., 2d sess., 1917, serial 7329.

House Committee on Indian Affairs. *Indians of the United States, Field Investigation*. H. Rept. 1133, 66th Cong., 3d sess., 1920, serial 7776.

Reorganizing the Indian Service. H. Rept. 1189 to accompany H.R. 15663, 66th Cong., 3d sess., 1921, serial 7776.

Senate Committee on Indian Affairs. *To Provide for the Disposition of Bonuses, Rentals, and Royalties from Unallotted Lands in Executive Order Reservations*. S. Rept.669 to accompany S. 876, 68th Cong., 1st sess., 1924, serial 8221.

Committee of One Hundred on Indian Affairs. *The Indian Problem*. Resolution of the Committee of One Hundred Appointed by the Secretary of Interior and a Review of the Indian Problem. H. Doc. 149, 68th Cong., 1st sess., 1924, serial 8273.

Indian Affairs in Oklahoma. H. Rept. 1527, 68th Cong., 1st sess., 1925, serial 8392.

Cancellation, Under Certain Conditions, of Patents in Fee Simple to Indians for Allotments Held in Trust by the United States. S. Rept. 536 to accompany S. 2714, 69th Cong., 1st sess., 1926, serial 8525.

Message from the President of the United States Returning without Approval the Bill (S. 4152) to Authorize Oil and Gas Mining Leases upon Unallotted Land within Executive Order Indian Reservations, and for Other Purposes. S. Doc. 156, 69th Cong., 1st sess., 1926, serial 8558.

Senate Committee on Indian Affairs. *To Authorize Oil and Gas Mining Leases upon Unallotted Lands within Executive Order Indian Reservations.* S. Rept. 1240 to accompany S. 4893, 69th Cong., 2d sess., 1927, serial 8685.

House Committee on Indian Affairs. *Oil and Gas Mining Leases upon Unallotted Land.* H. Rept. 1791 to accompany H.R. 15021, 69th Cong., 2d sess., 1927, serial 8688.

House Committee on Indian Affairs. *Cancellation of Patents in Fee Simple to Indians for Allotments Held in Trust by the United States.* H. Rept. 1896 to accompany S. 2714, 69th Cong., 2d sess., 1927, serial 8689.

House Committee on Indian Affairs. *Deferring Collection of Construction Costs Against Indian Lands within Irrigation Projects .* H. Rept. 966 to accompany H.R. 5282, 71st Cong., 2d sess., 1930, serial 9191.

Senate Committee on Indian Affairs. *Cancellation of Certain Patents in Fee Simple Issue to Indians for Allotments without Their Consent.* S. Rept. 1595 to accompany H.R. 15267, 71st Cong., 3d sess., 1931, serial 9323.

House Committee on Indian Affairs. *Cancellation of Certain Patents in Fee Simple Issued to Indians for Allotments without Their Consent.* H. Rept. 2269 to accompany H.R. 15267, 71st Cong., 3d sess., 1931, serial 9326.

House Committee on Indian Affairs. *Relief of Indians Who Have Paid Taxes on Allotted Lands.* H. Rept. 2673 to accompany H.R. 10644, 75th Cong., 3d sess., 1938, serial 10235.

Congressional Hearings

House Committee on Indian Affairs. *Authorizing the Secretary of the Interior to Adjust or Eliminate Reimbursable Debts of Indians.* Hearings on H.R. 8898 and H.R. 10884, 72d Cong., 1st sess., May 25, 1932.

House Committee on Indian Affairs. *Indian Appropriation Bill for Fiscal 1910–1920.* Hearings. Washington: Government Printing Office, 1909–1919.

Senate Committee on Indian Affairs. *Indian Appropriation Bill for Fiscal 1910–1920.* Hearings. Washington: Government Printing Office, 1909–1919.

House Committee on Indian Affairs. *Investigation of Indian Affairs.* Hearings of a Joint Commission to Investigate Affairs. 2 vols. 63d Cong., 1–2d sess., 1914.

Senate Committee on Indian Affairs. *For the Opening and Settlement of a Part of the Crow Indian Reservation in the State of Montana.* Part II. Hearings on S. 2378, 64th Cong., 1st sess., December 6, 15, 1916, May 2, 6, 13, 18, 1916, and June 1, 7, 23, 1916.

Senate Committee on Indian Affairs. *Conditions on the Fort Peck (Montana) Indian Reservation.* Hearings on S. 8272, 64th Cong., 2d sess., February 16–17, 1917.

House Committee on Indian Affairs. *Indians of the United States.* Hearings. vol. I: *On the Condition of Various Tribes of Indians.* 66th Cong., 1st sess., 1919, vol. III: *Investigation of the Field Service,* 66th Cong., 3d sess., 1920.

Senate Committee on Indian Affairs. *Leasing of Crow Indian Lands.* Hearings on S. 2890, 66th Cong., 1st sess., 1919.

Senate Committee on Indian Affairs. *To Provde for the Allotment of Lands of the Crow Tribe, for the Distribution of Tribal Funds, and for Other Purposes.* Hearings on S. 2890, 66th Cong., 1st sess., 1919.

House Committee on Indian Affairs. *Complaint of the Pine Ridge Sioux.* Hearings. 66th Cong., 2d sess., April 16, 1920.

House Committee on Indian Affairs. *On the Crow Tribe of Indians in Montana.* Hearings. 66th Cong., 2d sess., March 17, 19, 1920.

House Committee on Appropriations. *Interior Department Appropriation Bill for Fiscal 1921–1934.* Hearings. Washington: Government Printing Office, 1921–1933.

House Committee on Indian Affairs. *Crow Indians of Montana.* Hearings on H.R. 8185, 69th Cong., 1st sess., January 21, 1926, and February 4, 1926.

Senate Committee on Indian Affairs. *Development of Oil and Gas Mining Leases on Indian Reservations*. Hearings on S. 1722 and S. 3159, 69th Cong., 1st sess., February 27, 1926, and March 5, 9, 10, 1926.

House Committee on Indian Affairs. *Leasing of Allotted Indian Lands*. Hearings on H.R. 8823, 69th Cong., 1st sess., April 10, 14, 16, 1926.

House Committee on Indian Affairs. *Leasing of Executive Order Reservations*. Hearings on H.R. 9133, 69th Cong., 1st sess., February 19, 1926.

House Committee on Indian Affairs. *Leasing of Executive Order Reservations*. Hearings on H.R. 15021, 69th Cong., 2d sess., January 6, 12, 13, 1927.

Senate Committee on Indian Affairs. *Survey of Conditions of Indians in the United States*. Hearings pursuant to S. Res. 341, 69th Cong., 2d sess., February 23, 1927.

Senate Committee on Indian Affairs. *Survey of Conditions of Indians in the United States*. Hearings pursuant to S. Res. 79, 70th Cong., 1st sess., January 10, 13, 1928.

Senate Committee on Indian Affairs. *Authorizing the Secretary of the Interior to Adjust or Eliminate Reimbursable Debts of Indians*. Hearings on H.R. 8898 and H.R. 10884, 72d Cong., 1st sess., May 25, 1932.

Senate Committee on Indian Affairs. *To Grant Freedom to Indians Living Under Federal Tutelage*. Hearings on S. 2755 and S. 3645, 73d Cong., 2d sess., 1934.

House Committee on Indian Affairs. *Condition of Indians in the United States*, Part 1. Hearings on H.R. 8360, 74th Cong., 2d sess., March 11, 1936. Washington: Government Printing Office, 1936.

Senate Committee on Indian Affairs. *Survey of Conditions of Indians in the United States*. Hearings pursuant to S. Res. 79, 1928–1943. 43 vols. Washington: Government Printing Office, 1928–1943.

Indian Office Publications

Office of Indian Affairs. *Annual Report of the Commissioner of Indian Affairs to the Secretary of the Department of Interior for Fiscal 1900–1934*. Washington: Government Printing Office, 1901–1935.

Office of Indian Affairs. *Regulations Governing the Execution of Leases on Indian Allotted Tribal Lands for Farming, Grazing and Business Purposes*. July 20, 1923. Washington: Government Printing Office, 1923.

Office of Indian Affairs. *Regulations Governing Indian Allotments on the Public Domain Under Section Four of the Act of February 8, 1887 as Amended by the Act of February 28, 1891 and as Further Amended by the Act of June 25, 1910*. April 15, 1918. Washington: Government Printing Office, 1918.

Office of Indian Affairs. *Regulations Governing Indian Allotments on the Public Domain Under Section Four of the Act of February 8, 1887 as Amended by the Act of June 25, 1910*. February 1, 1928. Washington: Government PrintingOffice, 1928.

Office of Indian Affairs. *Rules and Regulations Relating to the Issuance of Patents in Fee and Certificates of Competency and the Sale of Allotted and Inherted Lands*. October 12, 1910. Washington: Government Printing Office, 1910.

Office of Indian Affairs. *Rules and Regulations Relating to the Issuance of Patents in Fee and Certificates of Competency and the Sale of Allotted and Inherited Lands*. May 1, 1922. Washington: Government Printing Office, 1922.

Other Published Government Sources

Biographical Directory of the American Congress, 1774–1971. Washington: Government Printing Office, 1971.

Board of Indian Commissioners. *Annual Report of the Board of Indian Commissioners, 1913–1929.* Washington: Government Printing Office, 1914–1930.

Congressional Record. vols. 49–70.

Isreal, Fred L. *The State of the Union Messages of thePresidents*. 3 vols. New York: Chelsea House, 1966.

Kappler, Charles J., compiler. *Indian Affairs: Laws and Treaties.* 5 vols. Washington: Government Printing Office, 1904–1941.

Reed, W. M. *Irrigation Work of the United States Indian Service.* Washington: Government Printing Office, 1919.

U.S. Department of Interior. *Indian Policies.* Comments on the resolution of the Advisory Council on Indian Affairs by Hubert Work. Washington: Government Printing Office, 1924.

U.S. Deparment of Interior. *Report of the Secretary of the Interior for Fiscal 1900–1930.* Washington: Government Printing Office, 1900–1930.

U.S. Department of Interior. Natural Resources Board. *Indian Land Tenure, Economic Status, and Population Trends,* Part X of *The Report on Land Planning.* Washington: Government Printing Office, 1935.

U.S. Statutes at Large.

Contemporary Writings

Books and Articles

Austin, Mary. "The Folly of Officials." *Forum* 71 (March 1924): 281–88.

Blanchard, Frances A. "The Deplorable State of Our Indians." *Current History* 18 (July 1923): 630–36.

Collier, John. "Are We Making Red Slaves?" *Survey* 57 (January 1, 1927): 453–55, 474–80.

———. "The Accursed System." *Sunset* 52 (June 1924): 15–16, 80–82.

———. "America's Treatment of Her Indians." *Current History* 18 (August 1923): 771–81.

———. *From Every Zenith: A Memoir.* Denver: Sage Books, 1963.

———. *Indians of the Americas.* New York: W. W. Norton and Co., 1947.

———. "Our Indian Policy." *Sunset* 50 (March 1923): 13–15, 89–93.

Corey, Herbert. "He Carries the White Man's Burden." *Collier's* 17 (May 12, 1923): 13.

Dawes, Charles G. *The First Years of the Budget of the United States.* New York: Harper and Bros. Publishers, 1923.

Grammer, Carl E. *Responsibilities for Indian Management.* Indian Rights Association Publication. Second Series. No. 94, 1914.

Hemphill, James. "Franklin Knight Lane." *North American Review* 206 (August 1917): 251–60.

Jacob, Harvey D. "Uncle Sam—The Great White Father." *Case and Comment* 23 (February 1917): 703–709.

Lane, Franklin K. "From the Warpath to the Plow." *National Georgraphic* 27 (January 1915): 73–87.

———. *The Letters of Franklin K. Lane.* Edited by Anne W. Lane and Louise H. Wall. Boston and New York: Houghton Mifflin Co., 1922.

Leupp, Francis E. *The Indian and His Problem.* New York: Charles Scribner's Sons, 1910; reprint ed., New York: Arno Press, 1971.

Moorehead, Warren K. *The American Indian in the United States.* Andover, Mass.: Andover Press, 1914; reprint ed.,Freeport, N.Y.: Books for Libraries Press, 1969.

"A New Question: Can the State Protect the Indians." *Outlook* 108 (September 9, 1914): 62–63.

"A New Step in Our Indian Policy." *Outlook* 116 (May 23,1917): 136.

Oskinson, John M. "In Governing the Indian, Use the Indian." *Case and Comment* 23 (February 1917): 272–76.

Sells, Cato. "The 'First Americans' as Loyal Citizens." *Review of Reviews* 57 (May 1918): 523–24.

————. "Land Tenure and the Organization of Agriculture." *International Review of Agricultural Economics* 77 (May 1917): 63–67.

Seymour, Flora Warren. "Our Indian Problem." *The Forum* 71 (March 1924): 273–80.

Smythe, William. "Franklin Knight Lane, American." *Review of Reviews* 61 (April 1920): 416–20.

Sniffen, Matthew K. *A Man and His Opportunity.* Indian Rights Association. Second Series. No. 94, 1914.

Sweeney, Marian Hopkins. "Indian Land Policy since 1887 with Special Reference to South Dakota." *South Dakota Historical Collections* 13 (1926): 250–83.

Tydings, Thomas J. "Rights of Indians on Public Lands." *Case and Comment* 23 (February 1917): 734–47.

Valentine, Robert. "Making Good Indians." *Sunset* 24 (1910): 599–611.

Willsie, Honore. "Mr. Lane and the Public Domain." *Harper's Weekly* 58 (August 23, 1913): 6–8.

Woehlke, Walter V. "Let 'Em Die." *Sunset* 51 (July 1923): 14–15.

Work, Hubert. "Our American Indians." *Saturday Evening Post* 196 (May 31, 1924): 26–27, 92, 94, 98.

Young, E. Marshall. "Leaders of Men." *Investors'* November 1919, pp. 5–6.

Newspapers and Periodicals

Indian Truth, 1924–1929.
New York Times.

Reports of Reform Organizations

Indian Rights Association. *Annual Report of the Executive Committee of the Indian Rights Association.*

Lake Mohonk Conference of Friends of the Indian and Other Dependent Peoples. *Annual Reports of Proceedings.*

Secondary Works

Books and Articles

Alexander, Thomas G. *A Clash of Inerests: The Interior Department and the Mountain West, 1863–1896.* Provo, Utah: Brigham Young University Press, 1977.

Baird, W. David. "William A. Jones (1897–1904)." In *The Commissioners of Indian Affairs, 1824–1977*, pp. 211–20. Edited by Robert M. Kvasnicka and Herman Viola. Lincoln: University of Nebraska Press, 1979.

Bates, J. Leonard. *The Origins of Teapot Dome: Progressives, Parties, and Petroleum, 1909–1921.* Urbana: University of Illinois Press, 1963.

Benedict, Murray R. *Farm Policies of the United States, 1790–1950* . New York: Twentieth Century Fund, 1953.

Bennett, J. E. *Laws of Titles to Indian Lands*. Oklahoma City: Harlow Publishing Co., 1917.

Berkhofer, Robert F. *The White Man's Indian: Images of the American Indian from Columbus to the Present*. New York: Random House, 1979.

Berthrong, Donald J. "Legacies of the Dawes Act: Bureaucrats and Land Thieves at the Cheyenne-Arapaho Agencies of Omaha." In *The Plains Indians of the Twentieth Century*, pp. 31–54. Edited by Peter Iverson. Norman: University of Oklahoma Press, 1985.

Brownlee, W. Elliot. *The Dynamics of Ascent: A History of the American Economy*. New York: Alfred A. Knopf, 1974.

Carlson, Leonard A. *Indians, Bureaucrats, and Land: The Dawes Act and the Decline of Indian Farming*. Westport, Conn.: Greenwood Press, 1981.

Chamberlin, J. E. *The Harrowing of Eden: White Attitudes toward North American Natives*. New York: Seabury Press, 1975.

Cohen, Felix S. *Handbook of Federal Indian Law*. Charlottesville, Virginia: Mitchee, Bobbs-Merrill, 1982.

Controneo, Ross R., and Dozier, Jack. "A Time of Disintegration: The Coeur d'Alene and the Dawes Act." *Western Historical Quarterly* 5 (October 1974): 405–19.

Dale, Edward Everett. *The Indians of the Southwest*. Norman: University of Oklahoma Press, 1949.

Debo, Angie. *A History of the Indians of the United States*. Norman: University of Oklahoma Press, 1970.

————. *And Still the Waters Run*. Princeton: Princeton University Press, 1940.

Deloria, Vine, Jr. ed. *American Indian Policy in the Twentieth Century*. Norman: University of Oklahoma Press, 1985.

Dippie, Brian W. *The Vanishing American: White Attitudes and United States Indian Policy*. Middletown, Conn.: Wesleyan University Press, 1982.

Downes, Randoph C. "A Crusade for Indian Reform, 1922–1934." *Mississippi Valley Historical Review* 32 (December1945): 331–54.

Dunbar, Robert G. *Forging New Rights in Western Waters*. Lincoln: University of Nebraska Press, 1983.

Ewers, John C. *The Blackfeet: Raiders on the Northwestern Plains*. Norman: University of Oklahoma Press, 1958.

Fey, Harold, and McNickle, D'Arcy. *Indians and Other Americans*. New York: Harper and Bros., 1959.

Hagan, William T. *United States-Comanche Relations: The Reservation Years*. New Haven: Yale University Press, 1976.

————. "Justifying the Dispossession of the Indian: Land Utilization Argument." In *American Indian Environments: Ecological Issues in Native American History*, pp. 65–80. Edited by Christopher Vecsey and Robert Venables. Syracuse: Syracuse University Press, 1980.

————. "Private Property: The Indians' Door to Civilization." *Ethnohistory* 3 (Spring 1956): 126–37.

Hargreaves, Mary W. *Dry Farming in the Northern Great Plains, 1900–1925*. Cambridge: Harvard University Press, 1957.

Harper, Allen G. "Salvaging the Wreck of Indian Land Allotment." In *The Changing Indian*, pp. 84–102. Edited by Oliver LaFarge. Norman: University of Oklahoma Press, 1942.

Hibbard, Benjamin H. *A History of the Public Land Policies*. New York: Peter Smith, 1939.

Hicks, John D. *Republican Ascendancy, 1921–1933*. New York: Harper and Row, 1960.

Holford, David M. "The Subversion of the Indian Land Allotment System, 1887–1934." *Indian Historian* 8 (Spring 1975): 11–21.

Hoxie, Frederick E. *A Final Promise: The Campaign to Assimilate Indians, 1880–1920*. Lincoln: University of Nebraska Press, 1984.

_____ . "From Prison to Homeland: The Cheyenne River Reservation Before World War I." In *The Plains Indians of the Twentieth Century*. pp. 55–76. Edited by Peter Iverson. Norman: University of Oklahoma Press, 1985.

Hundley, Norris J. "The Winter's Decision and Indian Water Rights: a Mystery Reexamined." In *The Plains Indians of the Twentieth Century*, pp. 77–99. Edited by Peter Iverson. Norman: University of Oklahoma Press, 1985.

Ise, John. *The United States Oil Policy*. New Haven: Yale University Press, 1926.

Kelley, Klara B. *Economic Development in American Indian Reservations*. University of New Mexico, Native American Studies, Development Series No. 1, 1979.

Kelly, Lawrence C. "Cato Sells (1913–21)," "Charles Henry Burke (1921–29)," and "Charles James Rhoads (1929–33)." In *The Commissioners of Indian Affairs, 1824–1977*, pp. 243–72. Edited by Robert M. Kvasnicka and Herman Viola. Lincoln: University of Nebraska Press, 1979.

_____ . *The Assault on Assimilation: John Collier and the Origins of Indian Policy Reform*. Albuquerque: University of New Mexico, 1983.

_____ . *The Navajo Indians and Federal Indian Policy, 1900–1935*. Tucson: University of Arizona Press, 1968.

Kickingbird, Kirke, and Karen Ducheneaux. *One Hundred Million Acres*. New York: Macmillan, 1973.

Kinney, J. P. *A Continent Lost—A Civilization Won: Indian Land Tenure in America*. Baltimore: Johns Hopkins University Press, 1937; reprint ed., New York: Arno Press, 1975.

Lagone, Stephen A. "The Heirship Land Problem and Its Effective Utilization." In *Toward an Economic Development for Native American Communities*. A Compendium of Papers Submitted to the Subcommittee on Economy in Government of the Joint Economic Committee, pp. 519–48. Washington: Government Printing Office, 1969.

Laidlaw, Sally Jean. *Federal Indian Land Policy and the Fort Hall Indians*. Occasional Papers of the Idaho State College Museum, No. 3. Pocatello, Idaho, 1960.

Link, Arthur. *Wilson*. vol. II: *The New Freedom*. Princeton: Princeton University Press, 1956.

Lipps, Oscar H., compiler. *Laws and Regulations Relating to Indians and Their Lands*. Lewiston, Idaho: Lewiston Printing and Binding Co., 1913.

Macgregor, Gordon. *Warriors without Weapons*. Chicago: University of Chicago Press, 1946.

McCool, Daniel. *Command of the Waters: Iron Triangles, Federal Water Development, and Indian Water*. Berkeley: University of California Press, 1987.

McDonnell, Janet A. "Land Policy on the Omaha Reservation: Competency Commissions and Fee Patents." *Nebraska History* 63 (Fall 1982): 399–412.

McLane, Alfred E. *Oil and Gas Leasing on Indian Lands*. Denver: Bradford-Robinson Printing Co., 1955.

Mead, Margaret. *The Changing Culture of an Indian Tribe*. New York: Columbia University Press, 1932; reprint ed., New York: Capricorn Books, 1966.

Meriam, Lewis, et al. *The Problem of Indian Administration*. Baltimore: Johns Hopkins University Press, 1928.

Meyer, Roy W. *History of the Santee Sioux*. Lincoln: University of Nebraska Press, 1967.

_____ . *The Village Indians of the Upper Missouri*. Lincoln: University of Nebraska Press, 1977.

Noggle, Burle. *Teapot Dome: Oil and Politics in the 1920s*. Baton Rouge: Louisiana State University Press, 1962.

Olson, Keith. *Biography of a Progressive: Franklin K. Lane, 1864–1921*. Westport, Conn.: Greenwood Press, 1979.

Otis, D. S. *The Dawes Act and the Allotment of Indian Lands*. Edited by Francis Paul Prucha. Norman: University of Oklahoma Press, 1973.

Parman, Donald L. "Francis Ellington Leupp (1905–1909)." In *The Commissioners of*

Indian Affairs, 1824–1977, pp. 221–32. Edited by Robert M. Kvasnicka and Herman J. Viola. Lincoln: University of Nebraska Press, 1979.

Paxson, Frederick L. *Postwar Years, Normalcy, 1918–1923*. Berkeley: University of California Press, 1948.

Peffer, E. Louise. *The Closing of the Public Domain: Disposal and Reservation Policies, 1900–1950*. Stanford: Stanford University Press, 1951.

Pfaller, Louis L. *James McLaughlin: The Man with an Indian Heart*. New York: Vantage Press, 1978.

Philp, Kenneth R. "Albert Fall and the Protest from the Pueblos, 1921–1923." *Arizona and the West* 12 (Autumn 1970): 273–54.

————. *John Collier's Crusade for Indian Reform, 1920–1954*. Tucson: University of Arizona Press, 1977.

Pisani, Donald J. "Irrigation, Water Rights, and the Betrayal of Indian Allotment." *Environmental Review* 10 (Fall 1986): 157–76.

Prucha, Francis Paul. *American Indian Policy in Crisis: Christian Reformers and the American Indian, 1865–1900*. Norman: University of Oklahoma Press, 1976.

————. *The Great Father: The United States Government and the American Indians*. Lincoln: University of Nebraska Press, 1984.

————. "Thomas Jefferson Morgan (1889–93)." In *The Commissioners of Indian Affairs, 1824–1977*, pp. 193–204. Edited by Robert M. Kvasnicka and Herman J. Viola. Lincoln: University of Nebraska Press, 1979.

Robbins, Roy M. *Our Landed Heritage: The Public Domain, 1776–1946*. Princeton: Princeton University Press, 1942; reprint ed., Gloucester, Mass.: Peter Smith, 1960.

Saloutos, Theodore, and Hicks, John D. *Agricultural Discontent in the Middle West, 1900–1939*. Madison: University of Wisconsin Press, 1951.

Schmeckebier, Laurence F. *The Office of Indian Affairs: Its History, Activities and Organization*. Baltimore: Johns Hopkins University Press, 1927.

Shepard, Ward. "Land Problems of an Expanding Population." In *The Changing Indian*, pp. 72–83. Edited by Oliver LaFarge. Norman: University of Oklahoma Press, 1942.

Shideler, James H. *Farm Crisis, 1919–1923*. Berkeley: University of California Press, 1957.

Smith, Burton M. "The Politics of Allotment: The Flathead Indian Reservation as a Test Case." *Pacific Northwest Quarterly* 70 (July 1979): 131–40.

Smith, Frank E. *The Politics of Conservation*. New York: Pantheon Books, 1966.

Stein, Gary C. "The Indian Citizenship Act of 1924." *New Mexico Historical Review* 47 (July 1972): 257–74.

Stern, Theodore. *The Klamath Tribe: A People and Their Reservation*. Seattle: University of Washington Press, 1965.

Stuart, Paul. *The Indian Office: Growth and Development of an American Institution, 1865–1900*. Ann Arbor: UMI Research Press, 1978.

Sutton, Imre. *Indian Land Tenure: Bibliographical Essays and a Guide to the Literature*. New York: Clearwater Publishing Co., 1975.

Swain, Donald C. *Federal Conservation Policy, 1921–1933*. Berkeley: University of California Press, 1963.

Szasz, Margaret G. "Indian Reform in a Decade of Prosperity." *Montana, Magazine of Western History* 20 (Winter 1970): 16–27.

Trani, Eugene P. "Hubert Work and the Department of Interior, 1923–1928." *Pacific Northwest Quarterly* 61 (January 1970): 31–40.

————. *The Secretaries of the Department of the Interior, 1849–1969*. Washington: National Anthropological Archives, 1975.

Trenholm, Virginia, and Carley, Maurine. *The Shoshones: Sentinels of the Rockies*. Norman: University of Oklahoma Press, 1964.

Tyler, Lyman S. *Indian Affairs: A Study of Changes in the Policy of the United States Toward Indians*. Brigham Young University, a publication of the Institute of American Indian Studies, 1964.

Washburn, Wilcomb E. *The Assault on Indian Tribalism: The General Allotment Law (Dawes Act) of 1887*. J. B. Lippincott Co., 1975.

_____ . *Red Man's Land/White Man's Law*. New York: Charles Scribner's Sons, 1971.

Worster, Donald. *Rivers of Empire: Water, Aridity and the Growth of the American West*. New York: Pantheon Books, 1985.

Wyant, William K. *Westward in Eden: The Public Lands and the Conservation Movement*. Berkeley: University of California Press, 1982.

Dissertations

Fitch, James B. "Economic Development in a Minority Enclave: The Case of the Yakima Indian Nation." Ph.D. dissertion, Stanford University, 1974.

Powell, Burt Edward. "Land Tenure on the Northern Plains Indian Reservations." Ph.D. dissertation, Duke University, 1975.

Trosper, Ronald. "The Economic Impact of the Allotment Policy on the Flathead Indian Reservation." Ph.D. dissertation, Harvard University, 1975.

INDEX

Allotment of land: procedure for, 7–8; for farming, 7; for mineral deposits, 10–11; for timber resources, 11–13; in public domain, 13–18; of poor quality, 19–20; allotting agents for, 19–20; resistance to, 21–23; effects of, 121–23
Allotting agents: 19–21
American Indian Defense Association (AIDA): and leasing on executive order reservations, 54; and fee patents, 115, 118, 119
Appropriations. *See* House Committee on Appropriations
Arapaho: and irrigation projects, 76; and allotment of land, 123
Arizona: allotment of land in, 14–15; farming programs in, 33; leasing land with mineral deposits in, 50; irrigation projects in, 71; and the Reclamation Service, 74; irrigation projects in, 76
Assiniboine: and protection of water rights, 74

Blackfeet reservation: and allotment of land, 10, 11; and stockraising programs, 38; and Five Year Programs, 40, 41, 42; and abuses of leasing land, 67; and irrigation projects, 72, 76, 82; and the Reclamation Service, 74; and liberalizing of fee patents, 105–06; and allotment of land, 122
Board of Indian Commissioners, 12; and executive order reservations, 16; and leasing land, 44, 70; and irrigation projects, 76, 82; and competency commissions, 94; and fee patents, 105, 109, 111–12; and federal Indian land policy failure, 124
Burke, Charles: and fee patents, 4–5, 111–13, 114–15, 117–18, 120; and allotment of land, 8–9, 12, 22–23, 24; and farming and stockraising programs, 35–36, 38, 40–41; and stockraising programs, 38, 40–41; and leasing land, 48–50, 52, 66–67, 70; and sale of land, 57, 58; and funding for irrigation projects, 81; and Burke Act, 88; and federal Indian land policy failure, 124, 125

California: allotment of land in, 8, 14, 19, 22; leasing land with mineral deposits in, 51; abuses of leasing land in, 61
Cameron bill, 54–55
Cameron, Ralph: and leasing on executive order reservations, 54
Carter, Charles: and issuance of fee patents, 107
Cheyenne River reservation: and allotment of land, 10, 123; farming on, 33; and Five Year Programs, 40; and abuses of leasing land, 61; and competency commissions, 95; and citi-

zenship ceremonies, 96–97; and fee patents, 100, 106–07, 113
Chippewa. *See* Turtle Mountain Indian reservation
Citizenship ceremonies, 95–96
Coeur d'Alene reservation: and competency commissions, 95; and cancellation of fee patents, 116
Collier, John, 23, 24–25; and leasing on executive order reservations, 54; and fee patents, 115, 118, 119, 120
Colorado River reservation: and allotment of land, 19, 20; during World War I, 33; and irrigation projects, 71, 76
Colville reservation: and allotment of land, 8
Commissioners of Indian affairs. *See* Burke, Charles; Collier, John; Jones, William A.; Leupp, Francis E.; Morgan, Thomas J.; Rhoads, Charles J.; Sells, Cato; Valentine, Robert G.
Competency commissions, 90–91, 93–99, 102, 104
Congress: and fee patents, 3–4, 102, 103, 107, 108–10, 111–12, 117, 118, 119–20; and allotment of land, 10–13, 21–25, 123; and farming and stockraising programs, 26, 28, 32, 33–34, 42; and leasing of land, 43–44, 47, 50–51, 64; and leasing on executive order reservations, 51, 52, 53, 54–55; and Indian Oil Leasing Act of 1924, 53–55; and Cameron bill, 54; and sale of land, 55–56, 58; and irrigation projects, 71, 76–79, 81, 82–83, 85; and protection of Indian water rights, 72–74; and the Reclamation Service, 74; and competency commissions, 94, 98, 102; and Burke Act of 1906, 115–116. *See also* House Committee on Appropriations; House Committee on Indian Affairs; Senate Committee on Indian Affairs
Coolidge, Calvin, 4–5; and allotment of land, 11; and leasing on executive order reservations, 54–55; and abuses of leasing land, 69
Creek: and competency commissions, 97
Crow Creek reservation: and allotment of land, 25; and farming programs, 28; and fee patents, 101
Crow reservation: and allotment of land, 8, 10, 19, 122; farming on, 33; and stockraising programs, 38; and Five Year Programs, 40; and sale of land, 57; and abuses of leasing land, 61, 64–65, 67, 68–69; and irrigation projects, 76; and competency commissions, 95; and citizenship ceremonies, 96; and fee patents, 100, 106, 114

"Declaration of policy" for fee patents: support

Janet A. McDonnell is a historian for the U.S. Army Corps of Engineers. She has taught history at the University of South Dakota and Yankton College and has published several articles on Indian history in the twentieth century.